# 101 Ways to Promote Your Tourism Web Site

# Other Titles of Interest From Maximum Press

## <u>Top Internet Business Books</u>

- *101 Ways to Promote Your Web Site*

- *3G Marketing on the Internet*

- *Podcasting for Profit*

- *Protecting Your Great Ideas for FREE*

- *101 Internet Businesses You Can Start From Home*

- and many more...

For more information go to *maxpress.com*
or e-mail us at *info@maxpress.com*

# 101 Ways to Promote Your Tourism Web Site

*Filled with Proven Internet Marketing Tips, Tools, and Techniques to Get Visitors to Your Site and Your Destination*

## Susan Sweeney, C.A.

MAXIMUM PRESS
605 Silverthorn Road
Gulf Breeze, FL 32561
(850) 934-0819
maxpress.com

Publisher: Jim Hoskins

Production Manager: Gina Cooke

Cover Designer: Lauren Smith

Copyeditor: Phyllis Stern

Proofreader: Jacquie Wallace

Indexer: Susan Olason

Printer: P.A. Hutchison

*Library of Congress Cataloging-in-Publication Data*

Sweeney, Susan, 1956-
101 ways to promote your tourism web site : filled with proven internet marketing tips, tools/Susan Sweeney. — 2nd ed.
p. cm.
Rev. ed. of: Internet marketing for your tourism business, 2000.
Includes bibliographical references and index.
ISBN 978-1-931644-62-4 (alk. paper)
1. Internet marketing. 2. Tourism—Marketing. I. Sweeney, Susan, 1956-. Internet marketing for your tourism business. II. Title. III. Title: One hundred one ways to promote your tourism web site. IV. Title: One hundred and one ways to promote your tourism web site.
HF5415.1265.S934 2008
910.68'8—dc22
2008002258

## Acknowledgements

Many thanks to Stephanie Strathdee, my right hand, for all the help with this edition of *101 Ways to Promote Your Tourism Web Site*. This book was definitely a team effort.

Thanks to the very talented Kaitlyn Sweeney for her assistance in research and her writing contribution.

Thanks to my great team at Verb Interactive (*http://www.verbinteractive.com*): Ed Dorey and Andy MacLellan who have been with me since their university days, and our whole team of Internet marketing experts.

The Internet is a fascinating and vast publicly accessible resource from which we can learn a great deal. I'd like to thank all those people who share their information so freely on the Net with sites like "WilsonWeb" (*www.wilsonweb.com*) by Dr. Ralph Wilson, "SearchEngineWatch" by Danny Sullivan, and newsletters like "I-Search" by Detlev Johnson.

Many thanks to my large network of experts whom I know I can always call on to get the latest scoop on what's really happening. Joe Mauro of inBox360.com and Ken Teeter of nTarget.com are always extremely knowledgeable and helpful in terms of the ever-changing world of private mail list marketing.

Thanks to Jim Hoskins and Gina Cooke at Maximum Press. This is our fifteenth book together. It's always a pleasure to work with you. One of these days we're going to have to meet face to face!

Special thanks to my absolutely wonderful husband, Miles, who makes all things possible. I wouldn't be able to do what I do if not for you. Also thanks to our three amazing children—Kaitlyn, Kara, and Andrew—for their love, encouragement, and support. Love you more than the last number!

Special thanks to my mom and dad, Olga and Leonard Dooley, for always being there and for instilling in me the confidence to know that I can do anything I set my mind to. It's amazing what can be done when you "know you can."

## Disclaimer

This book is not intended to replace the manufacturer's product documentation or personnel in determining the specifications and capabilities of the products mentioned in this book. The manufacturer's product documentation should always be consulted, as the specifications and capabilities of computer hardware and software products are subject to frequent modification. The reader is solely responsible for the choice of computer hardware and software. All configurations and applications of computer hardware and software should be reviewed with the manufacturer's representatives prior to choosing or using any computer hardware and software.

## Trademarks

The words contained in this text which are believed to be trademarked, service marked, or otherwise to hold proprietary rights have been designated as such by use of initial capitalization. No attempt has been made to designate as trademarked or service marked any personal computer words or terms in which proprietary rights might exist. Inclusion, exclusion, or definition of a word or term is not intended to affect, or to express judgment upon, the validity of legal status of any proprietary right which may be claimed for a specific word or term.

## Your "Members Only" Web Site

The online tourism world changes every day. That's why there is a companion Web site associated with this book. On this site you will find the latest news, expanded information, and other resources of interest.

To get into the Web site, go to *tourism.maxpress.com*. You will be asked for a password. Type in:

*mom*

and you will then be granted access.

Visit the site often and enjoy the updates and resources with our compliments—and thanks again for buying the book. We ask that you not share the user ID and password for this site with anyone else.

## Susan Sweeney's Internet Marketing Mail List

You are also invited to join Susan Sweeney's Internet Marketing Bi-weekly Internet Marketing Tips, Tools, Techniques, and Resources Newsletter at *http://www.susansweeney.com*.

# Table of Contents

## Chapter 2:
## Designing Your Site to Be Search Engine Friendly    23

## Chapter 6:
## Great Content                                                  94

## Chapter 7:
## Landing Pages                                                 102

## Chapter 8:
## Search Engine and Directory Submissions       108

## Chapter 9:
## Developing Your Pay-to-Play Strategy      125

## Chapter 10:
## The E-mail Advantage      135

## Chapter 11:
## Utilizing Signature Files to Increase Web Site Traffic  149

## Chapter 12:
## Autoresponders  158

## Chapter 13:
## Consumer Generated Media  164

## Chapter 14:
## Establishing Your Private Mailing List      172

## Chapter 15:
## Effective Promotion Through Direct Mail Lists      196

## Chapter 16:
## Developing a Dynamite Link Strategy      202

## Chapter 17:
## Maximizing Promotion with Meta-Indexes     217

## Chapter 18:
## Winning Awards, Cool Sites, and More     224

## Chapter 19:
## Online Advertising     230

## Chapter 20:
## Maximizing Media Relations                                    252

## Chapter 21:
## Increasing Traffic Through Online Publications      267

## Chapter 22:
## Really Simple Syndication      281

## Chapter 23:
## Blogs & Wikis                                                    293

## Chapter 24:
## Podcasting & Videocasting                                        303

## Chapter 25:
## Mobile Marketing            312

## Chapter 26:
## Interactive Mapping           319

## Chapter 27:
## The Power of Partnering        328

## Chapter 28:
## Web Traffic Analysis          333

# 1

# Planning Your Web Site

Travel is the most frequently sold thing on the Internet. With millions of travel and tourism Web sites competing for viewers, how do you get the results you're looking for? When asked if they are marketing on the Internet, many travel and tourism organizations say, "Yes, we have a Web site." However, having a Web site and marketing on the Internet are two very different things. Yes, usually you need a Web site to market on the Internet. However, a Web site is simply a collection of documents, images, and other electronic files that are publicly accessible across the Internet. Your site needs to be designed to meet your online objectives and should be developed with your target market in mind. Internet marketing encompasses all the steps you take to reach your target market online, attract visitors to your Web site, encourage them to visit your destination, buy your spa or ski or golf travel packages, and make them want to come back for more.

Having a Web site is great, but it is meaningless if nobody knows about it. Just as having a brilliantly designed travel product or destination marketing brochure does you little good if it sits in your sales manager's desk drawer, a Web site does you little good if your target market isn't visiting it. It is the goal of this book to help you take your Web site out of the desk drawer, into the spotlight, and into the hands of your target market. You will learn how to formulate an Internet marketing strategy in keeping with your objectives, your travel related products or services, and your target market. This chapter provides you with an overview of this book and introduces the importance of:

- Defining your online objectives

- Defining your target markets and developing your Web site and online marketing strategy with them in mind

- Developing the Internet marketing strategy that is appropriate for your travel and tourism organization or your destination.

## The Fundamentals—Objectives, Target Markets, and Products and Services

Things have changed dramatically over the past several years in terms of Web site design and development methodology. Back in the old days—a couple of years ago in Internet years—it was quite acceptable, and the norm, for a travel and tourism organization to pack up all of its brochures, ads, direct-mail pieces, news releases, and other marketing materials in a box, drop it off at the Web developer's office, and after a short conversation, ask when they might expect the Web site to be "done." The Web developer would then take the marketing materials and digitize some, scan some, and do some HTML programming to develop the site. By going through this process, organizations ended up with a Web site that looked just like their brochure, hence the term "brochureware." Brochureware is no longer acceptable on the Web if you want to be successful. Travel-related sites that are successful today are ones that are designed around:

- Objectives of the organization

- Needs, wants, and expectations of their target markets

- Travel-related products and services that are being offered.

Everything related to Internet marketing revolves around these three things—objectives, target markets, and products or services. It is critically important to define these things appropriately and discuss them with your Web developer. It is your responsibility, not your Web developer's, to define these things. You know (or should know) what your objectives are more clearly than your Web developer does. If you don't articulate these objectives and discuss them with your Web developer, it is impossible for him or her to build a site to achieve your objectives!

You know your target markets better than your Web developer does. You know what your visitors want, what they base their buying decisions on, and what their expectations are. You need to provide this information so that your Web developer can build a Web site that meets the needs, wants, and expectations of your target market.

Let's spend the remainder of the chapter on these fundamentals—objectives, target markets, and products and services—so you can be better prepared for the planning process for your Web site.

## Common Objectives

Before you even start to create your Web site, you must clearly define your online objectives. What is the purpose of your site? Brainstorm with people from all parts of your organization, from the frontline staff, to marketing and sales personnel, to customer support, banquet services, housekeeping, the bell desk, the concierge, and administration. You get the point—everyone has a different interaction with your customers and therefore should be included in this planning meeting.

Generate a comprehensive list of primary and secondary objectives. If you're going to build this Web site you might as well build it to achieve all of your online objectives. If you don't brainstorm with your stakeholders, document the objectives, and discuss these objectives with your Web developer, it will be impossible for the Web developer to build you a Web site that addresses all of your objectives.

Every element of your site should relate back to your objectives. When you decide to update, add, or change any elements on your Web site, examine how these changes relate to the primary and secondary objectives you have identified. If there is not a clear match between your objectives and your intended changes, you might want to reconsider the changes. It's amazing how many Web sites have been developed without adequate planning or without ensuring that the Web site ties in with the corporate objectives.

Some of the most common primary objectives include:

- Advertising your travel-related products, services, or destination

- Selling your destination, vacation packages, and travel-related products or services

- Providing customer service and support

- Providing destination, accommodation, product or corporate information

- Creating and establishing brand identity and brand awareness.

### Advertising Your Travel-Related Products, Services, or Destination

The objective of many Destination Marketing Organizations, or DMOs, is simply to promote but not directly sell a travel-related product, service, or destination. The objective is to create awareness or a "buzz," generate interest, and, ultimately, have a large number of people visit the destination. This type of site might include multimedia clips of the destination, pictures of the destination that appeal to the target market, viral marketing ("Tell a friend about this destination"), elements to encourage word-of-mouth marketing, an intriguing story about the destination, and other elements to help the DMOs achieve their objectives with their target market in mind.

### Selling Your Destination, Vacation Packages, and Travel-Related Products or Services Online

Selling products or services online is a common objective. The Internet provides a broad geographic reach and a huge demographic reach. Often travel and tourism organizations combine the objectives of advertising their travel packages and destination retreats with trying to sell them through their Web sites. This works well because visitors are not only given information about your packages, vacation specials, and your destinations, but they are given the option of easily booking online. The easier you make it, the more likely they are to buy or make a reservation.

### Providing Customer Service and Support

You might decide that the main reason for your business to have an online presence is to provide more comprehensive customer service. A great benefit of a Web site is that you can provide customer assistance 24 hours a day, 7 days a week, 365 days a year. By providing an easy way for your customers to solve their problems or get answers to their questions quickly and easily, you increase customer loyalty. Always include the appropriate contact information for customers to talk to a live person if they so choose.

## Providing Destination, Accommodation, Product, or Corporate Information

It is important for travel, tourism, and destination organizations to provide information on their vacation packages, accommodations, and products and services information to a particular target market. Some might also want to provide corporate information to potential investors. If your organization courts the media, it might include a media center, which can include all your press releases, corporate background, information on key company officials, articles that have been written about the company, and a gallery of relevant pictures that the media can use, as well as a direct link to the company's media person.

## Creating and Establishing Company Identity and Brand Awareness

Another objective might be to create and establish company identity and brand awareness. Based on the success of companies such as Orbitz.com, Yahoo!, Travelocity, Amazon, and eBay, it is apparent that branding a company or product on the Web can occur swiftly. Although they all had significant financial resources, each company used a combination of online and offline advertising to meet its objectives. Each of the sites features a prominent logo, consistent imagery, and a consistent color scheme. There is a lot we can learn from them.

When trying to establish corporate identity, any graphics developed for your Web site must be top-notch and reflect the colors associated with your corporate logo. A catchy slogan further promotes corporate identity. Your Web site must have a consistent look and feel and all offline promotional campaigns and material must be consistent with your online presence.

## Other Primary Objectives

Brainstorm with all the stakeholders in your organization to come up with other primary objectives for the organization. This process is critical to the organization's online success. Everything else revolves around your objectives—the elements included on your site and the Internet marketing techniques you use. If you were building new office space, you would want to include the input of all people working in your office to ensure that their needs were taken into consideration and the office was designed appropriately. The same is true when building a Web site—everyone must be included in the brainstorming session.

As much time should be spent in the planning stage as in the construction phase. By going through this process, you will be able to develop the best blueprint or storyboard for your proposed Web site.

## Other Objectives to Consider up Front

Although setting your primary objectives is vital, it is just as important to identify your secondary objectives. By setting appropriate secondary objectives, you will be more prepared to achieve all of your online goals. Many travel and tourism organizations identify only primary objectives for their Web site and completely neglect secondary objectives that can help them succeed online. If you're going to build a Web site, you might as well build it to achieve all of your objectives. Following are some common secondary objectives for travel and tourism organizations to consider:

- Your site should be designed to be search-engine friendly.

- Your site should be designed to encourage repeat traffic.

- Your site should have viral marketing elements that encourage visitors to recommend your destination, packages, and vacation specials to others.

- Your site should incorporate permission marketing, where visitors are encouraged to give you permission to send them e-mail, newsletters, e-specials, golf packages, etc., on a regular basis.

- Your site should be designed to encourage customer loyalty.

- Your site should incorporate stickiness, encouraging visitors to stay awhile and visit many areas of the site.

## Designing Your Site to Be Search Engine Friendly

Creating a site that is search engine friendly should be an objective of every travel and tourism company that wants to do business on the Internet. Search engines are the most common way for Internet surfers to search on the Net. In fact, 85 percent of all people who use the Internet use search engines as their primary way to look for information. By using keywords relating to your destination, packages, e-specials, and events in appropriate places on your site, you can improve how search engines rank you.

You want these chosen keywords in the domain name if possible, your page titles and page text, your Alt tags for graphics, and your page headers and keyword meta-tags as well as in each page's description meta-tag. Many search engines place a lot of emphasis on the number and quality of links to a site to determine its ranking. This means that the more Web sites you can get to link to your site, the higher your site will be in search engine results. (See Chapter 2 for more information on designing your site for high search engine ranking.)

### Including Repeat Traffic Generators on Your Site

Every travel, tourism, and destination Web site should be designed to entice its visitors to return again and again. Generating repeat traffic to your site is a key element of your online success and can be accomplished in a number of ways. Using contests, specials, packages, a calendar of events, and many other techniques, can increase your Web traffic. Chapter 3 describes many of these repeat traffic generators in much more detail.

### Getting Visitors to Recommend Your Site

The best exposure your travel and tourism Web site can get is a recommendation by a friend or unbiased third party. It is critical that you try to have elements of your Web site recommended as often as possible; therefore, you should have a way for people to quickly and easily tell someone about elements on your site.

The best way to encourage people to recommend your site is to include viral marketing techniques such as a "Tell a Friend" button on your site. You might want to include some variations on this as well. Under golf packages or specials you can have an "E-mail this golf package to a friend" button for people to refer their friends and associates to your site.

Virtual postcards are also a good way to get people to send more people to your Web site. There are many ways to encourage viral marketing. These are discussed in detail in Chapter 5.

### Using Permission Marketing

You always want your destination or travel organization to be seen as upholding the highest ethical standards and being in compliance with anti-spam legislation. Do not to send out unsolicited e-mail—known as spam—promoting your packages, destination, e-specials, or travel products. This is why it's important to develop a mailing list of people who have given you permission to send them messages, including company news and promotions.

When you're developing your Web site, an objective should be to get as many visitors to your site as possible to give you their e-mail address and permission to be included in your mailings. You can do this by having numerous ways for your visitors to sign up to join your e-club and to receive weekly spa or golf specials, vacation packages, coupons, or new giveaways. Chapter 3 has many examples of ways to encourage visitors to request to be added to your e-mail list and Chapter 4 provides all the details on permission marketing.

### Creating Loyalty among Visitors

The way to create loyalty among visitors is to provide them with some incentives for joining your online community, and provide them with proof that you really appreciate their business. You can do this by having a members-only section of your Web site or an e-club that has special offers exclusively for them, as well as discounts or freebies. People like to do business with people who appreciate their business. We are seeing a real growth in loyalty programs online.

### Including "Stickiness" Elements

To get your target market to visit your site often and have them visit a number of pages every time they visit, you need to provide interesting, interactive, and relevant content. You want your site visitors to feel as if they are part of your online community and to want to visit your site every day. You create "stickiness" by including many elements that keep your visitors' attention and by adding new content on a regular basis.

Your site can have a daily advice column or a new tip of the week on golf or skiing, descriptions of the different attractions at your destination, new packages and promotions that are constantly changing, a news section that is updated daily, as well as a weekly contest that site visitors can enter. The combination of these elements makes a site sticky. You want your site to be a resource people return to often and not a one-time event.

### Including Interactive Elements

The longer people stay on your site and the more pages they visit, the more your brand is reinforced. By utilizing interactive elements on your site you are more likely to engage your visitors and keep them around longer. The longer they stay, the more they feel a part of your community. The more they feel a part of your community, the more likely they are to give you permission to keep in contact with them, tell a friend about you and your site, and the more likely they are to do business with you—people like to do business with people they know and trust.

Interactive elements include such things as property videos or virtual tours, podcasts or videocasts (see Chapter 24 for more on podcasting and videocasting) or interactive maps (see Chapter 26 for more on interactive mapping). Check out your competition and see how they incorporate interactive elements on their sites. Whatever you decide to implement, make sure it relates to your target market.

## A Final Word on Objectives

Setting your Web site's objectives before you begin building your site is essential so that you can convey to your Web developer what you want your Web site to achieve. You obviously will have a number of different objectives for your site, but many of these objectives can work together to make your Web site complete.

Whatever your objectives might be, you must carefully consider how best to incorporate elements in your Web site and your Internet marketing strategy to help you achieve them. Successful marketing on the Web is not a simple undertaking. Before you begin to brainstorm over the objectives of your Web site, be certain you have read and studied all the information that is pertinent to the travel and tourism market. Read everything you can find and examine the findings of industry experts.

Your Web site objectives form a critical element in your Web site design and development, as you will see in the next section.

## Target Markets

It is important to define every one of your target markets. If you're going to build this Web site, you might as well build it for all of your target markets. For each and every one of your target markets, you need to determine:

- Their needs

- Their wants

- Their expectations.

For each and every one of your target markets, you should also try to determine an appropriate "WOW" factor. What can you provide for them on your Web site that will WOW them? Your objective should be to exceed the target market's expectations.

Your main target market might be your potential customer, but other target markets might include existing customers, or the media, or those who influence the buying decision for your potential customers.

When you look at—really look at—potential customers versus existing customers, you realize that what these two groups want and need from your Web site are probably different. Someone who is an existing customer knows your company. Learning about your vacation packages, destination information, accommodations, your business practices, and the like, are not a priority for this person. A potential customer needs to know about these things before giving you their business. "Customer" is such a huge target market; it needs to be broken down into segments. If you were a hotel, for example, your customer target market might be broken down further into:

- Business travelers

- Vacation travelers

- Family travelers

- Meeting planners

- Handicapped travelers

- Tour operators

- Golfers

- Outdoor adventure enthusiasts

- Eco-tourists.

You get the idea. You need to segment your customer target market and then, for each segment, you need to do an analysis of needs, wants, and expectations.

If you intend to market family getaways, your Web site should be colorful and the text simple and easy to understand, in keeping with what appeals to your target market. Chances are fun-looking graphics will be used extensively on your site to draw children further into it (see Figure 1.1).

**Figure 1.1.** Web sites designed to appeal to children include fun, colorful images.

Another aspect to consider when designing your Web site is your target market's propensity to utilize the latest technologies and the configurations they are likely to be using. Or it might be that your target market has yet to embrace the latest technologies and is still using a dial-up connection to the Internet, slower machines, and older software. They might still be using the Web browser that was originally installed on their system simply because they are uncomfortable downloading the latest version of the browser, are unaware of the more recent version, or are uninterested in downloading a large file. If your target market includes this demographic, be careful with your use of Java, Flash, and large graphic files.

## Travel-Related Products and Services

It is important to define what specifically you want to promote online. Web sites and Internet marketing strategies differ depending on the destination, attractions, packages, and products and services being sold. A destination that is marketing a theme park with roller-coasters and rides has to develop a fun and interactive Web site that is attractive to children and teens and the young at heart. The Web site should also give children a way to tell their friends about the site, as well as a reason to return to the site. This particular destination might want to offer an electronic postcard service where children can send a colorful and musical message to their friends to tell them about the site.

A travel agency's Web site might include features such as an opt-in mailing list to send people information on weekly vacation specials, or a page detailing the latest specials. The site might also include downloadable or streaming video tours of vacation resorts to entice visitors to buy resort vacation packages. Another idea is to have a system in place to help customers book vacations, rent cars, and check for available flights. The travel agency might also want to store customer profiles so they can track where particular customers like to sit on the plane, the type of hotel room they usually book, and their credit card information, to make bookings more efficient for the customer and the agency.

## The Fundamentals

Once you have clearly defined your online objectives, your target markets, and the travel related products or services you want to promote online, you are ready to move on to the next phase of planning your Web site—doing your competitive analysis.

## Using Competitor Sites to Your Advantage

You have to realize that your online competition is different from your offline competition. Online, you are competing with all organizations that have an online presence and sell the same types of products and services you do. When doing your competitive analysis online, you want to select the "best of breed"— those fantastic Web sites of the organizations selling the same products and services you do—no matter where they are physically located.

One of your Web site's objectives is to always meet and beat the competition in terms of search engine rankings and Web site content. To do so, you must understand exactly what it is your competition is doing. Take the time to research competitors and compare them on an element-by-element basis.

There are a number of ways you can identify your competition online. You can find them by conducting searches with the appropriate keywords, seeing which competing Web sites rank highly in the major search engines and directories. Similarly, there are many other online resources you can use to research your competition, including industry-specific Web portals and directories.

Once you have gathered a list of competing Web sites, analyze them element by element to determine which Web elements your competitors include on their sites and how their sites compare to one another. You want to look at what types of content they are providing to your target market. Other components you should analyze include the visual appeal of your competitors' sites, content, ease of navigation, search engine friendliness, interactivity, and Web site stickiness, or what they do to keep people coming back to their site. This information can provide you with details on what you need to incorporate into your site to meet and beat the competition.

When we do a competitive analysis for clients, we reverse-engineer (or dissect) the competing Web site from a number of different perspectives. Generally, you will choose five or six of the absolute best competing Web sites. Then you start to build a database using Excel or a table in Word.

Start with the first competing Web site, and from your review start to add database elements to the first column. Note any types of content, target markets defined, repeat traffic techniques used, viral marketing techniques used, search engine friendliness features used, download time for different types of Internet connections, cross-platform compatibility, cross-browser compatibility, and innovative elements. When you have dissected the first competing Web site and have noted appropriate database elements for comparative purposes, move on to the second competing Web site. Go through the same process, adding those elements new or different from what you already have in your database. Continue building the first column of your database by continuing through all the sites you want to include in your competitive analysis.

The next step is to develop a column for each of the sites you want to include in the competitive analysis. Then add two more columns—one for your existing Web site, to see how your site stacks against the competition, and the second for future planning purposes.

The next step is to go back and compare each site against the criteria for column 1, noting appropriate comments. For content information, you want to note whether the particular site has the same specific content, and how well it was presented. For download speeds, note specific minutes and seconds for each type of connection. For each repeat traffic generator, you may choose to include details, or just Yes/No. Continue with this process until you have completed the database, including your own existing site.

By this time, you should have a good feel for users' experiences when they visit your competitors' sites. Now you are ready to do your planning. In the last column of your database, review each of the elements in the first column, review your notes in your competitive analysis, and, where appropriate, complete the last column by categorizing each of the elements as one of the following:

- A—Need to have; essential, critical element; can't live without

- B—Nice to have if it doesn't cost too much

- C—Don't need; don't want at any price.

Remember that when users visit a number of sites that have certain elements incorporated, such as a virtual tour, that element becomes the norm. If your site does not have that virtual tour (or whatever that certain element is) they may feel as if you are not keeping up with industry standards, that you are not meeting their expectations. The bar is constantly being raised. Once a person sees something on three or four of your competitor sites, it becomes an expectation. The Internet has helped create very demanding consumers with very high expectations.

Having completed identification of your objectives, target markets, products and services, and now your competitive analysis, you are ready to develop your storyboard or architectural plan or blueprint for your site.

## Storyboarding Your Web Site

Before you start construction on your Web site there are many steps to be taken. First you must have the storyboard, or the blueprint of your site developed. In Web development, the majority of the time should be spent in the planning stage—integrate your objectives, your target market information, the findings of the competitive analysis, and your own ideas as well as those of others. This is done through the process of storyboarding.

The storyboard is the foundation of your Web site. Consider it the architectural plan or blueprint of your site. It should show you, on paper, the first draft of the content and layout of your site. It gives you the chance to review the layout and make changes before development begins.

A Web site storyboard can be thought of much like a hierarchical organizational chart in a business. In a typical business structure, the executives sit on top, followed by their subordinates, and so on.

Think of your Web site storyboard like this: You begin with your main page or home page at the top. Under the main page you have your central navigation bar. Each of the navigation options should be available on each page, regardless of where the user is on your site. Within each of the sections listed on your main navigation bar, you're going to have subsections, and so on. Figure 1.2 shows the storyboard of a hotel's Web site.

The storyboard can be created with a software program like Microsoft Visio, with sheets of paper, or with any other mechanism. Quite often when we begin storyboarding a project for a client, we'll start with yellow sticky notes on a wall. Very low tech, but it works! It is very easy to get a visual of the navigation structure and easy to fill in the content pages (one per sticky note) in the appro-

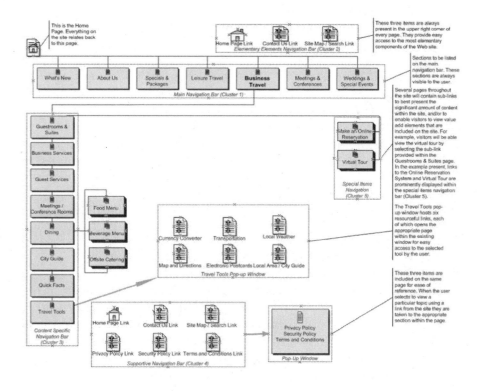

**Figure 1.2.** A storyboard for a hotel.

priate places. It is also very easy to edit—simply move a sticky from one section to another or add another sticky note for a new page.

In this section of the chapter we cover:

- Detailed planning of your travel or tourism site before a line of code is ever written

- Content guidelines

- Text guidelines

- Color guidelines

- Navigation guidelines

- Graphics guidelines

- Visual guidelines

- Other guidelines.

## Detailed Web Site Planning

Earlier in the chapter you learned how to develop your storyboard. Now you need to develop the specific content, text, and graphics for each page of your site.

The first draft of the text, for each page, should be developed by you. You know your target market better than anyone, you know what makes them book, you know what packages and specials they want and you know the buzz words for your industry far better than your Web developer.

Once you have the first draft of the text done, you want to have this text reviewed and edited by an online copywriter. Your online copywriter can be a person from your own organization, someone from a Web development organization, or an outsourced third party. Online copywriters often have a background in PR or advertising, and they know how to get the message across in as few words as possible. Online copywriters know how to grab the reader's attention and get them to do what it is you want them to do. Internet users don't want to read pages and pages of text—they want to get what they're looking for quickly. Online copywriters know that the text should be short, to the point, and written so it can be easily scanned.

Always review what the online copywriter has done. You want to make sure that the substance of your text has stayed the same and only the form has been changed.

After you have reviewed and approved the online copywriter's work, you want to have the content reviewed and edited by an Internet marketer. Again, the Internet marketer can be a person from your own organization, someone from a Web development organization, or an outsourced third party. Be sure that the Internet marketer you choose has expertise in search engines and their ranking criteria, repeat traffic generators, viral and permission marketing, as well as the latest trends in online marketing such as podcasts, blogs, and interactive maps.

The Internet marketer will review and edit the text and graphics making sure that the keywords are used in the appropriate places for high search engine ranking. The keyword assigned to a particular page should be used appropriately in the page title, the text throughout the page, the meta-tags for keyword and description, the headers, the Alt tags, and the comments tags. There is a real science to this so be sure to choose your Internet marketer carefully. You'll learn more about designing your site to be search engine friendly in Chapter 2.

The Internet marketer should also ensure that you have used the appropriate repeat traffic generators (see Chapter 3), appropriate permission marketing techniques (see Chapter 4), and appropriate viral marketing techniques (see Chapter 5). Again, you need to review and approve the changes to make sure your message is still presented appropriately for your target market.

Once you are satisfied with the Internet marketer's work, the next step is graphic design. The graphic designer will develop the "look and feel" for your site—the navigation bar, the background, and the separator bars. The graphic designer knows that your online and offline corporate identity should be consistent. Again, you review and approve the graphic design.

Once all this is done, and everything has been reviewed and approved, you are ready for the programming to start.

## Content Notes

Make all of your contact information readily available and easy to find and access. You always want to include your contact information on every page. Be sure to include your physical or mailing address, phone and fax numbers, and your e-mail address. It is important to make it easy for people to get in touch with you through every means possible.

Avoid "Under Construction" pages on your site at all costs. First of all, they are of no value to your visitors. When you have information, post it. Until then, don't mention it. Second, "Under Construction" pages can actually hinder your search engine placement with some of the more popular search engines and directories.

Be sure to include security information. Explain to your customers that when transactions or exchanges of information occur on your Web site they are secure.

Be sure to include your privacy policy as well. By telling your Web site visitors how their personal information (e.g., their name, e-mail address, etc.) will and will not be used, they will feel more comfortable and more willing to submit inquiries to your site or join your mailing list.

Minimize use of background sounds and auto-play sounds. Some people surf the Web from their office and wish to go discreetly from one site to the next. Background sounds and sounds that load automatically can compromise their discreetness. Give your visitors the option of listening to a sound, but do not force it upon them.

## Text Notes

To convey your intended image, your Web site uses the tone of your text and the design of your graphics. When determining the text content for your site, be mindful of excluding information on your site that is second nature to you, but important for your visitors. Review all text content on your site to ensure that you have not omitted anything crucial. Better yet, have your target market review and provide feedback—sometimes you are too close to the forest to see the trees.

Keep text brief. Almost 80 percent of Web users merely scan online text as opposed to actually reading it. Make your key points quickly and succinctly, and use lots of bulleted lists, headers, and horizontal rules to create visual breaks in the content. This helps keep visitors interested enough to read the information on your site. If they are faced with huge blocks of text, most visitors are overwhelmed by the quantity of the information and are either too intimidated to read your message or do not want to spend the amount of time it will take to read your message. Write for scanability.

Don't set your text size too small, as this is too hard to read. However, if your text is set too large, it looks like you are shouting. Also, avoid using ALL CAPS, WHICH ALSO COMES ACROSS AS SHOUTING.

## Color Notes

Keep your online and offline images consistent. Logos, corporate colors, and other marketing collateral associated with your company should all be consistent.

Choose your background and font colors carefully. You want to provide a pleasant viewing experience for your visitors, so be sure to use backgrounds that are not too busy and don't obscure your text. Only certain colors show up properly on certain backgrounds. A light background with dark text is easiest on the eyes, which is why most sites these days opt for a clear white background.

Use the default colors for links whenever possible. It is common knowledge by Web site visitors that blue text indicates an unvisited link, while purple, maroon, or darker blue usually represents a link that has not yet been visited, and red is the color of an active link. It should not be difficult for visitors to identify your links, so if you decide not to use the default colors, you must emphasize your links in a consistent manner through font size, font style, or underlines.

## Navigation Notes

Ease of navigation is very important to your site. You must provide a navigation bar in a consistent location on every page. You must make it easy for Web site visitors to get from one page to another so be sure to provide links to all of the major pages of your site on your navigation bar. Search engines can index any page from your site at any time, so your home page may not necessarily be the first page visitors come to. Never have dead ends. When viewers scroll down to the bottom of a page only to find that they must scroll all the way back to the top to move on (because you have no links at the bottom of the page) this is considered a dead end. A consistent-looking and well-positioned navigation bar with functioning links is the key to efficient site navigation.

A good rule of thumb is that your visitors should be able to get anywhere they want to go on your site in as little as three clicks or less. This is why it is important to develop an effective navigation bar as previously described. For very large sites (sites consisting of more than eight to ten major sections), it is a good idea to include a site map. Site maps, as shown in Figure 1.3, are usually

**Figure 1.3.**   Carlson Wagonlit's site map.

text-based lists that name all of the site's pages and their content. Site maps make it easy for users to access the information they are looking for without causing them much frustration—which is why it is important to make site maps accessible from any page on your site. Include a link from your main navigation bar to the site map for the easiest possible reference. Site maps are also great for submission to the search engines as they provide links to every page of your Web site, ensuring, as much as possible, that every page of your site gets included in the search engines' database.

An additional feature you might wish to include, if your site is fairly large, is an internal search tool. Internal search tools allow users to enter their query in a search box and have all relevant matches returned. This is a particularly useful feature for the travel and tourism market because you list many different types of destinations, package getaways, and travel specials on your Web site. This search tool will allow users to quickly search for their desired getaway or package—golfing in Miami or scuba-diving in the Maldives, for instance. Again, keep the design of your site consistent. Font types, headers, footers, navigational bars, buttons, bullets, colors, and so on, should be consistent throughout the site to maintain a polished, professional look.

## Graphics Notes

A good rule of thumb is to keep the combined size of the text and graphics on any Web page no more than 50 KB. Graphics that take too much time to download can cause visitors to leave your site before they get a chance to see it.

Some people even turn graphics off in their browsers to save time when searching, so you should provide all of your information in text format as well as graphics. To do this, use descriptive **Alt attributes** in your image tags. If for any reason the graphics do not display, the Alt text will load in place of the images. So visitors who choose not to browse with graphics turned on will have an easier time navigating your site. Another important reason for using descriptive attributes in your image tags is that Alt text is spidered and indexed by many of the major search engines. Therefore, using keywords in your Alt text for your image tags will improve your ranking in search engines and will provide a description of the images in the event that they are not loaded.

**Alt attributes**
Descriptive text associated with respective images on a Web site.

Use thumbnail graphics where applicable. Travel and tourism Web sites that have a page with a lot of large images should create small "thumbnail" versions of each image, then give visitors the option of clicking through to the larger versions they are interested in seeing. This is far superior to making your visitors wait for a series of large images to load.

Travel, tourism, and destination Web sites should be careful with the use of image maps as well. Image maps are large graphics with clickable "hot spots." Image maps are typically used for navigation purposes and usually have text embedded in the graphic. Search engines cannot read text embedded in a graphic, so from the standpoint of search engine friendliness, if you use image maps always ensure that you provide your appropriate text and Alt tags for the search engine.

Very often, when travel and tourism Web sites use a large graphic for an image map, visitors must wait for the entire image to load before it is apparent where they must click to begin navigating. Instead of using a large image map, it is a good idea to break the image into smaller sections so that visitors receive faster feedback without having to wait for a huge graphic to load. Also, always provide an alternate text link navigation system to assist people who surf with their graphics turned off.

It amazes me how often I see Flash intros as the **home page** for a Web site. The Flash intros are basically videos and the search engines have a difficult time indexing them as there is no text on the page, no Alt tags, no meta-tags, no headers, nor any of the other elements in the search engine ranking formulas.

**Home Page**
The main page of a Web site.

## Visual Notes

Check your site using different browsers. What viewers see when your site is downloaded depends on what browser they are using. Different browsers display the same Web site differently. Before you post your site online, check your site with the most popular browsers. You might want to check your Web traffic analysis to see what browsers your Web site visitors are using.

Also make sure that you review your site on both a Mac and a PC, as sometimes your Web site looks different depending on the platform.

Design your site for various screen widths. Try to accommodate visitors regardless of the screen resolution they use. Some Web users still run their systems at 640 pixels by 480 pixels; keep this in mind when designing your site. Use your Web traffic analysis software to determine the screen resolution preferences of your visitors. See Chapter 28 for more information on Web traffic analysis software and the reports you can access.

Your Web site should steer clear of scrolling marquee text. Scrolling marquees are difficult to read and are not compatible with all browsers. Simply post text directly on your pages if you have something important to say.

## Other Notes

Your home page should be 50 KB or less and should be displayed on no more than one or two screens. Studies have shown that visitors rarely wait beyond 15 seconds to download a site. Test the download time of your site using different connection speeds to ensure that it is reasonable for all users.

Also avoid dead links. These are links that don't go anywhere and the viewer usually receives a "404—File not Found" error message from the Web server after clicking on a dead link. Ideally you can designate your site map, if you have one, as the default page rather than a "404—File not Found" error message. Verify periodically that all your links are still active.

## Internet Resources for Chapter 1

I have developed a great library of online resources for you to check out regarding planning your site. This library is available on my Tourism Internet Marketing University Web site *http://www.TourismInternetMarketingU.com/max* in the Resources section where you can find additional tips, tools, techniques, and resources.

I have also developed courses on many of the topics covered in this book. These courses are also available on my Tourism Internet Marketing University Web site *http://www.TourismInternetMarketingU.com/max*. These courses are delivered immediately over the Internet or can be ordered as a CD.

# 2

---

# Designing Your Site to Be Search Engine Friendly

**W**hen Internet users are doing their travel research on where they want to go, where they want to stay, and what they are going to do when they get there… how do they do it? The most common research tool used is the search engine—85 percent of people doing research online use search engines to find what they are looking for. Because search engines can bring significant volumes of traffic to your site, you must understand how the major search engines work and how the design of your site can influence the indexing of your site by the search engines. You must also know about the elements that are included in the search engines' algorithms, or formulas, that are outside your Web site and what you can do to ensure that you earn maximum points for those things you can influence.

When people conduct Internet searches, they rarely go beyond the first couple pages of results. If you want to be noticed, you need to appear in the top 10 or 15 search results—ideally you want to appear on the top half of the front page of search results. But before you submit to the search engines, you have to be sure your site has been designed to be search engine friendly. In this chapter, we cover:

- The methodology to make your travel and tourism site search engine friendly

- The key elements of Web site design to accommodate search engines

- The all-important content

- The importance of keywords in all aspects of your Web site

- The elements that are in the search engine algorithms or formulas that are outside your Web site

- The importance of link popularity and link relevancy to your search engine placement.

## Methodology to Make Your Site Search Engine Friendly

To make your site search engine friendly you have to:

- Decide which search engines are critical for your success

- Learn as much as you can about their ranking criteria and the weighting given to each criteria in their algorithm. It is also important to know which databases they are using.

Then you must:

- Determine the keywords that your target market is using in the search engines to find what you have to offer

- Assign those keywords to specific pages throughout your site, and then

- Populate the pages with the assigned keywords in the appropriate places given the ranking criteria for your targeted search engines.

The remainder of this chapter walks you step-by-step through this process.

## Understanding Search Engines

Search engines use programs or intelligent agents, called bots, to actually search the Internet for pages which they index using specific parameters as they read the content. The agent reads the information on every page of your site and then follows the links. For example, Google's spiders continually crawl the Web looking for sites to index and, of course, index sites upon their submission. Google is obviously very important in the search engine community, so be sure your site is easily accessible to its spider. A detailed discussion on submissions to search engines and directories can be found in Chapter 8.

Registering with search engines is fairly simple. In most cases, you simply have to submit your URL or Internet address on their submission form. Even if your URL is not registered with search engines, a number of the major search engines will eventually find you as their **bots** are continually roaming the Internet looking for new sites to index. Your odds of being indexed increase significantly if you have a well-developed links strategy. There are millions of sites out there, so I suggest that you be proactive and register your site to ensure a speedier listing. Once you are registered, some

**BOTS**

Programs used by search engines to search the Internet for pages to index.

of the bots will periodically visit your site looking for changes and updates.

A common problem faced by Internet marketers is how to influence search engines to index their site appropriately and how to ensure that their site appears when people use relevant search criteria. Many of the interesting and creative sites on the Internet are impossible to find because they are not indexed with the major search engines. The majority (85 percent) of Internet users employ search engines or directories to find what they are looking for on the Web. They do this by typing in a keyword or phrase that represents what they are looking for. Usually people use a two or three keyword phrase. The following sections explore how to make your travel or tourism Web site more search engine friendly.

Many search engines and directories either partner with or license the use of the search technology of another search engine or directory. If you submit your site to a search engine that uses Google's index, then the design of your site influences how you're indexed in all search engines that rely on Google for their search results. For example, Google's results can be found on AOL, Netscape, HotBot, Lycos and more. Google's paid advertising results appear on many other sites as well.

In a similar fashion, you often find other search engine and directory data intermixed or included in some form with the data of another search engine or directory. To take this example further, some search engines are built on the premise of pooling the search results of many search providers and presenting the results to the end user—they do not maintain their own index, but rather manipulate the results of many other search engines in hopes of providing a better search experience. This type of search tool is called a meta-search engine. Dogpile is an example of a meta-search engine.

When designing your site, you must always keep the search engines in mind. Something as simple as a DHTML drop-down menu on your site or a Flash intro can cause problems with the search engines and the indexing of your site if implemented incorrectly. You want to do everything you can to ensure that your site is designed to meet the needs of your target audience while remaining completely search engine friendly. Search engines can produce a significant amount of traffic to your site if you can manage to be placed in the top search results.

## Decide Which Search Engines Are Important

To start this process, you want to decide which search engines you are going to be concerned about when taking steps necessary to rank high in their search results. For this section we are talking about **organic listings** rather than pay-per-click or sponsored listings.

Organic listings are the search results that are displayed to the left of the page and below the sponsored listings. Organic listings are free listings and are gained by how your site is ranked based on a unique formula, or algorithm, for each search engine. Pay-per-click or sponsored listings on the other hand are listings that are paid for and gained through a bidding process. Sponsored listings are always displayed at the top of the results and down the right hand side of the page. Ranking high in the pay-to-play search engines is discussed more in Chapter 9. See Figure 2.1 for organic and pay-per-click positioning on the search engine results page.

**Organic Listing**
A free listing of a site in the search results ranked by the search engine's ranking formula or algorithm.

You want to select a number of the most popular search engines for your concentration. You also want to be indexed in topic-specific search engines for your industry. You can find the most popular search engines by doing your research online through sites such as Search Engine Watch (*http://www.searchenginewatch.com*). You can keep up with what's happening in the search engines by joining one of the many discussion lists on the topic.

As it stands at the time of this writing, the major players in the search engine industry are:

- Google (*http://www.google.com*)

- Yahoo! (*http://www.search.yahoo.com*)

- MSN Search (*http://search.msn.com*)

**Figure 2.1.** Pay-per-click or sponsored listings appear at the top of the search results and along the right hand side of the page where as organic listings appear on the left hand side of the page and under the sponsored listings.

- AOL (*http://www.aol.com*)

- Ask (*http://www.ask.com*).

## Learn the Search Engine Ranking Criteria

Each search engine has its own unique ranking criteria and its own unique algorithm, or formula, giving different weighting to each of the criteria in its formula. For the search engines that you have decided to focus on, you have to learn as much as you can about their ranking criteria and relative weighting. See Figure 2.2 for a breakdown of how the search engines score sites. The site with the highest score appears at the top of the results and the rest appear in descending order of their score.

The search engines are all fighting for market share. The more market share a search engine has, the more valuable the company is. To gain market share a search engine has to provide better results than its competition. It is for this reason that the search engines are changing and improving their formulas on an

## How the Search Engines Rank Sites

Keyword Phrase Placement Points

+

Link Popularity/Link Relevancy Points

+

Miscellaneous Points

=

Total Score

**Figure 2.2.**   Formula for how the search engines rank Web sites.

ongoing basis. You have to keep up with changes in these formulas, tweak your site accordingly, and resubmit when necessary.

The search engines use different databases for their search results. They have different algorithms or formulas for their ranking. They have different weighting for the various elements within their formula. They change their formulas over time and they change their ranking over time. Sound complicated?

Things have changed quite a bit from the early days. Elements that used to have significant weighting may now have very little weight. You have to remember that it is the highest total score you are looking for so even if an element has reduced weighting, if the element has any points at all you want to incorporate the element to maximize your total score. Sometimes the top sites are within a small number of points of each other.

It is not as daunting as it might sound because the major search engines tend to look at similar information but weigh the relevancy for particular items differently in their algorithms. That having been said, here are the most important areas on a Web page that you must address when performing organic search engine optimization:

- Title tags (page titles)

- Keyword meta-tags

- Description meta-tags

- Alt tags

- Hypertext links (e.g., anchor text)

- Domain names and file names

- Body text (beginning, middle, and end of page copy)

- Headers

- Between the "NOFRAMES" tag of framed Web sites.

Page titles and text-based page content are the most important of the noted placement areas. Keyword meta-tags are not as critical as they once were, but are still applicable for some engines. Remember—it is the absolute highest score you are looking for—if there are any points available you want to design your site to take advantage of them.

Because Google is the favorite search engine for the time being, let's take a closer look at how it ranks pages. Google uses its internal index for its primary search listings. Google has many other features as well, some of which include:

- An images search

- Usenet news data database

- A news search feature

- Froogle (a shopping search tool)

- A local search

- A blog search

- A video search

- A product search

- A directory search

- A news search

- A catalog search

- Advertising services through the Google AdWords programs.

The ranking formula for Google's main search function looks for the keywords in the visible body text, headers tags, title tags, hypertext links, and Alt tags. Google gives a very heavy weighting to the link popularity with extra points for quality of links and relevancy of text around the links. Google also has miscellaneous points available for such things as:

- Age of domain/site—The longer you've registered your domain name the more likely that you are serious about being online for the long term.

- File size—Try not to exceed 100 k. A recent study found that the body section of your site ranks best between 50–70 k in size. Less than 100 k in size might not be cached unless it is considered exceptional content.

- Freshness of content—Goolge is always looking for sites that are updated on a regular basis. The more frequently you update your site the more frequently Google's spiders will visit your site.

- Links from directories—Google awards points if directories such as Yahoo!, Looksmart, DMOZ and About provide a link to your site.

Most of the search engines are giving heavy weighting to link popularity—that is, the number of links to your site from other sites on the Internet. The search engines are getting very sophisticated in the weighting of link popularity, with the search engines giving extra points for link relevancy—that is, how high the site with the link to your site would rank for the same keyword. Other points are awarded based on the keywords in the text around the link pointing to your Web site. For strategies on generating significant links to your site, see Chapter 16.

## Keywords Are Critical

Keywords are the terms and phrases that your target market uses when searching for the products and services you sell in the major search engines and directories. Your keywords are used in everything you do and are the key determining factor in how you rank in the search results among many of the major search engines.

A critical step in natural search engine optimization is to select the right keywords for your business, products or services (including descriptive words), and your target market. Understand whom you are targeting and build your search engine optimization efforts around your audience.

You need to choose keyword phrases that are going to bring sustainable targeted traffic consisting of potential customers—not just anything and everything. What you may think is the perfect keyword phrase may not be used at all by your target market in their search queries, which is why it is so critical to research and validate your keywords.

Ideally, each page of your Web site is going to focus on a different set of keywords that are specific to the content at hand. If you were to focus on the same set of keywords on every page, then you would hit only one small portion of your market potential because you are only going to hit those same keywords over and over again—it is self-defeating.

First, you want to gather a master list of all possible keyword phrases. To make the data easier to manage, you can create different keyword list profiles that represent individual topics as opposed to trying to cover all topics in a giant master list. For example, if you have two product lines, you can create a keyword list for each. Naturally, some keywords are shared across the lists, but it is important to understand that the people looking for one topic (for instance, "jobs") are not necessarily the same people looking for another topic (let's say, "cabins"), and as such they are going to use different keyword combinations in their searches.

How do you create your master keyword list? Here are four solid techniques for generating a list of potential keyword phrases:

1. Brainstorm, survey, and review promotional material.

2. Review competing and industry-leading Web sites.

3. Assess your Web site traffic logs.

4. Use keyword suggestion and evaluation tools.

Be sure to record the keywords you gather in a text document in your word-processing program or in a spreadsheet. Including them in a spreadsheet or database makes them much easier to sort when it comes time to prioritize the keywords and weed out the junk.

As you work your way through the list of techniques, you want to cycle back to some of the techniques because you will come across search terms that can expand the scope of your original efforts and open the door to new, more targeted phrases that you might have missed the first time around.

## Brainstorming, Surveying, and Reviewing Promotional Material

At this stage, the idea is to gather all the keyword phrases you can, within reason. Sit down with a pen and paper and jot down all keywords that come to mind. Bring other members of your team in on this process to fuel ideas. There is nothing scientific or technical to be concerned with here—the sky's the limit, but try to put yourself in your customers' shoes.

Try to think as your target market would if they were to do a search for information on a topic contained within your site. Do not just think about what people would do to find your site, but what they would do if they didn't know your business existed and were looking for the types of travel and tourism products and services you sell.

Here are several questions to help you with your brainstorming process:

1.  What business are you in (for instance, accommodations, travel agency, outdoor adventure)?

2.  What is the focus of your Web site (is it a resource, a guide, a store)? What would people search for if they were looking for a Web site like yours?

3.  If your customer were to take a guess at your Web address, what would it be? Remember, they do not know who you are, but they know what kind of products or services they are looking for.

4.  What travel and tourism-related products and services do you sell? What are some of the descriptive words or benefits of your products and services that might be familiar to your target market? For example, if your site offers information on all the different things to see and do in Topeka, Kansas, then one descriptive keyword phrase you might choose could be *Topeka attractions*.

Your current corporate materials, brochures, and other marketing collateral can be a valuable source of keyword phrases. Begin by indiscriminately highlighting any words that people might search for if they were looking for products or services your company has to offer.

To assist you in developing your keyword list, consider asking your customers for their input. Ask what keywords they might use to find a site like yours. You can always turn to a thesaurus for additional ideas if you get stumped.

## Review Competing and Industry-Leading Web Sites

Check out your online competition. The term *competition* is referenced quite loosely in that industry leaders with whom you may not directly compete are also included here. Look at the sites for which you have a record and look for sites in the major search engines using some of the keyword phrases you have gathered so far.

You want to see what sites are in the top 10 positions and understand them. By reviewing top-ranking Web sites, you can look for themes and patterns in the sites that give you a good indication of what they are going after and how they are doing it. You can then turn around and apply this newfound knowledge to your own travel or tourism Web site.

When reviewing competing Web sites, you should look at the same general areas you would optimize on your own Web site. As mentioned above, the most critical keyword placement areas include:

- Title tags (page titles)

- Keyword meta-tags

- Description meta-tags

- Alt tags

- Hypertext links (e.g., anchor text)

- Domain names and file names

- Body text (beginning, middle, and end of page copy; headers)

- Between the "NOFRAMES" tag of framed Web sites.

By searching for your most important keywords and observing what the top-ranking sites are using with respect to their page content, title tags, description meta-tags, keyword meta-tags, and so on, you can formulate a good plan of attack. Remember that if you don't appear in the first two or three pages of search results, it is unlikely that prospective visitors will access your site through the search engine.

Check to see what meta-tags your competitors have. Not only can you learn from the sites that catch your eye, you can also learn from your competitors' mistakes. After you have done a thorough job of this market research, you are in a good position to develop a description that is catchy and adequately describes your site.

To check your competition's meta-tags in Microsoft Internet Explorer, you simply go to their site, then click "View" on your menu bar and select "Source" from the drop-down menu. This brings up the source code for that respective page in whatever your default text browser is.

Pay special attention to the title tag of the top-ranked Web sites. To get a little more specific, you can narrow your search to keywords in a title tag. The reason for doing this is that optimizing a title tag is a given when it comes to search engine optimization, so it only makes sense to look at who else is doing it as well. On Google you can enter "allintitle: keyword phrase," without the quotes, to search for all pages with the noted keywords in their title tag. This approach is a little more focused than simply looking for all pages with a certain set of keywords because the keywords might just be there in passing, as a part of an article, and not something the site is intentionally trying to target. If the keywords are found in the title tag, there is a better chance their reason for being there is intentional.

As noted earlier, you can learn not only from the sites that catch your eye, but also from your competitors' mistakes.

### Assess Your Web Site Traffic Logs

Your Web site traffic logs can be a source of pertinent keyword information. You can view your traffic logs to see what search terms and search engines people are using to locate your Web site and to help you fine-tune future search engine optimization efforts.

If you are not sure whether you have access to a Web site traffic analysis program, check with your current Web site host to see if they provide one to you. If not, there are plenty of tools available to you. See Chapter 28, "Web Traffic Analysis," for helpful information.

Understand that the search terms displayed may not be the most relevant; they just happen to be the search terms people are executing to find your site during the selected time frame. Applying new search engine optimization techniques with relevant keywords changes how people find your Web site. The Web site traffic analysis package you use gives you the power to measure the impact of your optimization efforts.

Your traffic logs can be a source of inspiration for generating your master keyword list. Note the search terms people are currently using and add them to your list. For a more complete look at the search phrases reported on your Web site, expand the date range to cover a larger spread—say, over the period of a year.

When your site is optimized, your Web traffic analysis tool will become your best friend in monitoring your success.

## Keyword Suggestion and Evaluation Tools

There are a number of services available that can help you with selecting the most appropriate keywords for your site. These services base their suggestions on results from actual search queries. Wordtracker is an example of such a service.

Keyword research tools can help meet your current needs, whether you're looking for a place to start, are plum out of ideas, or simply feel like you're missing something. See the Resources section of my Web site at *http://www.TourismInternetMarketingU.com* for a list of keyword research tools.

## Fine-Tuning Your Keyword Phrases

Now that you have your master keyword list, probably with a few hundred keyword phrases, you have to drill down and figure out which keywords you are going to target for each page of your Web site that you want to optimize. Keep in mind that each page you optimize should lean toward a different set of keywords. Why? What good is buying 100 lottery tickets for the next drawing if they all have the same number? It is the same idea here.

Your efforts should focus around those keyword phrases that bring in a fair volume of traffic and that are highly targeted. The return on investment for such keywords will be much higher. When reviewing your keyword list, you need to consider:

- Which keywords are vital to your objectives

- Which keywords are popular enough to generate reasonable, sustainable traffic

- Which keywords do not have so much competition that it would be counterproductive considering the time and effort necessary to target them.

For a hotel to have the keyword *travel* stand alone on the hotel's Web site would prove a waste of effort. *Travel* is a vastly popular keyword, which is good, but it is too generic and too competitive to be worthwhile. You have to make judgment calls from time to time. In some cases a word is relevant and popular, but also competitive to the point of being intimidating. If this word is essential to your business, however, then go for it.

Organize your keywords according to their level of importance. When completed, you will have a refined master keyword list that you can refer to when optimizing your Web site. Also, different directories allow different numbers of keywords to be submitted. Because you have organized the list with the most important words first, you can simply include as many of your keywords as the directory allows.

You can begin editing the list by deleting words that either are too generic (for example, *business*) or are not appropriate for keyword purposes. Review each word and ask yourself, "Would people search using this word if they were looking for the products and services available through my Web site?"

For each page that you are optimizing, take a copy of the comprehensive master list and delete words that are not appropriate for that particular page. Reprioritize the remaining keywords based on the content of the page you are indexing. Now take the keyword phrase you have assigned to this page and put it at the top of the list. This is the keyword list for that particular page. Repeat this procedure for every page you are optimizing. This is also a great procedure when you are developing the keyword meta-tag for each page of your site.

What I covered above is a very basic approach to organizing keywords. If you are up to the challenge, you can take it further by adding weights and multipliers to your keyword list to further refine it.

You can choose to keep it basic while you are learning the ropes, but as you become more familiar you might want to be more critical in selecting your keywords to boost your performance in the search engines. The more knowledge you are armed with, the better prepared you are to optimize your Web site. Here are some additional tips to keep in mind when refining your keywords master list:

- **Plural and singular keywords**—There is some debate about whether it is better to use only the plural version of a keyword or whether it is best to use both the plural and singular forms. Is your target market looking for both? As an example, some people might search for *Los Angeles hotel,* and others might search for *Los Angeles hotels.* Google matches exactly what the user searches for, so it is important to use both where possible.

- **Using the names of your competitors**—There is often the question as to whether to include your competitor's name in your keywords. The idea here is that if someone looks for your competitor, they are going to find you as well. Never include a competitor's name in your keywords. Because several search engines read only a small amount of content for keywords, you lose valuable page real estate to irrelevant keywords when you use your competitor's name. In addition, there have been recent legal battles regarding the use of competitors' names within one's keywords.

- **Common misspellings of words**—There are many words that people misspell on a frequent basis. The question here is, do you include those misspelled keywords in your site or not? My stance is "No." Although people use them in their searches, it hurts your credibility in that you come off as a company incapable of spelling its own products and services. There are exceptions to every rule. Canadian sites often have U.S. customers as their target market and U.S. sites often have Canadian customers as their target markets. There are a number of words that are spelled differently by these countries—*theatre* in Canada is *theater* in the United States, *centre* in Canada is *center* in the United States, *colour* in Canada is *color* in the United States, are just a few examples. If you are caught with one of your important keywords spelled differently by your target market, you might want to optimize a page of your site to accommodate this. Perhaps you might offer a page that is designed for "Our Canadian Friends" or for "Our American Friends."

- **Case sensitivity**—Some search engines are not case-sensitive and others are. Regardless, most people search in lowercase, so to keep the process simple, for now you should record your original keyword master list using lowercase. Once you begin finalizing your keyword list, you might notice that people are actually searching for the proper spelling of a word, in which case you would reflect the changes in your keyword list.

- **Stop and filter words**—Filter words are words that search engines simply ignore during searches. Stop words are extremely common words that search engines use as triggers to stop grabbing content on a given page, such as "and," "a," and "the." Some search engines view stop words and filter words as the same thing, but you need to remember only one thing: search engines bypass these words to save time as these words are not considered to add any value to the search. It is best to try to avoid using stop words where possible in your keyword phrases. Following is a sample list of some of the more common stop words:

| | | | | | |
|---|---|---|---|---|---|
| a | aa | about | above | according | across |
| actually | ad | adj | ae | af | after |
| afterwards | ag | again | against | ai | al all |
| almost | alone | along | already | also | although |
| always | am | among | amongst | an | and |
| another | any | anyhow | anyone | anything | anywhere |
| ao | aq | ar | are | aren | aren't |

| | | | | | |
|---|---|---|---|---|---|
| around | arpa | as | at | au | aw |
| az | b | ba | bb | bd | be |
| became | because | become | becomes | becoming | been |
| before | beforehand | begin | beginning | behind | being |
| below | beside | besides | between | beyond | bf |
| bg | bh | bi | billion | bj | bm |
| bn | bo | both | br | bs | bt |
| but | buy | bv | bw | by | bz |
| c | ca | can | can't | cannot | caption |
| cc | cd | cf | cg | ch | ci |
| ck | cl | click | cm | cn | co |
| co. | com | copy | could | couldn | couldn't |
| cr | cs | cu | cv | cx | cy |
| cz | d | de | did | didn | didn't |
| dj | dk | dm | do | does | doesn |
| doesn't | don | don't | down | during | dz |
| e | each | ec | edu | ee | eg |
| eh | eight | eighty | either | else | elsewhere |
| end | ending | enough | er | es | et |
| etc | even | ever | every | everyone | everything |
| everywhere | except | f | few | fi | fifty |
| find | first | five | fj | fk | fm |
| fo | for | former | formerly | forty | found |
| four | fr | free | from | further | fx |
| g | ga | gb | gd | ge | get |
| gf | gg | gh | gi | gl | gm |
| gmt | gn | go | gov | gp | gq |
| gr | gs | gt | gu | gw | gy |
| h | had | has | hasn | hasn't | have |
| haven | haven't | he | he'd | he'll | he's |
| help | hence | her | here | here's | hereafter |
| hereby | herein | hereupon | hers | herself | him |
| himself | his | hk | hm | hn | home |
| homepage | how | however | hr | ht | htm |
| html | http | hu | hundred | i | i'd |
| i'll | i'm | i've | i.e. | id | ie |
| if | il | im | in | inc | inc. |
| indeed | information | instead | int | into | io |
| iq | ir | is | isn | isn't | it |
| it's | its | itself | j | je | jm |
| jo | join | jp | k | ke | kg |
| kh | ki | km | kn | kp | kr |

| | | | | | |
|---|---|---|---|---|---|
| kw | ky | kz | l | la | last |
| later | latter | lb | lc | least | less |
| let | let's | li | like | likely | lk |
| ll | lr | ls | lt | ltd | lu |
| lv | ly | m | ma | made | make |
| makes | many | maybe | mc | md | me |
| meantime | meanwhile | mg | mh | microsoft | might |
| mil | million | miss | mk | ml | mm |
| mn | mo | more | moreover | most | mostly |
| mp | mq | mr | mrs | ms | msie |
| mt | mu | much | must | mv | mwmx |
| my | myself | mz | n | na | namely |
| nc | ne | neither | net | netscape | never |
| nevertheless | new | next | nf | ng | ni |
| nine | ninety | nl | no | nobody | none |
| nonetheless | noone | nor | not | nothing | now |
| nowhere | np | nr | nu | nz | o |
| of | off | often | om | on | once |
| one | one's | only | onto | or | org |
| other | others | otherwise | our | ours | ourselves |
| out | over | overall | own | p | pa |
| page | pe | per | perhaps | pf | pg |
| ph | pk | pl | pm | pn | pr |
| pt | pw | py | q | qa | r |
| rather | re | recent | recently | reserved | ring |
| ro | ru | rw | s | sa | same |
| sb | sc | sd | se | seem | seemed |
| seeming | seems | seven | seventy | several | sg |
| sh | she | she'd | she'll | she's | should |
| shouldn | shouldn't | si | since | site | six |
| sixty | sj | sk | sl | sm | sn |
| so | some | somehow | someone | something | sometime |
| sometimes | somewhere | sr | st | still | stop |
| su | such | sv | sy | sz | t |
| taking | tc | td | ten | text | tf |
| tg | test | th | than | that | that'll |
| that's | the | their | them | themselves | then |
| thence | there | there'll | there's | thereafter | thereby |
| therefore | therein | thereupon | these | they | they'd |
| they'll | they're | they've | thirty | this | those |
| though | thousand | three | through | throughout | thru |
| thus | tj | tk | tm | tn | to |

| | | | | | |
|---|---|---|---|---|---|
| together | too | toward | towards | tp | tr |
| trillion | tt | tv | tw | twenty | two |
| tz | u | ua | ug | uk | um |
| under | unless | unlike | unlikely | until | up |
| upon | us | use | used | using | uy |
| uz | v | va | vc | ve | very |
| vg | vi | via | vn | vu | w |
| was | wasn | wasn't | we | we'd | we'll |
| we're | we've | web | webpage | website | welcome |
| well | were | weren | weren't | wf | what |
| what'll | what's | whatever | when | whence | whenever |
| where | whereafter | whereas | whereby | wherein | whereupon |
| wherever | whether | which | while | whither | who |
| who'd | who'll | who's | whoever | whole | whom |
| whomever | whose | why | will | with | within |
| without | won | won't | would | wouldn | wouldn't |
| ws | ww | wx | y | ye | yes |
| yet | you | you'd | you'll | you're | you've |
| your | yours | yourself | yourselves | yt | yu |
| z | za | zm | zr | | |

- **Modifiers**—A modifier is a keyword you add to your primary keyword phrase to give it a boost. Who simply searches for a hotel at random? It doesn't make sense. You look for a hotel in combination with a destination. In this case, the destination is the modifier. As a side note, local search is becoming increasingly popular, so if the local market plays a significant role in the success of your business, be sure to use geographic modifiers accordingly.

- **Multiple-word keyword phrases**—Two- or three-keyword phrases perform better than single keywords. According to OneStat.com (*http://www.onestat.com*), people tend to use two- and three-word phrases when performing a search online. Here is a list of the most popular number of words used in a search phrase:

  – two words—28.38%

  – three words—27.15%

  – four words—16.42%

– one word—13.48%

– five words—8.03%

– six words—3.67%

– seven words—1.36%

– eight words—0.73%

– nine words—0.34%

– ten words—0.16%

Not only are multiple keyword phrases used more often by searchers, but using them also enables you to be more descriptive in the modifiers to your keyword phrases.

## Assign Specific Keywords to Specific Pages

The next step is to allocate specific keywords to specific pages of your site for search engine optimization. You then populate each page in the appropriate places with the assigned keyword. You do this because you want to ensure that no matter which keyword or keyword phrase your target market decides to search on, one of the pages on your site is likely to rank in the first couple of pages of search results.

Many sites populate all their pages with the same keywords in the hopes that one of their pages will rank high in the search results. They use the same meta-tags for every page on their site. Again, this is the same as buying 100 tickets on the lottery but selecting the same numbers for every single ticket.

Some search engines rank sites by how early the keyword appears on the site. The earlier a keyword is mentioned on your site, the more points earned and the higher your site may be positioned in search results. And remember what was stressed earlier: though you don't want to repeat a keyword hundreds of times (some search engines are on to this), you do want to repeat the keywords assigned to that particular page a number of times on that page of your site.

When you have allocated your keywords to the various pages on your site, you will populate or include the keyword phrases assigned in the appropriate places for that particular page. Let's take a closer look at all those appropriate places.

## Title Tags—Use Descriptive Page Titles

It is extremely important that all Web pages have titles. Title tags are viewed as one of the most important elements of search engine optimization when it comes to keyword placement. Each of the pages on your Web site should be given a title.

The title is inserted between the title tags in the header of an HTML document. <HEAD> indicates the beginning of the header and the ending of the header is marked by </HEAD>. A simplified version might look like:

- <HTML>

- <HEAD>

- <TITLE>Document Title Here</TITLE>

- <META-NAME="keywords" CONTENT="keyword1, keyword2, keyword3">

- <META-NAME="description" CONTENT="200-character site description goes here">

- <META-NAME="robots" CONTENT="index, follow">

- <!—Comments tag, repeat description here>

- </HEAD>

Title tag information identifies and describes your pages. Titles tell readers where the information contained on a page originated. Most Web browsers display a document's title in the top line of the screen. When users print a page from your Web site, the title usually appears at the top of the page at the left. When someone bookmarks your site or adds it to their "Favorites," the title appears as the description in his or her bookmark file. These are all reasons that it is important that a page's title reflects an accurate description of the page. More importantly, the title tag is typically what the target market sees in search results in some of the major search engines. In Figure 2.3 you can see that a typical search result consists of the title tag as the link to the Web site, a brief description of the Web site, and the URL.

Every page of your Web site should have a unique title tag and each title tag should accurately describe the page content. Your target market should be able to read the title tag and understand what the page they are about to view contains.

**Figure 2.3.** Typical search result consisting of the title tag as the link to the Web site, a brief description of the Web site, and the URL.

Keep your title tags brief—in the realm of five to ten words. The longer your title tag is, the more diluted your keywords become and the more likely your title tag is to be truncated by a search engine. Google displays a maximum of 66 characters. Yahoo!Search, on the other hand, permits up to 120 characters for a title tag. Presently Google and Yahoo!Search are the two most important search engines; use their requirements as an approximation when designing your title tag.

My advice is to include your most important keyword phrases first, within Google's 66-character range. Overspill, or less important keywords, can run into the excess space Yahoo!Search allows. By including your most important keywords first, you secure their position for use by the search engines and for browser bookmarks.

The shorter and more accurate the title tag is, the higher the keyword density and relevancy for that title tag. Try to keep your use of a keyword phrase to a single instance if possible, unless the title tag truly warrants duplication. In the case of a hotel, the word *hotel* might appear twice in a title—once for the hotel's proper company name and once in a descriptive term such as a targeted geographic area.

Match the keywords you use in your meta-tags with the words you use in your page titles. Search engines check page titles, meta-tags, and page content for keywords. For certain keywords, your pages will be more relevant and, therefore, will place higher in the search engines if these keywords appear in each of these three sections. Position your keywords near the beginning of your page titles to increase your keyword relevancy.

Some of the search engines retrieve your page, look at your title, and then look at the rest of your page for keywords that match those found in the title. Many search engines use title tags as one of the elements in their algorithm to determine search engine ranking. Pages that have keywords in the title are seen as more relevant than similar pages on the same subject that don't, and may thus be ranked in a higher position by the search engines. However, don't make your title a string of keywords such as *Atlanta accommodations, Atlanta hotel cuisine, Atlanta hotels,* because this is often considered spam by the search engines and you end up worse off in the rankings or removed altogether. Also keep in mind that people will see that title in the search results, and they're more likely to click on a site that has a title that flows and is descriptive—not a list.

## Keywords Meta-Tag

As we noted earlier in this chapter, a common problem faced by Internet marketers is how to influence search engines to index their site appropriately and how to ensure that their site appears when people use relevant search criteria.

Retaining a certain measure of control over how search engines deal with your Web site is a major concern. Often Web sites do not take advantage of the techniques available to them to influence search engine listings. Most search engines evaluate the HTML meta-tags in conjunction with other variables to decide where to index Web pages based on particular keyword queries.

Although in recent years fewer points have been allocated to content in the keywords meta-tags, it is important to keep your eyes on the total score—if there are any points at all allocated to this element, you want them all. As we've already mentioned, the site with the highest total score appears at the top of the search results, so you are going after every point you can get.

The Web Developer's Virtual Library defines an HTML meta-tag as follows:

The META element is used within the HEAD element to embed document meta-information not defined by other HTML elements. The META element can be used to identify properties of a document (e.g., author, expiration date, a list of keywords, etc.) and assign values to those properties.

An HTML tag is used in the HEAD area of a document to specify further information about the document, either for the local server or for a remote browser. The meta-element is used within the HEAD element to embed document meta-information not defined by other HTML elements. Such information can be extracted by servers/clients for use in identifying, indexing, and cataloging specialized document meta-information. In addition, HTTP servers can read the contents of the document HEAD to generate response headers corresponding to any elements defining a value for the attribute HTTP-EQUIV. This provides document authors with a mechanism for identifying information that should be included in the response headers of an HTTP request.

To summarize this lengthy definition, meta-information can be used in identifying, indexing, and cataloging. This means you can use these tags to guide the search engines in displaying your site as the result of a query. There are many meta-tags, including:

- Abstract

- Author

- Copyright

- Description

- Expires

- Keywords

- Language

- Refresh

- Revisit

- Robots.

Most of the above meta-tags are not useful for optimization purposes. The most recognized meta-tag is the keywords meta-tag.

<META-NAME="keywords" CONTENT="..."> tells search engines under which keywords to index your site. When a user types one of the words you listed here, your site should be displayed as a result. A space or comma can be used to separate the words. Do not repeat the keyword frequently; rather, repeat the keyword about five times in different phrases. You do have the option of using more than 1,000 characters in your keywords meta-tag, but be wary of keyword dilution. You should create a unique keywords tag for each page of your site that lists the appropriate keywords for that particular page.

## Description Meta-Tag

<META-NAME="description" CONTENT="..."> should be included on every page of your Web site. The description meta-tag is used to supply an accurate overview of the page to which it is attached. The description meta-tags can influence the description in the search engines that support them.

It is best to keep the description meta-tag to somewhere in the realm of 200 to 250 characters in total. Be sure to use the same keywords applied elsewhere on the page being optimized in the description meta-tag for consistency and relevancy; however, do not duplicate your title tag in your description meta-tag, or you may run the risk of being accused of keyword stacking. Also, it helps to include a call to action encouraging the target market to visit your Web site or take some other action.

## Alt Tags

Some search engines use the information within Alt tags when forming a description and determining the ranking for your site. Alt tags are used to display a description of the graphic they are associated with if the graphic cannot be displayed, such as in text-only browsers. Alt tags appear after an image tag and contain a phrase that is associated with the image.

Ensure that your Alt tags contain the keywords assigned to the particular page wherever you can. This gives your page a better chance of being ranked higher in the search engines. For example:

<image src="images/logo.gif" height="50" width ="50" alt="Best Western Hotel Orlando">

You do not want your Alt tags to look something like "Best Western" or "Company Logo" because this does not include any keywords. Be sure you apply proper Alt tags to all images on your site to achieve best results. Keep in mind that users who browse with graphics disabled must be able to navigate your site, and proper use of Alt tags assists them in doing so.

## Hypertext Links

A hypertext link consists of the description of a link placed in between anchor tags. Here is an example of an absolute link, where the link includes the total path to where the document can be found:

<a href="http://www.DomainName.com/HotelOrlando">. This is the anchor text for the sample link </A>.

The text inside a hyperlink, or anchor text, is increasingly important for search engine optimization. The major search engines have points available for including the keyword phrase being searched on in the text around the link pointing to your Web site. There is a strong relevancy pattern.

Good places to use links include the primary and sub-navigation aspects of a Web site, as well as links to external resources from within the page copy. Likewise, if links on other Web sites pointing to your Web site include the same string of keywords, your site's relevancy gets a boost. When you encourage other Web sites to link to yours, be sure to provide them with the link text they should use and make sure you get the keyword phrase you have assigned to that particular page in the text around the link. Similarly, when you submit your Web site to directories and other link sources, provide the comparable link or title text.

## Domain Name and File Names

Use of keywords within your domain name and file names can help with search engine positioning. Some professionals argue that including dashes to separate keywords makes it easier for search engines to distinguish keywords, which can help boost your rankings. Personal experience leads me to believe that if it actually does make a difference, the difference is so small that you are better off spending your time optimizing your Web site in areas that really count. This also applies to file names.

Examples of domain names are:

1. www.thisisadomainname.com

2. www.this-is-also-a-domain-name.com.

Examples of file names are:

1. www.thisisadomainname.com/samplepage.html

2. www.thisisadomainname.com/samples-page.html.

It does not take much effort to give your images and file names meaningful names—names that include the keyword phrase you have assigned to that page—so take the time to do it. For example, instead of the MGM Grand Hotel and

Casino in Las Vegas, NV using *http://wwwmgmgrand.com/index.html* for a page that is focusing on its restaurants, it would be much better to use *http://www.mgmgrand.com/lasvegasshows.*

### Body Text—Header Tags and Page Copy

The body text of a Web page consists of all the visible text between the <body> and </body> tag, such as headings and the page copy encased in paragraphs. Along with page titles, body text is the next important area on which to focus your search engine optimization efforts. Body text is where you want to spend the bulk of your time.

#### Headings—<H1>Header Tags</H1>

Use your HTML <H1> header tags effectively to indicate the subject and content of a particular page. Most people use them only as a method of creating large fonts. Some search engines, including Google, use the content included within the header text in their relevancy scoring. The H1 tag is the most important, followed by H2. Include your most important keywords in your header tags. If you can, work a couple of H2 tags into your page and get the keyword phrase you've assigned to that page within the header tag.

#### Page Copy

You want to ensure that the keyword you have assigned to a specific page appears in the first 200 characters on that page and as close to the beginning as possible. The higher up on a page, the greater the keyword prominence. Search engines tend to lend more weight to page content above the fold. The fold is where your browser window ends and where vertical scrolling begins, if necessary.

The assigned keyword should appear at the beginning of the text on the page, in the middle, and again at the end. You want to build a theme on your page, and to do so you have to spread your keywords throughout the page, not just focus on the first paragraph.

Always have a descriptive paragraph at the top of your Web page that describes what can be found on the page for your target market and for the major search engines. Search engines use this as their source for a site description and keywords on your site. In addition, search engines use the content found within the opening paragraph in influencing the ranking of your site among search results. Again, be sure to use the most important keywords first, preferably within the first two or three sentences. This is enormously important. Make sure that the keywords you use flow naturally within the content of the opening paragraph and relate to the content and purpose of your site. You don't want the search engines to think you're trying to cram in words where they don't fit.

As you can tell, textual HTML content is extremely important to the search engines, which brings me to my next point. Never create a page with excessive graphics as content. For example, don't display information that should be displayed in text as a graphic file. I've seen this done numerous times. A site may have the best opening statement in the world, but the search engines can't use it because the information is presented in the form of a graphic. No matter how great it looks, the search engines can't read text embedded in your graphics for content. Very often I see a site that has the company name used every time in a graphic logo. If someone were to do a search on the company name, they may not earn enough points to score on the first page of results.

Do not make your home page excessively lengthy. The longer your page is, the less relevant the information on the page becomes to the search engines. I recommend that you keep your home page short and to the point. A page consisting of between 250 and 800 words provides the major search engines with the information they need.

Little things such as how often you update your site can have an effect on how well your site places in search engine results. Spiders can determine how often a page is updated and will revisit your site accordingly. This may lead to higher rankings in some of the major search engines. Fresh content is good for your target market and for search engine rankings. After all, who wants to view stale content?

As a final note, before you submit your site, be sure the content on the page you are submitting is complete. Some of the major search engines will ignore your submission if you have an "under construction" or similar sign on your page.

Do not get too muddled down in the science of search engine optimization. No two search engines' formulas or algorithms are identical, so if you spend all of your time tailoring your site for just one engine, you may have many missed opportunities on your hands. You generally will do just fine if your application of relevant keywords is related to your page at hand, tied together with the different optimization elements that make-up a Web page, and is used consistently and creatively enough to build a theme. A tool such as Web Position (*http://www.webposition.com*) can assist you in analyzing your pages for keyword density and relevancy.

Keyword density is the number of times a keyword, or keyword phrase, is used on a Web page, divided by the total number of words on that particular page. Your keyword density should be between 3 and 11 percent. If your keyword density is below 3 percent, it is not there often enough to count. If your keyword density is above 11 percent, it may appear as if you are attempting to manipulate the search engines.

## Spamming

Search engines want to provide the most accurate and complete search results they can to their target market. After all, this is what drives all aspects of their business model. If people have no faith in a search engine, the traffic dries up and the sponsored listing fees as well as other advertising fees cease to exist.

In the olden days, Internet marketers used various techniques to trick the search engines into positioning their sites higher in search results. These tricks do not work with the search engines today, and if it is discovered that you are trying to dupe the search engines, some may not list you at all. Search engines are programmed to detect some of these techniques, and you will be penalized in some way if you are discovered. A few of the search engine tricks that used to work—BUT DO NOT WORK TODAY, SO DON'T USE THEM—pertaining to Web site design are included below. I include them so you can go back to look at your site to see if they have been used on your site, and if they are, this is probably the reason you are having difficulty with search engine placement.

- **Repeating keywords**—Some Web sites repeat the same keywords over and over again, by hiding them in the visible HTML, in invisible layers such as the <NOFRAMES> tag, and in meta-tags. Repeating keywords over and over again by displaying them at the bottom of your document after a number of line breaks counts as well! For example:

  - . . . cabins, cabins, cabins, cabins, rental cabins, cabins, cabins, forest cabins, lakeside cabins, cabins, cabins, cabins, cabins. . .

- **Keyword stacking**—It is quite obvious when a site is using this ill-fated technique. Its not so obvious cousin is called keyword stuffing, which is when you exercise the same stacking techniques on aspects of the Web site that should not be optimized, such as spacer images. A spacer image is used by Web developers for just that—properly spacing items on a page. It is not good practice to include descriptive text in an Alt tag for a spacer image.

- **Jamming keywords**—If you are displaying keywords on your Web pages using a very small font, then you are jamming keywords. Why would you even do this unless you were specifically trying to manipulate search results? Don't do it. This spam technique is called "tiny text."

- **Hidden text and links**—Avoid inserting hidden text and links in your Web site for the purpose of getting in more keywords. For example, you can hide keywords in your HTML document by making the text color the same as the background color. Another example is inserting keywords in areas not visible to the end user, such as the hidden layers in style sheets.

- **Misleading title changes**—Making frequent and regular title changes so that the bots think your site is a new site and list you again and again is misleading. In the case of directories, you could change the name of your site just by adding a space, an exclamation mark (!), or "A" as the first character so that you come up first in alphabetical lists.

- **Page swapping**—This practice involves showing one page to a search engine, but a different one to the end user. Quite often you find people hijack content from a top-ranking site, insert it on their page to achieve a top ranking, then replace that page with a completely different page when a desired ranking is achieved.

- **Content duplication**—Say you have one Web page and it is ranking pretty well. You decide it would be nice to improve your ranking, but hey, it would be good to keep your current position too. You decide to duplicate your page, fine-tune a few things, and call it something different. You then submit that page to the search engine. Your ranking improved and now you have two listings. Not bad! Why not do it again? And so on and so forth. If you are caught duplicating Web pages, you will be penalized. Search engines want to provide unique content, not the same page over and over again.

- **Domain spam (mirrored sites)**—Closely related to content duplication, this is when an entire Web site is replicated (or slightly modified) and placed at a different URL. This is usually done to dominate search positions and to boost link popularity, but in the end all it does it hurt you when you get caught. You will get banned for practicing this technique.

- **Refresh meta-tag**—Have you ever visited a site and then been automatically transported to another page within the site? This is the result of a refresh meta-tag. This tag is an HTML document that is designed to automatically replace itself with another HTML document after a cer-

## Refresh Meta-tag
A tag used to automatically reload or load a new page.

tain specified period of time, as defined by the document author—it's like automatic page swapping. Do not abuse this tag. Additionally, don't use a redirect unless it is absolutely necessary. A permanent redirect (HTTP 301) can be used to tell the search engines that the page they are looking for has a new home; this tells them to go there to index it.

If you do use a refresh meta-tag to redirect users, then it is suggested that you set a delay of at least 15 seconds and provide a link on the new page back to the page they were taken from. Some businesses use refresh meta-tags to redirect users from a page that is obsolete or is no longer there. Refresh meta-tags also may be used to give an automated slideshow or force a sequence of events as part of a design element.

- **Cloaking**—This technique is similar to page swapping and using the refresh meta-tag in that the intent is to serve search engines one page while the end user is served another. Don't do it.

- **Doorway pages**—Also known as gateway pages and bridge pages, doorway pages are pages that lead to your site but are not considered part of your site. Doorway pages lead to your Web site but are tuned to the specific requirements of the search engines. By having different doorway pages with different names (e.g., indexy.html for Yahoo! or indexg.html for Google) for each search engine, you can optimize pages for individual engines.

Unfortunately, because of the need to be ranked high in search engine results and the enormous competition among sites that are trying to get such high listings, doorway pages have increasingly become more popular. Each search engine is different and has different elements in its ranking criteria. You can see the appeal of doorway pages because this allows you to tailor a page specifically for each search engine and thus achieve optimal results.

Search engines frown upon the use of doorway pages because the intent is obvious—to manipulate rankings in one site's favor with no regard for quality content. Do not use them.

- **Cyber-squatting**—This term refers to stealing traffic from legitimate Web sites. If someone were to operate a Web site called "Gooogle.com" with the extra "o" or "Yahhoo" with an extra "h," that would be considered cyber-squatting. Domain squatting is when a company acquires the familiar domain of another company, either because the domain expired or the original company no longer exists. The new company then uses the familiar domain to promote completely unrelated content. Google, in particular, frowns on cyber-squatting.

- **Links farms**—These are irrelevant linking schemes to boost rankings based on achieving better link popularity. Having thousands of irrelevant links pointing to your Web site does more damage than good. The search engines are on to this technique and they don't like sites that try to manipulate placement. For best results, only pursue links that relate to your Web site and are of interest to your target market.

How do you know if you are spamming a search engine? If the technique you are employing on your Web site does not offer value to your end user and is done solely for the intention of boosting your search engine rankings, then you are probably guilty of spam.

Search engines post guidelines for what they consider acceptable practices. It is advised that you read each search engine's policy to ensure that you conform to their guidelines. Following is Google's policy (*http://www.google.com/ webmasters/guidelines.html*) on quality:

## Quality Guidelines—Basic Principles

- Make pages for users, not for search engines. Don't deceive your users, or present different content to search engines than you display to users.

- Avoid tricks intended to improve search engine rankings. A good rule of thumb is whether you'd feel comfortable explaining what you've done to a Web site that competes with you. Another useful test is to ask, "Does this help my users? Would I do this if search engines didn't exist?"

- Don't participate in link schemes designed to increase your site's ranking or PageRank. In particular, avoid links to Web spammers or "bad neighborhoods" on the Web as your own ranking may be affected adversely by those links.

- Don't use unauthorized computer programs to submit pages, check rankings, etc. Such programs consume computing resources and violate our terms of service. Google does not recommend the use of products such as WebPosition Gold that send automatic or programmatic queries or submissions to Google. WebPosition is a great software program to monitor your positioning and has great tools to tweak your search engine optimization—just don't use these types of tools for submission. Both Yahoo! and Google have implemented dynamic characters that must be replicated in the submission form. These dynamic characters are embedded in a graphic and software programs, such as WebPosition, are unable to read the text and input the code.

See Chapter 8 for more on search engine and directory submission.

## Quality Guidelines—Specific Recommendations

- Avoid hidden text or hidden links.

- Don't employ cloaking or sneaky redirects.

- Don't send automated queries to Google.

- Don't load pages with irrelevant words.

- Don't create multiple pages, subdomains, or domains with substantially duplicate content.

- Avoid "doorway" pages created just for search engines or other "cookie cutter" approaches such as affiliate programs with little or no original content.

These quality guidelines cover the most common forms of deceptive or manipulative behavior, but Google may respond negatively to other misleading practices not listed here (for example, tricking users by registering misspellings of well-known Web sites). It's not safe to assume that just because a specific deceptive technique isn't included on this page, Google approves of it. Webmasters who spend their energies upholding the spirit of the basic principles listed above will provide a much better user experience and subsequently enjoy better ranking than those who spend their time looking for loopholes they can exploit.

If your Web site is mistakenly penalized for spam, your best course of action is to contact the search engine and discuss remedies. If you are applying a technique that is considered spam, get rid of it. Know what is considered search engine spam and avoid it before it ever becomes a problem for you.

## Other Important Design Factors

It is not always possible to have a Web site that meets all requirements of a search engine and your target market. Perhaps you are coming in on the tail end of a Web development project or simply want to make your Web site as search engine friendly as possible, without having to do a significant redesign. Here are some common issues and how you should deal with them to improve the search engine friendliness of your Web site, whether you are building a new site or are improving your current one:

- Frames

- Robots.txt, meta-robots tag

- Clean code is king

- Navigation techniques

- Revisit meta-tag

- Cascading style sheets

- Dynamic pages and special characters

- Splash pages and the use of rich media

- Use of tables

- Custom error pages

- Image maps

- Optimization for search localization.

## Frames

From a marketing perspective, you should avoid building a Web site entirely based on **frames** when you develop your Web site. This is probably the most recognized hurdle when it comes to search engine optimization.

## Frames
The division of a browser's display area into two or more independent areas.

Frames may result in some search engines being unable to index pages within your site, or they can result in improper pages being indexed. Also, many people simply prefer sites that do not use frames. Frames also cause problems when someone wants to bookmark or add to their favorites a particular page within a framed site. Usually only the home page address is shown.

What I mean by "improper pages being indexed" is that content pages will be indexed, and when the search engines direct users to these content pages, they will likely not be able to navigate your site because the navigation frame probably will not be visible. To prevent this one technique from being used, you can insert a robots meta-tag in the header section of your HTML that does not allow bots to proceed beyond your home page. As a result, you can really submit only your home page, which means you have less of a chance of receiving the high rankings you need on the major search engines. Alternatively, you should include textual links to all major sections within your site to accommodate those users who enter your site on a page other than a home page, and to assist the search engines with indexing your site.

Some search engines can read only information between the <NOFRAMES> tags within your master frame. The master frame identifies the other frames. All too often the individuals who apply frames ignore the <NOFRAMES> tags, which is a big no-no. If you do not have any text between the <NOFRAMES> tags, then the search engines that reference your site for information have nothing to look at. This results in your site being listed with little or no information in the indexes, or you are listed so far down in the rankings that no one will ever find you anyway. To remedy this situation, insert textual information containing your most important descriptive keywords between the <NOFRAMES> tags. This gives the search engines something they can see, and it also helps those users who are using browsers that are not frame-compatible.

Now that the search engines have found you, you still have a problem. They can't go anywhere. Create a link within your <NOFRAMES> tags to allow search engines and users with browsers that aren't frame-compatible to get into your site. Frames are a headache when you are designing your site to be search engine friendly. To make your life easier and from a marketing perspective, it's better to avoid them altogether.

## Robots.txt, Meta-Robots Tag

<META-NAME="robots" CONTENT=" "> tells certain bots to follow or not follow hypertext links. The W3 Consortium white paper on spidering (spiders are defined below) offers the following definition and discussion:

- <META-NAME="ROBOTS" CONTENT="ALL | NONE | NOINDEX | NOFOLLOW">

- default = empty = "ALL" "NONE" = "NOINDEX, NOFOLLOW"

- The filler is a comma-separated list of terms:

  - ALL, NONE, INDEX, NOINDEX, FOLLOW, NOFOLLOW.

Note: This tag is for users who cannot control the robots.txt file at their sites. It provides a last chance to keep their content out of search services. It was decided not to add syntax to allow robot-specific permissions within the meta-tag. INDEX means that robots are welcome to include this page in search services.

FOLLOW means that robots are welcome to follow links from this page to find other pages. A value of NOFOLLOW allows the page to be indexed, but no links from the page are explored. (This may be useful if the page is a free entry point into pay-per-view content, for example. A value of NONE tells the robot to ignore the page.)

The values of INDEX and FOLLOW should be added to every page unless there is a specific reason that you do not want your page to be indexed. This may be the case if the page is only temporary.

## Clean Code Is King

Clean code is essential to search engine success. You want to ensure that you do not have stray tags, HTML errors, or bloated code. Problematic code is bad for the user experience and bad for search engine placement.

## Navigation Techniques

JavaScript embedded in anchor tags, drop-down menus, and pull-down menus can cause many headaches for a Web site looking to be indexed by the major search engines. The rollover effect on navigation links is quite common and can add visual appeal to a Web site. A problem arises when JavaScript is encased within the anchor tag, which can cause problems for the search engines.

The rollovers look good, so odds are that if your site is using them you are not going to want to get rid of them. A quick and simple solution to ensure that your site is indexed is to include text-based navigation along the bottom of your Web page as supportive navigation. This approach also gives you the opportunity to get in your keywords twice—once in the Alt tag for your main navigation and the second time around the anchor tag for the supportive text links. In addition, it is to your benefit to include all your JavaScript material in external files to keep the Web site code as clean as possible.

Drop-down menus (DHTML, for example) and pull-down menus pose similar concerns because of the coding script necessary for them to execute. If you choose to use them, be sure to have an alternative means of navigation available.

### Revisit Meta-Tag

You cannot tell a search engine when to visit your Web site, though the theory behind the revisit meta-tag is that you can define how often you want a search engine to come back to your Web site. Use the revisit meta-tag if you like, but it is not needed.

### Cascading Style Sheets (CSS)

CSS is common practice in the Web development world. It gives developers more control over how they want their Web page to be laid out, plus it requires less coding. Less coding means less room for error and better site performance. Like JavaScript, CCS benefits from being stored in external files as opposed to being embedded in each page's individual source code.

### Dynamic Pages and Special Characters

Dynamic content has historically caused many problems for search engines because they do not like to be fed duplicate content and the query strings can cause spiders confusion. Times are getting better, but these elements can still cause some difficulties.

Dynamically driven content typically has a query string in the URL such as question marks (?), an ampersand (&), or the percent sign (%). The lengthy URL contains a number of calls to database information and to a template to put together the Web page you see in your browsers. Search engines struggle to figure out what exactly they are supposed to index because they have difficulty understanding what information is actually meaningful and how to present it.

There is no question that dynamically driven sites are common. Your challenge is to work around the needs of the search engines and include pure HTML-based information pages that the search engines can index as a standard part of your Web site. Likewise, there are methods of reducing the complexity of URLs into a form the search engines can process—Amazon.com has been very successful at this. Amazon.com has eliminated all stop symbols from its page URLs.

Depending on the technology used to create your Web site (such as ASP, CFP, or PHP), tools exist to help you rewrite your URLs at the server level to make them more friendly for search engine indexing. This is the same logic applied behind services such as *http://www.tinyurl.com.*

## Splash Pages and the Use of Rich Media

A splash page is basically an opening page that leads into a site. Often splash pages consist of a Java or a Macromedia Flash intro that can be slow to load for some users and contain little meaningful content for search engines.

Some Web sites use splash screens that consist of an eye-pleasing image and an invitation to enter the site. Many splash pages implement techniques that automatically send you to the home page once you've seen the splash page, and others invite you to "Click here to enter" in some form or another. Why do people use splash pages on their sites? For one, they usually look nice. Another reason is to provide the user with something to look at while images or content for the home page loads in the background. Individuals also use splash pages as a means of advertising. Splash pages are usually very attractive in appearance, but they often lack content relevant to search engines.

If you do use a splash page on your site, be sure you include the proper meta-tags within your HTML header. This is necessary for search engines that use meta-tags to access this information. This ultimately affects your ranking and how your site is displayed to users in the search results.

Include a paragraph or statement on your splash page that pertains to your site's content. This can help boost your rankings on some of the major search engines that both do and do not use meta-tags. Some search engines will review your opening paragraph and use this information when developing a description for your site that is presented in their search results.

Lastly, include a link into your Web site for the target market and the search engines. Many splash pages implement the refresh meta-tag, and this should be avoided.

## Use of Tables

**Tables** can pose indexing problems with some of the search engines. Tables are a common feature found on many Web sites to display information and position content, but if implemented incorrectly, they can cause the search engines some confusion. Also, by using tables close to the top of a page, you are potentially forcing

**Tables**
Information arranged in columns and rows.

the content you want search engines to see farther down on your page. Because some search engines look only so far, you might be hurting your chances of receiving a high ranking. If you are using tables, place any important information pertaining to the page content above the table, if possible, to help prevent any potential problems.

Here's an interesting problem with some search engines. Assume you have a Web site where the main color of the background is white, and you have a table on the page with a dark background. If you were to use white text in the table, some of the major search engines would pick this up as you using text that is the same color as the background and ignore your site's submission because it is considered spam to search engines. Using tables is okay—many people do it—just be careful with your choice of colors.

## Custom Error Pages

A custom 404 error (page not found) page should be created for your Web site. This page is displayed when a user attempts to access a page that does not exist. The custom error page should contain your company's branding and contain links to all major pages of your Web site, similar to the site map.

If you redesign or rework your Web site, then odds are pages are going to get moved or no longer exist. It is possible that people have pages of the old Web site bookmarked and those pages may no longer be a part of the new Web site. Also, search engines index select pages of the current Web site, and those pages may also no longer exist under the new design. The custom error page allows people and search engines to easily make updates to their references.

## Image Maps

Image maps are single graphics that are split into "hot spots" or sensitive areas that when clicked lead you to different pages or resources within the Web site. The problem with image maps is they basically lock search engines out and prevent them from indexing your Web site properly.

If you do decide to implement image maps, always include text hyperlinks so that the search engines trying to give you a more accurate index can use them. Another option is to include a site map, which is basically the entire layout of your Web site in the form of hypertext links. Submitting your site map to the search engines is also a good idea as it can assist the search engine in making sure it indexes all the pages within your Web site.

## Optimization for Search Localization

A recent study by comScore Networks (*http://www.comscore.com*) discovered that 60 percent of consumers search for local content. Much of the local searches surround such topics as restaurants, travel, hotels, and car rentals. With the introduction of Google Local, optimizing your site for local searches has become important.

Search localization is simply when searchers put in their keyword phrase and hit the Local tab while searching on Google, or when they simply add a geographic modifier to their query in any search engine in order to get more accurate results from a search engine. If you want to go out to dinner, then odds are you're going to want to go to some place in your area. Common modifiers include:

- ZIP or postal code

- Street

- City or town, along with descriptive words such as "Northern," "Central," "East," "West," and "Southern"

- State or province, entirely spelled out as well as the abbreviation

- Country, entirely spelled out as well as the abbreviation

- Area code and phone number

- Recognizable landmarks and destinations (such as, right next door to ...).

Search localization presents a good opportunity for companies optimizing their Web site. Naturally, any company looking to speak to a local market should be considering search localization when optimizing its Web site.

Optimizing your Web site to speak to the local market is no different from regular search optimization; it just requires a bit of creativity. The same optimization areas, such as page titles, page copy, and meta-tags, are relevant to search localization. Here are some examples to get you started:

- Include geographic keywords in page headers and footers. For example, you can insert a copyright notice at the bottom of each page of your Web site that includes your location: "© 2008, Prince George Hotel, a Centennial Hotels Property. 1725 Market Street in downtown Halifax,

Nova Scotia B3J 3R9. Hotel Reservations 1-800-565-1567 • tel 902-425-1986 • fax 902-429-6048."

- Include geographic-related keywords in your page titles. Instead of Fine Italian Dining—il Mercato Restaurant, you could have Fine Italian Dining in Downtown Halifax—il Mercato Restaurant.

- Include geographic-related keywords in your page copy. For example, a paragraph can include a statement such as "Come visit us on the Halifax waterfront, right next door to Historic Properties" to capture high-profile local destinations. You could also have "Just south of Halifax in Peggy's Cove" or "Ten minutes from Halifax." In this case you are adding a modifier to include a nearby city to capitalize on a market that might not think to look for your exact location.

- Include comprehensive geographic-related information throughout your Web site, on your contact page, maps and directions page, and in your Frequently Asked Questions (FAQs).

- Pay-to-play or PPC is covered in another chapter, but you can use the same geographic modifiers in your paid search placement campaigns to zero in on local markets and increase your return on investment. Yahoo!, Google, SuperPages.com, Findwhat.com and AskJeeves are all examples of search providers that offer some means of search localization.

- Add your GPS coordinates to your site as well. With more and more mobile devices equipped with GPS, as well as the likelihood that the search engines will include this information in their search query, this will become standard practice. I know that we at Verb Interactive are incorporating this information in most of our client sites these days.

## Monitoring Results

As with any business endeavor, you want to know how successful you are. There are a number of ways to measure your search engine placement success.

*Web site traffic analysis*—You can check the effectiveness of your keyword placement and utilization by using Web traffic analysis reports. This is discussed fully in Chapter 28. You can use Web traffic analysis reports to determine what sites are referring people to you and how often the search engine spiders are visiting your Web site looking for new content. You can strip down this information further to view only search engine referrals. By looking at this information, you can also see exactly what keywords people are using to find you and you can alter the keywords used based on this information. Refining your keywords is one of the key elements to success—you're letting the search engines tell you what you're doing right and what you could be doing better.

Early in the chapter we looked at how Web traffic analysis can contribute to your master keyword list. The amount of targeted traffic and the return on investment (ROI) achieved through your optimization efforts are the true measures of success. How much business you generate online ultimately depends on how well constructed your Web site is. Just because you perform well in the search rankings does not mean the target market automatically does business with you. Once the target market reaches your Web site, it is up to your Web site to sell your business.

Also look at entry pages and paths through your Web site. Because you optimized specific pages for specific keywords, people should be entering your Web site on those pages. If the page is designed to meet the needs of your target market, it should push them deeper into the Web site or to a point where a transaction takes place, which you can monitor by looking at paths through your Web site and entry pages. For example, say you created a Web page to address a particular special at a hotel with a goal of having the target market fill out a reservation request form. If the specials page is performing well in the engines, but people are staying on the page only a few seconds and are then leaving the Web site, you know it is the page itself that is not performing. Odds are the copy and images do not have the right appeal to the target market, so you can tweak it. The page may not require a complete redesign—it could be that the call to action to fill out the reservation form is not obvious, so make minor changes and monitor performance.

*Search engine rankings*—You can check the performance of your Web site for a particular keyword phrase by hand or through the use of an application such as WebPosition (*http://www.webposition.com*). If you are checking your results by hand, then you simply need to go to the search engine in which you're interested, enter your keyword phrases, and observe where your Web site ranks. You can hire someone to do this for you as well. Using an application to check your rankings allows you to check more rankings faster by automating the process. Search engines tend to frown on this because of the added stress it puts on their system when you have many people using these automated packages to run many searches.

Checking your search rankings tells you how well your Web site is ranking for particular keyword phrases. You can use this information to keep your rankings current and target your optimization efforts toward gaining increased ratings on any particular engines you wish.

*Paid inclusion accounts*—The search engines that have paid inclusion features usually give the customer the means to track some search information. This includes basic information such as the keywords searched for and the number of referrals the search engine sent through to the destination Web site.

*Pay-to-play accounts*—At the heart of all pay-to-play campaigns (PPC) is the tracking functionality. You are paying for each and every click, so it is important to know which search terms are working and which are not. One of the most well known pay-to-play providers is Yahoo! Search Marketing. When you sign up with Yahoo! Search Marketing, you can track all aspects of your campaign, including conversion rates, click-throughs, and revenue generated.

## Internet Resources for Chapter 2

I have developed a great library of online resources for you to check out regarding designing your site to be search engine friendly. This library is available on my Tourism Internet Marketing University Web site *http://www.TourismInternetMarketingU.com/max* in the Resources section where you can find additional tips, tools, techniques, and resources.

I have also developed courses on many of the topics covered in this book. These courses are also available on my Tourism Internet Marketing University Web site *http://www.TourismInternetMarketingU.com/max*. These courses are delivered immediately over the Internet or can be ordered as a CD.

# 3

# Web Site Elements That Keep 'Em Coming Back

There are many little things that will spice up your Web site to "keep 'em coming back." Learn the tips, tools, and techniques to get visitors to return to your site again and again. In this chapter, we cover:

- Attractive Web site content

- How to have your own What's New page, Tip of the Day, and Awards page

- Ensuring that you are bookmarked

- Trivia

- Contests

- Calendar of events and reminder services

- Blogs, podcasts, and RSS feeds

- Special guests or celebrity appearances

- Giveaways and awards

- Offline tactics for promotion.

## Rationale for Encouraging Repeat Visits

Just as you would want customers to visit your tourism operation, or your destination frequently, so too in cyberspace you want present and potential customers to visit often. The more often people visit your site, the more likely they are to purchase something or make a reservation. You want to ensure that the techniques you use to get repeat traffic are appropriate for your target market. For example, if you were having a contest on your site targeted toward children, you would not want to give away a bread-maker as the prize. That would be fine, however, if your target market was families or homemakers. You want to offer something of interest to the market you are targeting. If your target market is skiers, then a weekend in Vail, or your destination, might work.

I am a big proponent of leveraging everything you do for maximum marketing results. Almost every repeat traffic generator provides an opportunity for permission marketing and also for viral marketing. Make sure you review the repeat traffic generators you use on your site and incorporate the appropriate permission and viral marketing elements.

The more often a person visits your site:

- The more your brand is reinforced

- The more your target market feels a part of your community, and people do business with people they know and trust

- The more likely they are to give you permission to stay in touch

- The more likely they are to tell others about you, your packages, and your destination

- The more likely you will be first in mind when they go to buy or make a reservation.

## Use a What's New Page for Repeat Visits

A What's New page can mean different things to different sites. For some, this page updates users with summaries of the most recent travel packages, specials, or promotions. Of course your What's New page could also include any awards you or your company have received and new additions to your Web site, such as a package builder, or news and events. Your What's New page should be accessible from your home page so that when people visit your site they do not have to search through your entire site to find out what is new. If visitors repeatedly find interesting additions in the What's New section, they will come back to your site on a regular basis to check out what's new. Here you can leverage this repeat-traffic generator with permission marketing by asking if visitors would like to be notified via e-mail when you've added something to the What's New section. It's all about getting their permission to send them e-mail and therefore include them in your community.

Other approaches for the What's New page could be What's New on your site, What's New in your company or What's New in your location. Whatever it is, you should always make sure that it is of interest to your target market. Again, you can ask your visitors if they would like to be notified when updates are made to this section of your Web site. This, once again, gives you permission to e-mail them and present them with new information that might make them want to come back to your site again.

## Free Stuff—Everyone Loves It

Offering free things is a great way to increase traffic—everybody likes a freebie. If you provide something for free that is valuable to your target market you are sure to have a steady stream of repeat traffic. When you have freebies or give-aways on your site, your pages can also be listed and linked from the many sites on the Internet that list places where people can receive free stuff. To find these listings of free stuff, simply go to a search engine and do a search on "Free Stuff Index" or "Free Stuff Links." You will be amazed at how many people are giving things away online.

You don't have to give something away to everyone. You could simply have a drawing every week. You could then ask entrants if they would like you to notify them of the winner, which again, gives you permission to e-mail them.

To get people into your restaurant you could offer a free dessert with an entrée coupon. To get a number of people to visit your attraction you might have a buy three, get one free coupon. You might also have a free gift upon arrival for a hotel or a cruise.

You should change your freebie often and let your site visitors know how often you do this. Something like, "We change our free offer every single week! Keep checking back," or "Click here to be notified by e-mail when we update," also works well.

Freebies provide ideal viral marketing opportunities as well. Have a "Tell a friend about this" button near the freebie so site visitors can quickly and easily tell their friends.

## Everyone Wants the Best Price—Coupons and Discounts

Offer coupons and discount vouchers that can be printed from your site. By partnering with non-competing travel and tourism businesses, such as luggage or appropriate clothing stores, and offering their coupons to your visitors you can get people to come back to your site again and again. You can change the coupon daily or weekly to encourage repeat visits. People will come back to your site again and again if they know they can find good deals there. You can ask people if they want to be notified by e-mail when you update the coupons on your Web site. This once again gives you the opportunity to present them with new information about your business. Offering coupons is a great idea if you have a physical location as well as a Web site. These can be your loss leaders to get customers to come into your tourism operation.

You can develop a coupon banner ad that links to your site, where the coupon can be printed. The banner ads should be placed on sites frequented by your target market. You can trade coupons with non-competing sites that target the same market you do; your coupon on their site links to your site, and their coupon on your site links to their site.

By offering coupons from your Web site, you also cut down your overhead cost because people are printing the coupons on their own printers, thus not using your paper. Remember that you should have terms and conditions on the coupons that are available for printing. For example, you should have an expiration date. Someone could print a coupon, then visit your operation in a year and try to use it. You should try to have the expiration date close to the release of the coupon. This will create some urgency, enticing the visitor to use the coupon more quickly and then come back for more coupons.

We are seeing an increase in the number of coupon-related sites that are appearing on the Internet. CoolSavings.com (*http://www.coolsavings.com*) is an online coupon network where businesses can advertise and place coupons for their products and services, as seen in Figure 3.1. Sites like this are a good way to promote your business, for they receive a high amount of traffic. Another benefit is that the traffic is already in a buying mood. CoolSavings.com has been a household name since it launched its national advertising campaign in the late 1990s. If you offer coupons from your site, it benefits you to be listed on these types of sites. If you are not aiming for a national appeal, you should search to find out if there are coupon networks in the geographic location that you are targeting. Destination marketing organization sites that promote your area are another great place to provide your coupons. There are meta-indexes to sites with coupons or discounts from which you can be linked for greater exposure.

Coupons provide ideal viral marketing opportunities—for example, "Send this coupon to a friend."

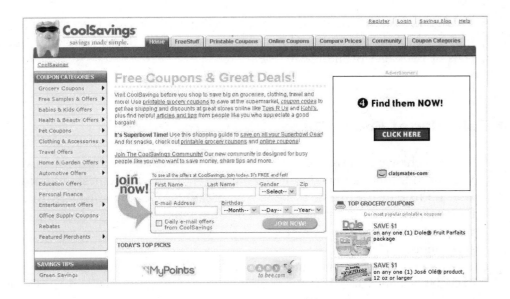

**Figure 3.1.** CoolSavings.com offers coupons from businesses to people all over the USA.

## Specials, Promotions, and Packages

Everyone likes to get a deal. You might consider having a special travel promotions or vacation packages section on your Web site. You'll want to change your promotion fairly frequently and let your site visitors know: "We change our specials every week. Bookmark our site and keep checking back!"

You might employ permission marketing here as well: "We change our vacation packages every week. Click here if you'd like to be notified when we update," or "Click here to join our e-club and receive our e-zine, advance notice of deals, members only e-specials, and other great stuff every week." If you send e-specials via e-mail, make sure you give viewers a reason to visit your site and provide the appropriate hypertext links in the e-mail.

Make it easy to have your site visitors tell their friends about your specials or vacation packages. Have a "Tell a friend about this special" or "Tell a friend about this package" button placed next to each one of your special promotions. You can leverage the viral marketing with an incentive: "Tell three friends about our special and be included in a drawing for (something appropriate for your target market)."

Again, look for other sites that are frequented by your target market when they are looking for travel related information to see if you can have your specials or packages promoted on their sites.

## A Calendar of Events Keeps Visitors Informed

A comprehensive, current calendar of events related to your tourism business or your destination can encourage repeat visits. Your calendar should always be kept up to date and be of value to your readers. When someone is planning a trip to a particular destination they are often interested in what's going on while they are there. Sometimes a great calendar of events can encourage a visitor to stay longer.

A calendar of events can encourage a lot of repeat traffic as long as the calendar is kept current and complete. Again, you can ask people if they'd like to be notified via e-mail when you update your calendar of events.

If you have a great calendar of events, you can encourage others to use it by providing a link to it from their Web site. This offer works well because it is win/win—you are providing them with great content that is kept current and they are providing you with traffic. This works well for destination marketing organizations.

If you don't have the time or inclination to develop your own calendar of events but one would be great content for your site, you might provide a link from your Web site to a calendar you consider top-notch. If you do this, make sure your link opens a new browser window rather than taking the visitor from your site to the referred site.

## Luring Customers with Contests and Competitions

Contests and competitions are great traffic builders. Some sites hold regular contests on a weekly or monthly basis to generate repeat visitors. Holding contests is also a great way to find out about your target market by requesting information on the entry form. See Figure 3.2.

Having a contest with your destination as the prize or part of the prize is great as all contest entrants are telling you that they are a potential customer. They wouldn't enter the contest if they didn't want the prize.

You can simply request that people fill out an electronic ballot to enter the contest. If you want to find out something about the people entering, ask them to answer an appropriate question or two. If you want to do some market

**Figure 3.2.** Contests are a great way to encourage repeat traffic.

research, again, ask a question or two. Make it easy and unobtrusive. The more fields they have to fill out, the fewer people will enter your contest. Be selective with the questions you ask.

If your destination is appropriate for a prize or part of the prize for other people's contests, the benefits can be many:

- Exposure for your operation if the contest site has a significant number of visitors.

- Link from the contest site will give you targeted traffic

- The link will help your search engine positioning (see Chapter 16 on links).

You might have contestants answer three questions relating to your tourism operation on the entry form. Of course, to find the answers to the questions, the visitor has to visit a number of pages on your site, and the three questions are marketing related; sending the visitor to pages that may influence the sale or get them to take a desired action. A question like, "What do you get when you join our e-club?" will take them to your e-club sign up page to find that they get 15 percent off their next stay when they join the e-club. Chances are they'll sign up while they are on the page.

You can have the contest be one where you get information about your target market. When contestants enter the contest, have them rank what influences their buying decision. The information you request can also provide you with demographic or psychographic information.

Allow site visitors to enter your contest often. It boggles my mind when I see these contests that limit the number of times a visitor can enter their contest. The objective of the contest is to get visitors back to your site on a regular basis! I'd suggest that to accomplish this objective it might be more appropriate to tell your Web site visitors to "Enter today! Enter often!" "Bookmark this site—The more times you enter the more chances you have to win!"

You might consider changing the information on the contest Web page around the entry form on a regular basis. Create Web site stickiness by providing links to other areas of your site—perhaps to other repeat-traffic generators you are using on your site, such as your coupons or your e-specials.

Whatever type of contest you determine best meets your marketing objectives, be sure you encourage permission marketing ("Click here to be notified when we have a new contest") and viral marketing ("Tell a friend about this great contest"). Leverage, leverage, leverage: "Tell five friends and receive five extra ballots for yourself."

Make your contest conditional: "Sign up to receive our weekly e-specials and be included in our drawing for (something of interest to your target market)."

Before you go ahead with holding any kind of contest, find out if any legal issues concern you. There may be restrictions that you are not aware of (for instance, you might be required to purchase a legal permit to hold lotteries). You should also remember to ask the entrants the e-mail address where they want to be notified of the winner. This, again, grants you permission to e-mail them to tell them who the winner was, and also to inform them of the new contest or specials that you might have on your site that month.

You want to promote your contest through public and private mail list postings, newsgroup postings, your e-mail signature file, press releases, and links from contest sites.

It always amazes me when I see an online contest where the winner is announced only on the Web site. What a missed opportunity! If your tourism operation is part of the prize, the people who entered the contest have identified themselves as a potential customer. Don't let them get away! As much as contest owners might like to think that all the people who entered the contest are anxiously awaiting the date the contest ends and the winner is announced (perhaps they have even put a reminder in their scheduler) so that they can beat a path back to your site to see if they were the winner—it's not going to happen! To take full advantage of having the contest and achieving your objectives, you want to send an e-mail to all contest participants notifying them of the winner and, in the same e-mail, offering them the contest prize at a discount only avail-

**Figure 3.3.** The Travel Industry Association of America provides useful links for travel industry professionals.

able to the contest entrants for a limited time, or for the first 20 respondents. In the same e-mail you may want to also tell them about your new contest and provide a link back to the new contest entry form.

## Creating Useful Links from Your Site

Provide visitors with links to other sites similar to yours or a meta-index of links that would be of interest to your target market (see Figure 3.3). If you are a hotel that caters to golfers you might develop a list and links to all the golf courses in your area. If your target market is skiers you might have a list and links to all the ski hills in your area.

Do not put outbound links on your home page. Place them down a level or two so your visitors have seen all the information you want them to see before you provide the links away from your site.

Links can be incorporated in two ways. The first is where clicking the link loads the new page in the same browser window (it replaces the content of your page with the content of the linked page). The second and preferred method is to have the link open a new browser window (your page stays where it is and the content from the linked page opens up in the new browser window). This is preferred because once visitors are finished with the new page, they can close the new browser window and your page is still there in the "old" browser window. Try exchanging links with others so you receive a link from their site to your site. As long as the links are of value to your visitors, people will come back to use your resource.

You might consider asking visitors if they are interested in being notified when you update your list of links or just make updates to your site in general. By offering this, if they choose to do so, you have the opportunity to send people an e-mail message and remind them about your site while presenting them with new information about what might be going on with your site.

## Providing a "Featured" or "Tip of the Day/Week" to Encourage Repeat Visits

Have a section that offers cool tips that relate to your tourism operation, your products or services, your destination, or your target market, as in Figure 3.4. These tips can be from one sentence to one paragraph long. In the example

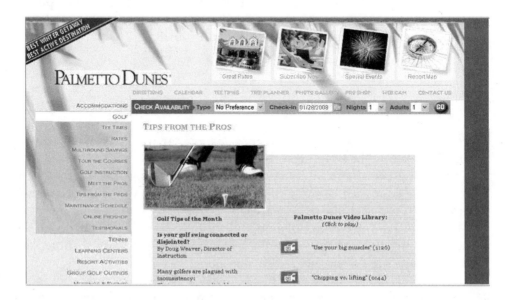

**Figure 3.4.** Palmetto Dunes provides Golf Tips of the Month. Tips of the day, week, or month can encourage repeat visitors.

**Figure 3.5.** When you see a "Bookmark this site now!" or "Bookmark us!" call to action, nine times out of ten you will at least consider it.

shown in Figure 3.4, Palmetto Dunes provides a golf tip of the month. This golf tip is provided as a video clip. You can be guaranteed that golfers will return to this site on a regular basis to view the video golf tip.

If visitors find your advice helpful, they will return repeatedly to see what interesting piece of information you have displayed that day. Ask your visitors if they would be interested in receiving the tip via e-mail or if they would like to be notified when the tip has been updated so they can then visit your Web site. Encourage people to send the tip to a friend. You can also encourage others to use your tip on their Web site as long as they provide a link back to your site as the source. You can go a step further and syndicate your content, putting it up on appropriate sites to be accessed and available by anyone looking for content for their newsletter, e-zines, or Web sites. You can also make it available to other sites by way of an RSS feed (see Chapter 22 on RSS feeds).

All of these techniques work equally well for a featured section on your site. What is featured will be different for different Web sites.

This technique has been used very effectively by a number of businesses— featured treatments by spas, featured destination of the week by travel agencies or destination marketing organizations, ski tip of the week by ski hills, golf tip of the week by golf courses, or fishing tip of the week for fishing camps. There are as many options for tips and featured sections as there are businesses.

## Ensuring Your Site Gets Bookmarked

Encourage visitors to add you to their bookmark list. At appropriate parts of your site, display the call to action: "Bookmark me now!" (see Figure 3.5). A call to action is often effective—it's amazing how often people do what they are told to do! Make sure the title of the page that has the "Bookmark me now!" clearly identifies your site and its contents in an enticing way, because the title is what appears in the bookmark file as a description. Whenever I see "Bookmark this site now!" I always consider it. Sometimes I do and sometimes I don't, but I always consider it. Often, when the call to action is not presented, I don't think about it and don't bookmark it. Then, days later when I want to go back there, I wish I had remembered to bookmark it.

## Encourage Repeat Visits with Your Site of the Day

Having your own Site of the Day or Site of the Week listing means a great deal of work, searching the Internet for a cool site to add or looking through all the submissions. However, if your picks are interesting to your audience, you might find that avid Internet users come back every day to see what great new site is listed. Remember that this must be updated on schedule; displaying a week-old Site of the Day reflects poorly on your site and your company. For more information, see Chapter 18 about hosting your own award site.

## MP3s/Podcasts

Many travel and tourism sites are incorporating downloadable audio content or podcasts (see Chapter 24 for more details on podcasting) and adding new content on a regular basis to encourage repeat visitors.

This is becoming very popular because people like to download and listen to this type of content at their own convenience; they can do an hour of travel research or travel planning while working out, or sitting on the beach, or riding the subway, or traveling by air.

If you plan to add podcasts on a regular basis, you will want to let people know on your Web site that you have new podcasts available every week, every two weeks, or every month, depending on how often you are prepared to develop these. Leverage it with permission marketing by asking them if they'd like to receive an e-mail when you have new downloads available or allow them to subscribe through RSS. Remember when you provide the RSS opportunity to also include links to social bookmarking (see Chapter 22 on RSS).

Once you have developed podcasts, you might want to make them available and downloadable through a number of the online podcast directories like Podcast.net (*http://www.podcast.net*).

## Distribution through RSS Feeds and Autoresponders

Many of the repeat traffic generators we have discussed in this chapter can be provided to others for their information by way of autoresponders (see Chapter 12 on autoresponders) or to be used as content on their Web sites by way of an RSS feed (see Chapter 24 on RSS feeds for more details).

## Internet Resources for Chapter 3

I have developed a great library of online resources for you to check out regarding repeat-traffic generators. This library is available on my Tourism Internet Marketing University Web site *http://www.TourismInternetMarketingU.com/ max* in the Resources section, where you can find additional tips, tools, techniques, and resources.

I have also developed courses on many of the topics covered in this book. These courses are also available on my Tourism Internet Marketing University Web site *http://www.TourismInternetMarketingU.com/max*. These courses are delivered immediately over the Internet or can be ordered as a CD.

# 4

---

# Permission Marketing

Permission marketing is an extremely important aspect of Internet marketing for the travel and tourism industry. While legislation imposes restrictions on what you can and cannot send via e-mail, permission marketing can be a valuable asset to any marketing campaign if it is used in the right way. This chapter provides details on what permission marketing is and how it can be incorporated into your travel, tourism, or destination site. Chapter 14 on private mail list marketing provides all the details on how it is sent, how to grow your database, and how to make sure your permission-based e-mail is not treated as spam.

## Permission Marketing Explained

Permission marketing boils down to asking your target market and Web site visitors for their permission to send them information on a regular basis. Many travel and tourism businesses compete for the attention of their target market on a daily basis, but it is very difficult to break through all of the advertising clutter the market is already receiving. The key to a successful permission marketing campaign is to get your target market to willingly volunteer to participate. In order to get your target market to do this, whatever it is you are proposing must be of value to them. Remember, before your target market agrees to participate in your permission marketing campaign they will stop and ask themselves, "What's in it for me?" If they see no benefit in participating, then they will not participate—it's that simple.

Chapter 3 discusses many ways to encourage repeat visits to your Web site. Repeat-traffic generators provide great opportunities for permission marketing. A few examples include:

- "We update our vacation packages every week! Click here to join our e-club to be notified as soon as we update."

- "Click here to join our e-club and receive our biweekly newsletter filled with coupons, new getaway packages, and travel tips."

- "We constantly update our calendar of events. Keep checking back or click here if you'd like to be notified by e-mail every time we update."

With the legislation rapidly evolving in the industry, I expect that the next round will allow you to send only those things that people have specifically requested. That is, if someone has given you permission to send them your e-specials, you don't have their permission to send your newsletter or your last minute getaway packages. It might be a good idea to consider integrating your permission marketing requests with an e-club. If you have an e-club and encourage people to "Join our e-club to receive our new golf packages, new coupon offers, and other great information available only to e-club members," you are essentially getting umbrella permission to send all types of marketing information.

Permission marketing is extremely effective because it's not intrusive. Your target market volunteered to receive your information because it is of interest to them. Because of this, your target market is expecting to receive your information and is more likely to take the time to view it and be receptive to it. When implemented correctly, permission marketing can be a valuable asset in acquiring new customers and maintaining relationships with existing ones.

## Uses of Permission Marketing

Permission marketing is a great way to increase your online success. There are many ways in which you can integrate permission marketing with many other Internet marketing tools like repeat traffic generators, customer loyalty programs, newsletters, surveys, contests, and so on. Chapter 3 covers many repeat-traffic and customer-loyalty-building tools that you can use on your Web site. Permission marketing is an excellent way to enhance and leverage the use of those tools—a few of which are covered in depth in this chapter.

Newsletters are one of the most popular resources for integrating permission marketing on travel and tourism sites. With newsletters you can ask visitors if they would like to receive notification of new spa treatments, family getaways, updates to your site, vacation planning tips, industry news, and so on—whatever might be of interest to your target market. People who sign up to receive your newsletter do so because they have a clear interest in the information you have to offer. In your newsletter you can integrate strategic promotional opportunities to encourage readers to come back to your site or to take some other course of action. If your newsletter is about recent happenings in the travel and tourism industry, or new activities happening at your destination, encourage readers to "follow this link" to see the updates or additional details. When they click on the link, take them to your Web site. A newsletter is a great way to keep in front of your target market and constantly remind them of your presence. Permission marketing opens the door for communication with your target market; this is an important step in building a long-lasting and profitable relationship with them.

Another ideal opportunity to put permission marketing to work on your Web site is through contests or sweepstakes. In this case, the contest is the primary motivator to encourage people to sign up. The e-mail sent out to notify each contestant of the winner can also include promotional material and can encourage people to visit your Web site. Remember, in order for people to sign up for your contest, it must be of significant interest to them.

Once users have filled out and sent in their contest entry, they should be sent an e-mail confirmation stating that the entry was received. You should also include in the confirmation e-mail a viral marketing call to action to tell others about the contest as well as a call to action for the reader to visit your site. It's not a bad idea to encourage visitors who are signing up for your contest to also sign up for your newsletter at the same time. A good way to encourage this is to present the newsletter sign up on the contest entry form. This is an excellent example of how to combine contests, newsletters, and permission marketing to maximize the opportunity. Not only is the target market encouraged to enter the contest, but they are also encouraged to sign up for the newsletter while their interest is piqued.

## Personalization

Make it easy, keep it simple! When asking permission to communicate with your target market, don't have them complete a long form where they have to provide all kinds of information. You want to make it as easy and as simple as possible for your target market to give you permission.

Have a simple form where they only have to provide their e-mail address and their first name. It is important to get their first name so that you can personalize your communication. You want to personalize the text in the body of the message as much as possible as well as the text in the subject line.

Most mail list software programs these days allow for easy personalization of all messages. You want to use a software program that manages all the permissions—the unsubscribes as well as the subscribes. See Chapter 14 on private mail list marketing for details.

## Sell the Benefits

You need to sell the benefits of your e-club and the communication they will receive when they are a member.

People are inundated with junk e-mail on a regular basis and need to be "sold" on why they should subscribe to or join your communication list. As stated before, they need to know what's in it for them. "Join our weekly newsletter" just doesn't cut it. Something that states "Join our e-club to receive our members only specials, coupons and sweepstakes" will get you more subscribers. You have to know your target market well and know what is enticing enough to get their permission (see Figure 4.1).

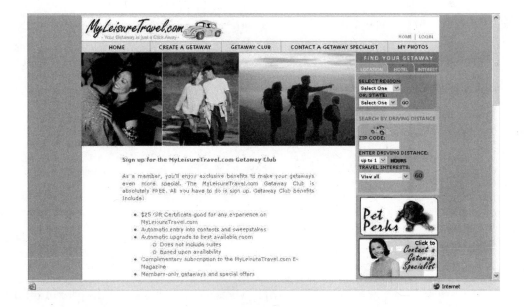

**Figure 4.1.** MyLeisureTravel.com provides a list of reasons to join its getaway club.

## Cooperative Permission Marketing

Cooperative marketing is starting to take hold on the Internet. Cooperative marketing is where you would form an alliance with other sites that are trying to reach the same target market as you. Once you have found the appropriate sites you would come up with a way to do some win-win marketing together. For example, if you have a monthly newsletter, you can allow subscribers to sign up to receive your alliance partners' newsletters at the same time they sign up to receive yours. In return, your alliance partners do the same. This same technique can be used for many other repeat-traffic generators like coupons, e-specials, e-zines, etc. Get innovative!

## Incentive-Based Permission Marketing

Increase the response to any permission marketing opportunity by offering an incentive. For example, "Join our e-club and be included in a drawing for a free Vegas vacation." This is exactly what Myer Hotels has done, as you can see in Figure 4.2.

**Figure 4.2.** Myer Hotels offers people who sign up for its e-club 15 percent off their next stay as an incentive.

You can also try offering a free gift to new e-members or subscribers. It could be a discount on a night's stay at a hotel, a free golf lesson at your resort, or extra reward points; just make sure it is of interest to your target market.

## A Closing Comment on Permission Marketing

Permission marketing adds leverage to your online marketing campaigns. Once you are in front of your target market, you want to take every opportunity to stay there and continue to communicate with them time and time again. Permission marketing helps you achieve this, but it is a game of give and take. You give them a reason to give you permission to send them e-mail—they give you the permission you are looking for; you take their personal information and they take your valuable content via your newsletter. There is a trade-off and the cycle continues. Over time, you will gain more knowledge about your target market, which will empower you to provide them with a better overall experience in dealing with your company through better targeted promotions and better fulfillment of customer needs.

To summarize, permission marketing can return a much higher response rate over intrusive advertising; it can increase sales, build your brand, and help develop relationships with your target market; all while being cost effective.

Visit Chapter 14 for more tips, tools, techniques, and resources related to permission marketing.

## Internet Resources for Chapter 4

I have developed a great library of online resources for you to check out regarding permission marketing. This library is available on my Tourism Internet Marketing University Web site *http://www.TourismInternetMarketingU.com/max* in the Resources section where you can find additional tips, tools, techniques, and resources.

I have also developed courses on many of the topics covered in this book. These courses are also available on my Tourism Internet Marketing University Web site *http://www.TourismInternetMarketingU.com/max*. These courses are delivered immediately over the Internet or can be ordered as a CD.

# 5

---

# Spreading the Word with Viral Marketing

Have you ever visited a Web site and found an article, a coupon, a special, or something else that impressed you so much that you immediately sent an e-mail to your friends about it? If you have, you've already been bitten by the viral marketing bug! Viral marketing, which is often referred to as "word-of-mouse" marketing, is a low-cost, highly effective way to market your tourism product or service using the Internet. Just like a flu virus in humans, viral marketing replicates and propagates itself online. Viral marketing enables you to capitalize on referrals from an unbiased third party—the consumer!

We know that most vacationers do not travel alone. Viral marketing is a must for tourism operators—you need to make it very easy for a vacation planner to tell others about your destination, your packages, and your specials right from your site.

The power that peers and reference groups have over the purchasing decision is phenomenal. Similar to how a positive testimonial from a reliable source can add credibility to a product or service, the opinions of friends, business associates, and family can also help influence a consumer's purchasing decision. By implementing various viral marketing techniques on your Web site, you are provided with a dynamite opportunity to leverage the opinions of your Web site visitors. In this chapter, we will cover:

- How you can use viral marketing to increase traffic

- Word-of-mouth viral marketing

  - Pass-it-on viral marketing

  - Tell-a-friend scripts

- Various ways to leverage your viral marketing campaigns

- Incentives to encourage viral marketing.

## Capitalizing on Viral Marketing Opportunities

Viral marketing can be one of your most powerful online marketing techniques, using the power of associations to spread the word. Viral marketing is still evolving, but today we see three common forms being used:

1. Word of mouth—such as "Tell a friend," "Send this coupon to a friend," or "Recommend this vacation package to a friend"

2. Pass it on—when we receive a travel e-zine, a destination newsletter, travel e-specials or a funny or branded video and then forward it to friends

3. Product or service based—when a free tool is used online and that tool includes an embedded marketing message, such as **VoIP** dialer.

> **VoIP**
> (voice over IP) is an IP telephony term for a set of facilities used to manage the delivery of voice information over the Internet.

### Word of Mouth

You can use viral marketing techniques in a number of different ways throughout your Web site. By placing a "Tell a friend about this vacation getaway" or "Share this golf package information with a friend" button on your site, you enable users to quickly and easily spread the word about your site, your destination, and your products and services. Visitors can click on the button, provide appropriate information in the "To" and "From" fields (including name and e-mail address of both the recipient and the sender), and a brief message. Although the message is personalized, you can include additional information, including details about the package, your destination, the price, and a link directly to the page where the recipient can make a reservation or purchase the package. Because the message is personalized from a friend, the recipient will see their friend's name in the FROM field. Because it comes from someone they know and trust, they are more apt to open the e-mail and visit the site to find out more about the product than they would be if the e-mail came from a traditional corporate e-mail campaign.

The CAT (see Figure 5.1) is a prime example of a company that has implemented viral marketing features throughout its site. When visitors browse through The CAT's travel packages, they are always presented with the opportunity to "Send this package to a friend." Providing this feature leverages the effectiveness of The CAT's Web site and ultimately results in increased sales for the company.

In addition to the aforementioned techniques, there are many different ways that you can implement viral marketing techniques on your Web site. If you have a newsletter on your site, you can add a "Tell a friend about this newsletter" button. You can also incorporate a message in the body of your e-mail

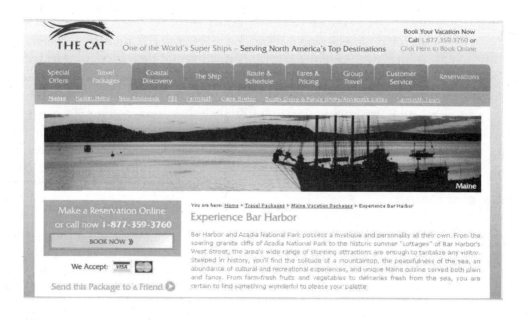

**Figure 5.1.**   The CAT leverages its viral marketing by incorporating a "Send this package to a friend" option for all of the packages on its site.

**Figure 5.2.** Including a "Send to a friend" button on your newsletter can encourage readers to forward a copy to their friends.

newsletter encouraging readers to forward a copy to friends they think would benefit from the information included in the newsletter. You should also include information in the message on how to subscribe to the newsletter for those recipients who receive the newsletter from a friend. The recipients will then be able to send a copy of the newsletter to their friends, who will in turn be presented with the opportunity to subscribe and regularly receive the newsletter (see Figure 5.2). The opportunities for viral marketing are endless.

A good word-of-mouth viral marketing strategy enables a visitor to your site or a recipient of your e-mail to share your site or e-mail content with others with just one click of a button or link. The design and placement of that link or button is critical to the success of the campaign. Most people don't scroll **below the fold**.

**Below the fold**
Content of a Web page that is not seen by the consumer unless the consumer scrolls down.

You should look to every repeat-traffic generator you have on your site for viral marketing opportunities. Repeat-traffic generators like coupons, newsletters, e-specials, and contests all provide ideal opportunities for "Tell a friend" or "Send a copy to a friend" links and buttons. Once you have determined the viral marketing techniques you are going to use, you want to make it easy for the site visitor or e-mail recipient to spread the word.

To be effective, you have to make it obvious what you want your visitors to do. Use a call to action to get them to do it. A button with "Send this coupon to a friend" or "Tell a friend about this e-special" works well. Don't assume that people will take the time to open their e-mail program and send an e-mail to a friend about your e-special or coupon or include the URL to the page on your Web site just because you have a great offer—it doesn't happen! You have to make it easy.

Here are some tips to make your viral campaign effective:

- Have a fantastic button or graphic that grabs their attention.

- Provide a call to action telling the visitors what you want them to do.

- Place the button in an appropriate place away from clutter.

- Have the button link to an easy-to-use "Tell a friend" script. The "Tell a friend" script accepts the name and e-mail address(es) of the friend(s) and the name and e-mail address of your site visitor who is sending the message to a friend. You need to provide a section for a message (see Figure 5.3). You might provide clickable options for this, such as "Thought this might be of interest" or "Knew you'd be interested in this."

- Give clear instructions on how to participate; make it simple, intuitive, and easy.

- Offer an incentive to encourage them to do what you want them to do: "Tell a friend and be included in a drawing for (something of interest to the target market)."

- Leverage, leverage, leverage: "Tell five friends and be included in a drawing for (something of interest to the target market)."

- Avoid using attachments in the message you want spread. This will avoid any potential technical problems with opening the attachments as well as allaying any fears related to viruses.

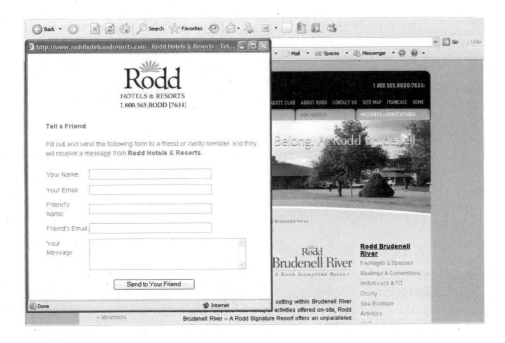

**Figure 5.3.** Rodds Hotels and Resorts uses the "Tell a friend" option as one of its viral marketing techniques.

- Have your privacy policy posted. If the user is going to pass along a friend's e-mail address, he or she wants to be assured that you will not abuse the contact information.

Viral marketing will only be successful if the content is good enough or valuable enough to be passed along.

## Pass-It-On Viral Marketing

When we find a great resource, a funny video, or a cool game, we usually forward it to our colleagues or friends who we know will be interested in it. This old "they tell two friends and they in turn tell two friends" formula works very effectively online to enable you (with the right content) to reach a tremendous segment of your target market.

For this type of viral marketing to be successful, you have to start with great content that recipients will want to share with others. It can take many forms:

- E-books

- Fun videos

- Checklists

- Podcasts

- A sound bite or **audiozine**

- Articles.

---
### Audiozine
A magazine in audio format.
---

The pass-it-on viral marketing methodology works best using small files that can easily be spread around.

### E-Books

E-books are very big these days. If you have great content an e-book can do wonders to create great exposure for you, your site, your destination, and your products and services. Ensure that you have clear references to you and links to your Web site that provide a reason for people to click through. You might provide additional resources on your site or encourage people to visit for copies of other e-books you have developed. Then market, market, market that e-book. Encourage e-zine and newsletter providers to send a copy to their subscribers, and promote it through your sig file, in newsgroups, and in publicly accessible mail lists.

### Fun Videos

Nothing seems to spread faster on the Web than funny video clips. We've all seen the bear taking salmon from the fisherman. Sometimes these video clips are cartoons, seen one slide at a time with embedded audio, and other times they seem to be full-scale productions. Savvy marketers are developing very innovative videos that incorporate their brand, their destination, or their products, with the objective of having a winner that will be passed on many times.

## Checklists

If you have a checklist that others might find useful, why not include links to your site in it and then provide it to your target market for use? For example, you might have a great checklist for travel planning, meeting planning, wedding planning, or cruise planning. Think about your target market and what they might find useful. Always remember to encourage them to pass it on through viral marketing.

## Podcasts, MP3, or Audiozine

Today's technology enables you to very quickly and easily forward podcasts, sound bytes, MP3s, or audiozines. As long as the content is relevant, pertinent, and of value to your target market or people in the industry you serve, people will pass it on. See Chapter 24 for more on podcasts.

## Articles

Writing articles that can be distributed as content for newsletters or e-zines is another form of viral marketing. Submit these articles to syndication sites so that they can be distributed to other sites to be used as Web site content as well. Just make sure that you have clearly stated that others are free to use your article as long as they include it in its entirety verbatim and include the Source box. The article should contain links to your site. The Source box should include information on you, your company, and your Web site.

You should track your viral marketing rate of infection. You want to know what is working and how fast it is working. You can always include a graphic in the article or e-book or digital game that is accessed from your site. Then you can use your Web traffic analysis to find information on the effectiveness of your pass-it-on viral marketing campaigns.

## Virtual Postcards

Today many tourism related businesses are increasing traffic to their sites by offering virtual postcards on their Web site, which enables them to capitalize on viral marketing opportunities. Visitors can send virtual postcards to their family and friends. The postcard should not actually be sent as an attachment, but

**Figure 5.4.**  The town of Mahone Bay offers free virtual postcards to generate exposure for its destination and its Web site.

rather, an e-mail notice is sent saying that a postcard is waiting for the recipient at a particular Web address. By clicking on the Web address, the recipient is sent to the Web site to view the personalized postcard.

An example of this is the very scenic seaport town of Mahone Bay *(http://www.mahonebay.com)*, a site that gives visitors the opportunity to send their friends colorful postcards depicting scenes of Mahone Bay via e-mail (see Figure 5.4). When you send a postcard to your friend, he or she receives an e-mail containing a link to the page where the postcard can be viewed. When your friend clicks through to view the postcard, there are links to other sections of the Web site. Offering electronic postcards is a great way to generate repeat visitors to your site and to spread the word about your site through the use of viral marketing.

## Internet Resources for Chapter 5

I have developed a great library of online resources for you to check out regarding viral marketing. This library is available on my on my Tourism Internet

Marketing University Web site *http://www.TourismInternetMarketingU.com/max* in the Resources section where you can find additional tips, tools, techniques, and resources.

I have also developed courses on many of the topics covered in this book. These courses are also available on my Tourism Internet Marketing University Web site *http://www.TourismInternetMarketingU.com/max*. These courses are delivered immediately over the Internet or can be ordered as a CD.

# 6

## Great Content

Once Internet users have been drawn to your site using the key elements explained in this book, your next step is to keep them there and convert them from a visitor to a customer. You can achieve this by having a site with great content. A Web site with great content is one that not only meets the expectations of the Internet user, but exceeds them.

If something is seen on the Internet three times, it then becomes an expectation. For example, if a consumer is searching the Internet for an all inclusive golf vacation and three of the five sites they visit have a virtual tour of the golf course, club house, and/or resort rooms, the consumer suddenly expects to see a virtual tour on all golf resort sites. Any site that does not have a virtual tour will be seen as not keeping up with the latest trends.

By providing great content on your site you will ensure a higher conversion rate among your Web site visitors and position yourself to be seen as a leader in your industry. Great content keeps visitors on your site longer. The longer they stay the more they feel like they know you, the more they feel they are a part of your community, the more they trust you, and the more willing they are to do business with you—and as I've said before, and will say again, people do business with people they know and trust.

Exceeding customers' expectations, online and offline, should be part of every tourism operator's business culture. Some companies get it and some don't. I stayed at Outrigger Waikiki while speaking at a conference and this note was on the night stand:

*Aloha!*

*Ki-na'ole (flawlessness)—We do the right thing, the right way, at the right time, in the right place, for the right person, for the right reason, with the right feeling, the first time.*

They obviously get it.

Ultimately, as with everything related to your Web site and Internet marketing, what is considered to be great content depends upon your objectives and your target market. In this chapter I will give you an overview of a variety of elements which, if appropriate for your Web site and implemented correctly, will be successful in attracting and converting your target market, including:

- The "WOW" factor

- eBrochures and iBrochures

- Audio and video

- Podcasts

- Trip planners

- Interactive maps

- Interactive elements

- Blogs and wikis.

## The "WOW" Factor

Anyone can go on the Internet and quickly find sellers looking for buyers. But it is rarer to find a Web page that seems tailored to the viewer, drawing the individual in from the beginning and demonstrating why this person should want to be a buyer. The text tells, in detail, why they need your particular travel or tourism-related product or service, your travel packages, or your destination and how it can save time and money, solve a problem, or meet their very own specific needs. With such an introduction, the Web site is successful in laying out the foundation of the promise which your company offers to people who can use your travel packages or services. Everyone wins. The consumers' conscious is introduced to the positive changes this vacation or package will bring them, things they had not even dreamed of earlier. Followed by the guarantee of a safe transaction, and the reassurance of text which communicates a company that knows what it's doing and does it well, the consumer is supplied with a positive user experience, and the company can simultaneously gain leverage, profit, and a competitive advantage.

## eBrochures and iBrochures

eBrochures are simply electronic brochures. They are similar to paper brochures in that they contain all of the information you want your target market to read. An iBrochure is similar again, except that it implements elements of interactivity. iBrochures implement macromedia flash and page turning capability with a simple point-and-click format, as if the viewer is turning the pages of a brochure or magazine. iBrochures can also implement interactive maps and calendars.

Electronic brochures (see Figure 6.1) provide an easily accessible, easily updated way of communicating with existing and prospective customers. Both eBrochures and iBrochures complement your existing Web site and branding strategy and are covered in more depth in Chapter 21.

## Audio and Video

Audio and video are a great form of media which can be used to connect to potential customers and communicate why exactly your travel packages, services, or products are what they need.

Through audio and video, a certain feeling can be communicated which is difficult to attain through text alone—whether it be the blood pumping adventure of white water rapids or a warm, welcoming country bed and breakfast. Use these forms of media to your full advantage in communicating the character and customized value of your destination, travel packages, services, and related products to your potential customers.

**Figure 6.1.** Electronic brochures provide an easily accessible, easily updated way of communicating with existing and prospective customers.

## Podcasts

Podcasting, in its simplest form, relates to audio content that can be listened to on a Web site, on your personal computer, any MP3 player (not just the Apple iPod), and many mobile devices. When you make podcasts available on your travel and tourism site, your Web site visitors can listen to the content on your site, you can allow the podcasts to be downloaded on an individual basis, or you can allow visitors to subscribe to them through an RSS feed.

Podcasts are a great way of keeping your target markets up to date on special events, new package deals, industry news, etc. They are a great way of keeping communications with your target market open and a great way to establish yourself as an expert in the travel and tourism industry. Podcasting is covered in more depth in Chapter 24.

## Trip Planners

As I've stated many times throughout this book, Web site interaction is a key element in connecting with your Web site visitors and developing a stronger relationship. Many destination marketing organization Web sites are now offering their visitors the option of planning their own trip online. They are providing visitors a comprehensive list of all of the attractions available in their area, including hotels, restaurants, and shopping centers. This allows users to see at a glance what is available and book their trip accordingly.

More and more we are seeing these trip planners with interactive content including virtual tours, interactive maps (see Chapter 26), videos and podcasts (see Chapter 24), to provide visitors with all of the options available so that they can decide where and what they want to do on their vacation.

We are even seeing sites like Yahoo! Travel offering trip planners, as shown in Figure 6.2. These types of sites integrate consumer generated media including personal photos, videos, reviews and opinions (consumer generated media is discussed more in depth in Chapter 13). With these trip planners, users may be able to get tailored rates and packages for nearby golf courses, hotels, or events and put together their very own "dream vacation."

With so much interactivity, trip planners are a great way to meet and exceed your Web site visitors' expectations and at the same time deliver great content on your travel and tourism site.

**Figure 6.2.**   Trip planners, such as the one Yahoo! Travel uses, are great content for many travel and tourism sites.

## Interactive Maps

A fundamental component that is missing in many online travel and tourism transactions is being able to see where you are going and what is in the surrounding area. This is where the role of interactive maps comes in.

An interactive map is just that—a map that your Web site visitors can interact with. It is a map of a specified region that has integrated interactive multi-media functionality. These interactive multi-media capabilities give users the ability to explore the maps in much more depth. Interactive maps are great for the travel and tourism industry because they give you the opportunity to show consumers where your hotel is located, where the nearest golf courses are in relation to your hotel, where the nearest shopping centers are, what restaurants are in that same area, and links to content which could be useful to the consumer who is planning a trip. Interactive maps can link to visual images, a voice-guided tour, videos, or any other marketing component you can dream of. See an example of an interactive map in Figure 6.3. Interactive maps are covered in more depth in Chapter 26.

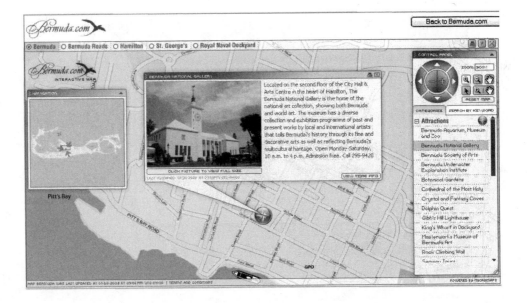

**Figure 6.3.**   Bermuda.com uses interactive maps as great content for its Web site visitors.

## Interactive Elements

Engaging your Web site visitors with interactive elements is not only a great way to get them to stick around your site longer, but also a great way to keep them coming back—and if you use the viral marketing techniques discussed throughout this book, you could get even more visitors to your site.

Take for example the Alibi Maker from VisitLasVegas.com pictured in Figure 6.4. Everyone knows the saying "What happens in Vegas, stays in Vegas." Well, with this Alibi Maker Web site visitors are presented with the opportunity to create their very own alibi. It's fun, it's interactive and it helps create a profile of your Web site visitors so that you can offer them their dream vacation.

Here's how it works: visitors are presented with a series of questions and multiple choice answers. All questions are related to shopping, golf, or shows and entertainment. Once the user has gone through all of the questions, they are presented with an alibi and the opportunity to book their Vegas dream vacation based on the answers they gave.

Through the Alibi Maker, VisitLasVegas.com is successful in narrowing down the ideal vacation it has to offer each of its users. After identifying themselves as

**Figure 6.4.**    VisitLasVegas.com's Alibi Maker makes great Web site content.

the "All I Did Was Shop" or "The Golfer," viewers are presented with their tailor-made array of ideal vacation elements and options, complete with links to the Web sites of the options listed, which they can then compile into their very own dream vacation package. What more could be asked?

## Blogs and Wikis

The same way other elements of great content are successful, blogs and wikis can be extremely useful in regaining that sense of connection between your travel and tourism operation and the buyer. Blogs and wiki's can help you keep your web site current, and keep your visitors informed, because they are an easy way to add new content to your site.

Blogs and wikis can be used to provide your potential and existing customers with the latest news on your products and services, industry news, updates, tips, or other relevant content. They are also a great way to open up communication between you and your customers and potential customers.

Some travel and tourism operations are even giving their customers the opportunity to create your own vacation blog. This provides an added bonus to the customer experience. For more information on blogs and wikis see Chapter 23.

By offering elements such as the ones above that go beyond the customary travel experience, you place your business ahead of the competition. Again, great content entails a Web site which not only meets the expectations of the Internet user, but exceeds them as well.

## Internet Resources for Chapter 6

I have developed a great library of online resources for you to check out regarding great content. This library is available on my Tourism Internet Marketing University Web site *http://www.TourismInternetMarketingU.com/max* in the Resources section where you can find additional tips, tools, techniques, and resources.

I have also developed courses on many of the topics covered in this book. These courses are also available on my Tourism Internet Marketing University Web site *http://www.TourismInternetMarketingU.com/max*. These courses are delivered immediately over the Internet or can be ordered as a CD.

# 7

---

# Landing Pages

When you do online promotion, whether it be through a banner ad, newsletter promotion, or pay-to-play campaign, you want to maximize the results of your effort. You want to take the interested person directly to the information they are looking for—not to your home page where they may have to navigate to get to the specific information. When done properly, creating a targeted landing page for an ad can greatly increase conversions, or the number of customers who act on your offer. In this chapter, we cover:

- What is a landing page?

- Considerations for landing page content

- Landing page layout

- Testing your landing page.

## What Is a Landing Page?

A landing page is a Web page that is created specifically to respond to a marketing campaign you are running. You can't provide all the details and the opportunity to make the purchase in the banner ad, so you develop a landing page to follow through from the banner ad. When your target market clicks on the banner ad, they are taken to the landing page that was developed specifically for that ad. The action you want the target market to take might be to make a reservation, join your e-club, view a virtual tour, or use your travel planner. The key is that the landing page is usually geared toward a conversion or converting the browsers into buyers.

The way your landing page is developed depends entirely on your business objectives, your target market, and your offer itself. The landing page should focus on the one thing you want the visitor to do—keep it focused.

The presentation and the content, or copy, of your landing page have a huge impact on the ability of the landing page to close the offer. We begin with a look at content for your landing page. There are a number of points to make note of when preparing content for a landing page:

1. Your landing page should be a continuation of your ad—repeat and expand on the offer presented in your ad. The ad is designed to generate interest and the landing page is designed to close the sale.

2. Your landing page should emphasize the benefits of your offer—this is what justifies the purchase.

3. Your landing page content should flow from the advertisement. If your ad promotes your virtual tour, then when visitors click through to the landing page they should be given the opportunity to take that virtual tour. Take your target market where you want them to go. Tell them what you want them to do.

4. Your landing page should "speak" to your target market. Use their language and buzz words. Use the appropriate tone for this particular target market.

5. Your landing page should have a dynamite headline. Grab their attention!

6. Your landing page should be written for scanability. Internet users don't read, they scan.

7. Your landing page should promote the "value-added" portion of the offer that will help with your objectives. Free gift on arrival, a coupon, a discount toward a future purchase, or the number of travel reward points earned with purchase—all of these add to the value of the offer.

8. Your landing page should create a sense of urgency—get your visitors to do what you want them to do NOW! If they leave your site without making the purchase or reservation, it is often unlikely you'll get an-

other opportunity. Using appropriate calls to action like "Book Today!," telling the target market that there are "limited quantities" or "limited space available," and techniques like time-stamping the offer with an expiration date, create a sense of urgency that encourages the target market to take immediate advantage of the offer.

9.  Your landing page content should minimize risk. If you have a money back guarantee, emphasize it! Anything that helps to close the deal should be prominently displayed.

10. Your landing page should ask for the sale—maybe multiple times and places. You don't get what you don't ask for.

11. Your landing page should include content that enhances your credibility. Things like client testimonials or product/service reviews. Content that helps establish credibility also helps build trust, which is key to doing business online.

12. Your landing page should be optimized for the search engines. If you are running a promotion for just a couple of days, then odds are you do not want your landing page indexed by the search engines. In this case you would use your robot's exclusion protocol in your robots.txt file to tell the search engines not to index the page. See Chapter 2 for search engine optimization and Chapter 9 for pay-to-play considerations.

Once you have developed a dynamite landing page, you will want to do some testing to maximize your conversion; very few people get it perfect the first time. You will want to test different page content, format and lengths, different jargon and tones, different layouts, different offers, and a number of other things to find the right balance to best sell your product, service, or destination.

## Considerations for Landing Page Content

Your most important information on the landing page should be above the fold. The fold is where the bottom of the browser window sits and additional scrolling is required to view the remaining content. This is what your target market sees when they land on your landing page. It is usually this content that encourages them to keep going or to click away.

Your landing page should focus on the one thing you want them to do. You want to eliminate anything that might distract the target market from doing what you want them to do.

Be wary of "banner blindness." People tend to not even notice the information that is in the standard banner ad areas. Stay away from having any content that looks like an ad in shape, size, and color.

Leverage the elements on this landing page. You want to give your visitors the option to sign up for your permission marketing-based newsletter or e-club. You want to make use of the viral marketing Tell-a-friend function. You do not want these elements to take over the page and distract the user, but you want to encourage these actions—be subtle!

Give your target market access to anything needed to get them to do what you want them to do. What information do they need? Pricing information? Privacy information? Your contact information? Make sure that they have access to whatever they need.

Make sure the landing page looks great. Choose things like font types, styles, and color to your best advantage. Photography should be professionally done; you can always tell the difference.

Provide your target customer with options on how to make the purchase or the reservation. Prominently display alternative purchase options. Your visitor might be extremely interested in your offer, but not so comfortable making the purchase online.

All of the best practice techniques that go into building a Web site apply to your landing page as well. The landing page still has to be cross-browser-compatible, easy to use, quick to load, have clean code and effectively brand your business. See Chapter 1 for best practices.

## Testing Your Landing Page

There is always something you can do a bit better to maximize your landing page results. There are any number of things you can test and tweak to refine your landing pages. Even the smallest changes can have a big impact. When running a marketing campaign, employ A/B testing to see which landing page techniques generate the best responses from your target market.

When performing A/B testing, you might do a split-run campaign where you run a marketing campaign that directs 50 percent of your target market to landing page A and the other 50 percent to landing page B.

Here are some items to consider when testing your landing pages:

## Landing Page Content

1. Is short or long copy more effective?

2. Is it better for you to use bulleted lists to emphasize key points as opposed to paragraphs of information?

3. Does separating content with tag lines or headers increase the number of responses?

4. What happens if you bold or otherwise emphasize key points in your copy?

5. What impact does changing the writing style or tone of your copy have on your landing page's ability to convert?

## Landing Page Layout and Presentation

6. What impact does changing the presentation of the offer itself have on results? "Buy one, get one free," "50% off," "1/2 price," "Save $100 off the list price," showing the original $200 price tag with a strikethrough and the new price next to it emphasized in bold red font as $100, are all different ways of presenting the same offer. Which method generates the best response from your target market?

7. Does your landing page perform better with vivid imagery, little imagery, or no imagery? Maybe showing different color shots of the same product if it is available in more than one color will boost sales. Try it.

8. What colors on the page elicit the most favorable responses from your target market? Does the contrast between the page copy and the background influence sales?

9. What font types, styles, and sizes are most effective?

10. How many navigation options work best on the landing page? Are you providing the target market with so many navigation options that they get distracted, or would the page be effective with more navigation options intact?

11. Where is the best position on the landing page to place the "buy," "order," or "reserve" buttons?

Capitalizing on any great campaign requires a great closing. Your closing is your landing page—a prime reason you never want to put all of your eggs in one basket. It is highly recommended that you test and refine your landing pages over time. This is by no means a complete list of items worth testing, but it is a good place for you to start.

It is best to test one element at a time so that you can measure results and determine the effectiveness of the new change. If you change too many items at once, it will be difficult to attribute how much of an impact the items you changed had on the effectiveness of that page. If you made three adjustments to your landing page at once, it might be that two of the three components have increased the response rate, but the third might have dragged it down a bit, so you are not quite reaching your potential. If you just change one element at a time, you can tell what impact your change has on the landing page's ability to convert.

This same testing logic applies to the online marketing campaigns you partake in as well. You want your marketing efforts and your landing pages to work together.

Today's Web traffic analytics and Web metrics software provide great information on what's working, what's not, and also the implications of testing elements (see Chapter 28).

## Internet Resources for Chapter 7

I have developed a great library of online resources for you to check out regarding landing pages. This library is available on my Tourism Internet Marketing University Web site *http://www.TourismInternetMarketingU.com/max* in the Resources section where you can find additional tips, tools, techniques, and resources.

I have also developed courses on many of the topics covered in this book. These courses are also available on my Tourism Internet Marketing University Web site *http://www.TourismInternetMarketingU.com/max*. These courses are delivered immediately over the Internet or can be ordered as a CD.

# 8

# Search Engine and Directory Submissions

There are billions of travel and tourism Web pages on the World Wide Web, so how can you increase your chances of being found? One method is to submit your Web site to the many search engines and directories. Once you've optimized your Web site to be search engine friendly, you are ready to face the challenge of submitting it to the most important search engines. By "search engines," I'm referring to the combination of search engines, directories, spiders, and crawlers. As already mentioned to ensure your best possible success online you need to be within the first two pages of search results. This is no easy feat, but this chapter will provide you with the knowledge necessary to get on the road to success. This chapter covers:

- Search engines, directories, and their ranking criteria

- Search engine and directory submission pointers.

## Submission Process

Although people often use the term *search engine* interchangeably for search engines and directories/portals, there is a major difference when it comes to submission protocols. The search engines (Google, Yahoo! Search, Ask, and MSN/Microsoft Search, to name a few) allow you to simply "Add your URL." Your URL is your uniform resource locator—also known as your Web address, your www.yourcompanyname.com. When you add your URL, it is put in a queue and when it is your turn, the search engine's spider or crawler visits your site and includes it in its database.

On the other hand, to submit to directories such as the Yahoo! Directory, Open Directory, and Business.com, you have to go to the directory site, select a category, and find the link to its submission form. For the directories, you generally have to complete a detailed form filling in all the blanks of required information.

Paid advertising placements and pay-per-click campaigns are covered in Chapter 9.

## A Closer Look at Search Engines and Directories

Search engines and directories share a common goal, that is, to provide the searcher with relevant, meaningful results; however, there are many differences in their functionality. In general, search engines have a much larger index than directories, and utilize spiders to add sites to their index. In contrast, directories typically have a smaller index and often are maintained by humans. When you're submitting to a site, you can usually tell the difference between a directory and a search engine by the information they request. A search engine typically asks only for the URL you wish to submit and sometimes your e-mail address. A directory usually asks for much more information, including your URL, the category you wish to be added to, the title of your site, a description, and your contact information.

When you do a search on the Internet, in seconds the search engine has digested what you are looking for, searches the millions of pages it knows about, and responds to your request with appropriate sites ranked in order of importance. Amazing! How do they do it?

Search engines use spiders to index your site. Some search engines are free, while others require you to pay for inclusion. Sometimes, a search engine's spider will include the pages on your site in its database without your even submitting a request to be added. Even though a number of spiders constantly crawl the Web looking for sites, I suggest you take a proactive approach and submit all appropriate pages on your site to the search engines to guarantee that all your important pages are properly listed. But before you submit, check the search engine's submission document to be sure submitting more than one page is permitted, because you don't want your site to be rejected. A search engine might also have restrictions on the number of pages you can submit in a single day—perhaps only five or ten pages are allowed to be submitted.

Many search engines and directories either partner with or license the use of another search engine's or directory's search technology. Being indexed by these engines means your Web site is likely to be found in other major search services. For example, Google's results can be found on AOL and Netscape. Google's paid advertising results appear on many other sites as well. Bruce Clay has a fantastic site that shows the relationship among the various search engines. See Figure 8.1 for the chart, which Bruce keeps updated on his site (*http://www.bruceclay.com*).

The ranking criteria of each search engine most often differ from each other in determining who gets top placement, so even though two search engines might use the same database, they most often provide different search results (see Chapter 2 for more on designing your site to be search engine friendly). For example, some search engines' ranking criteria are determined by how often a keyword appears on the Web page. It is assumed that if a keyword is used more frequently on a page, then that page is more relevant than other pages with a lower usage of that keyword. Some search engines' ranking criteria look for the keyword in the title of the Web page and assume that if the keyword is in the title, then that page must be more relevant than those that don't have the key-

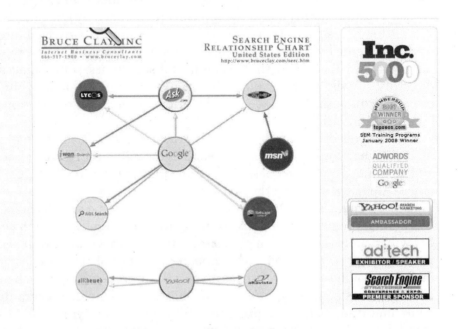

**Figure 8.1.**   Bruce Clay's search engine relationship chart.

word in their title. Some search engines determine where keywords are used and assume that pages with keywords in the headings and in the first couple of paragraphs are more relevant. Some search engines use the number of links pointing to a particular page as part of their ranking criteria. Some search engines use information contained in meta-tags; others don't look at the meta-tags at all.

To summarize, search engines all have different ranking criteria and this is why you receive different results when you search on the same keyword with different engines. You should learn as much as you can about each of the major search engines' ranking systems and make sure your site is optimized for the search engines before you submit. One particularly useful site with this information is SearchEngineWatch.com (*http://searchenginewatch.com*).

The remaining major players in the search engine industry are:

- Google (*http://www.google.com*)

- Yahoo! Search (*http://www.yahoo.com*)

- MSN (*http://search.msn.com*)

- AOL (*http://www.aol.com*)

- Ask (*http://www.ask.com*).

Let's turn our attention to directories now. Directories are maintained by human administrators. Some directories permit free submissions, while others require you to pay—just like the search engines. Popular directories include:

- Yahoo! (*http://www.yahoo.com*)

- LookSmart (*http://www.looksmart.com*)

- Open Directory (*http://www.dmoz.org*)

- About.com (*http://www.about.com*)

- Business.com (*http://www.business.com*).

You can expect to wait a longer period of time when submitting your Web site to a directory before seeing your page appear in its index. In general, you can expect to wait from two to eight weeks unless you pay a fee for an expedited review.

For example, Yahoo! Directory charges US$299 for an expedited review. When you pay the fee, Yahoo! will review your site for inclusion within seven business days. There is no guarantee they will include you; just a guarantee they will review your site and consider including you.

In contrast to a search engine, your site's position in directories depends much less on its design and much more on the initial submission process itself. For this reason, you will be asked for much more information when you submit to a directory.

Directories catalog a smaller number of pages than search engines. Search engines are known for their enormous databases of indexed Web sites. Google currently claims that it has the largest index, with an excess of 8 billion indexed pages! Open Directory, Yahoo!, and LookSmart are popular directories, and each has a few million indexed Web pages.

## Submitting to the Search Engines

Registering with search engines is fairly simple. In most cases, you simply have to submit your URL or Internet address on their submission form. Figure 8.2 shows Google's search submission page.

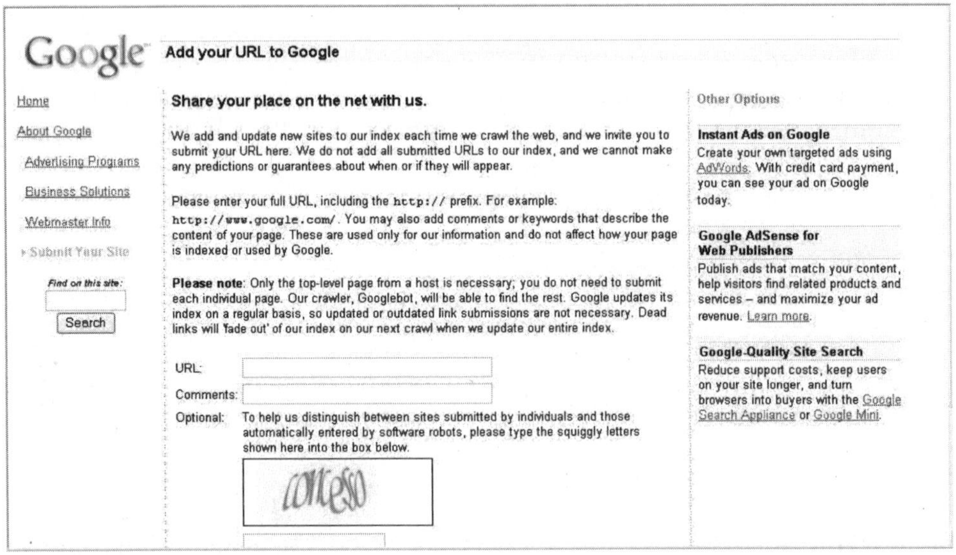

**Figure 8.2.**   Google's Web page submission form.

Even if your URL is not registered with search engines, a number of the major search engines may eventually find you, since their bots are continually roaming the Internet looking for new sites to index. There are millions of sites and billions of travel, tourism and destination-related pages out there, so I suggest that you register your site to ensure a speedier listing. Once you are registered, some of the bots will periodically revisit your site looking for changes and updates. How high you rank depends largely on how well your Web site is optimized, along with other proactive marketing activities, such as links strategy development (links are discussed more in Chapter 16) and updated content.

Outside of pay-to-play advertising options covered in Chapter 9, you will basically encounter two search submission options:

1. Free submission

2. Paid inclusion.

## Free Submissions

Most of the major search engines have free submission and each has its own set of guidelines that indicate how many pages and how often you can submit from a single site. It might be one page in total, one page per day, five pages at a time, or even 50 pages at once. Take the time to read their guidelines to improve your chances of being indexed. Your home page is the most important page on your Web site to be indexed, so if you can submit only one page, be sure that is the one.

## Paid Inclusion

With paid inclusion you have more control over your destiny, but it comes at a price, which implies the need to create a search submission budget based on your available resources and the submission fees requested by the search engines.

With paid inclusion you are guaranteed to be indexed by the search engine, up to the number of pages you have paid for, within a short, defined period. Paid inclusion options tend to offer other perks as well, such as guaranteed revisits to update your listings (e.g., every 24 hours), guaranteed inclusion on any partners' Web sites, reporting to track your performance, and in some cases a review of your Web site to ensure its relevance. Just because you paid to have your site indexed does not mean it will rank well. How well your Web site performs depends on how well it is optimized for a particular search engine.

## Automated versus Manual Submission

Search engine submissions need to be handled manually rather than by an automated application. Google and Yahoo! Search both require you to type in your Web address as well as a code that is embedded in a graphic on the submission form page. The text that is embedded on that page is dynamically generated, meaning it is different for each visitor. Submission software would be unable to read the text embedded in the graphic and, therefore, would be unable to input the required code into the submission form.

All of the submission suggestions assume you are interested in being indexed by the major U.S.-based search engines. If you plan to submit your Web site to international search engines or international editions of the major search engines, then you need to take into consideration search engine optimization for specific languages and cultures.

## Is Your Page Already Indexed?

Before you submit or resubmit to a search engine, check to see if your page is already indexed. Perform a search using the most important keywords you think people will use to find your page. Also, perform a search using your company name.

With many of the search engines, you can narrow the search to your specific domain. Check out the help files for each search engine for more information on how to verify that your URL is included in their index. To check for your Web site in Google, all you have to do is enter the following information into the search field, where "yourwebsite" is replaced by the name of your real Web site:

*site:yourwebsite.com*

If your page is found and you're happy with the results, you need not submit or resubmit.

## Submitting to the Directories

When you submit to a directory, you have to take the time to find the best category for your site. Submitting your site to the wrong category could mean a minimal increase in traffic if no one thinks to look for you in the category you submitted to. Also, your site might not be added if you select an inappropriate category.

When choosing categories you want to pick one (or two if the directory permits you to do so) that consistently gets listed near the top of results for popular searches and that accurately represents your tourism Web site. Use the keyword phrases you have gathered to help you identify good categories. If local traffic is important to your travel and tourism business, you should look at submitting to the regional categories found on most directories. You can also look at where your competitors are listed in the directory for an indication of where you should be focusing your efforts.

LookSmart's travel category contains subcategories including activities, destinations, lodging, transportation, and so on. These categories are then often broken down further into other categories within the subcategories. The deeper you go, the more specific the category becomes.

Your site's ranking in a directory depends on the information you provide them on the directory submission form. As such, it is critical that you review each directory's submission procedure and tips. Compared to a search engine, you will be asked for much more information when you submit to a directory. The title, description, and any other information you give them during submission are what is used to rank your site. Figure 8.3 illustrates Open Directory's submission form.

**Site URL:**
http://
What type of link is this? ⊙ Regular ○ PDF ○ RSS ○ Atom

⚠URL stands for Uniform Resource Locator, which means your site address. Example: http://dmoz.org

- Do not add mirror sites.
- Do not submit an URL that contains only the same or similar content as other sites you may have listed in the directory. Multiple submissions of the same or related sites may result in the exclusion and/or deletion of those and all affiliated sites.
- Do not disguise your submission and submit the same URL more than once. Example: http://www.dmoz.org and http://www.dmoz.org/index.html.
- Do not submit any site with an address that redirects to another address.
- The Open Directory has a policy against the inclusion of sites with illegal content. Examples of illegal material include child pornography; libel; material that infringes any intellectual property right; and material that specifically advocates, solicits or abets illegal activity (such as fraud or violence).
- Do not submit sites "under construction."
- Submit pornographic sites to the appropriate category under Adult.
- Submit non-English sites to the appropriate category under World.
- Don't submit sites consisting largely of affiliate links.

**Title of Site:**

⚠Please supply a short and descriptive title.

- Always opt for the official name of the site.

**Figure 8.3.** Open Directory's submission form.

The keyword research you performed for optimizing your Web site is every bit as important when it comes to directories. You must use your important keyword phrases when filling out the directory submission forms. Again, for best results be sure to review each directory's submission guidelines.

## Preparing Your Directory Submission

Before submitting to the directories, you should go to each one you are interested in submitting to and print the submission form. Then develop a Word file with all the required fields for all the submission forms you will be completing. Take the time up front to develop the submission material carefully. Organize the information in a logical order in a text file. Then, when you go to submit, you can copy and paste the content to the appropriate fields on each of the submission forms.

This approach gives you a starting point and will save you time when submitting your Web site. You may need to adjust your information for each directory submission, though, because they all have unique submission requirements. You need to be careful to follow them to the letter to reduce the risk that a directory editor might change your submission entry. You want your listing to appear in your words, with no editing.

Be sure to spell-check, check, and recheck everything before you start. Spell-checkers won't pick up misspelled "works" if that word is also in the dictionary.

After you print the submission forms, you'll find that there are many common elements requested by the different directories. The information prepared for each page on the site to be indexed should include:

- URL

- Page title

- Ten-word, 25-word, 50-word, and 100-word descriptions for the page (different engines allow different lengths of description)

- List of keywords for each page (based on the master keyword list you generated in Chapter 2)

- Description of the ideal audience for the site

- Categories and subcategories you should be listed under for the different directories you plan to submit to

- Contact information:

  - Company name

  - Contact name

  - E-mail address

  - Company address

  - Telephone and fax numbers.

## Pay Careful Attention to Titles and Descriptions

Pay careful attention to your titles and descriptions. When it comes to supplying a page title, a directory typically wants you to restrict it to your company name. In some cases, they will provide you with additional direction on supplying a descriptive tag line; however, your company name will be required to accurately represent your travel, tourism, or destination company or organization. Proper punctuation and capitalization are a must.

It is a good idea to create a number of different descriptions of varying lengths because the different directories allow different description sizes. Start off by creating descriptions consisting of 10, 25, 50, and 100 words. Make sure that you use the right length for each directory, because you won't want it to be altered when it is displayed in the search results. Editors are notorious for editing descriptions if your submission does not meet the directory's guidelines, or even a particular editor's style. When submitting to a specific directory, it does not hurt to read the other entries in your category to look for a common theme in the descriptions and then modify yours to follow suit.

Your description should be compelling. When you get your site to appear in the first page or two of results for a search, the description is what differentiates your site from the rest. It is the description that entices a prospective visitor to click and visit—or pass by and go to a more exciting travel or destination site.

Always use your important keywords or keyword phrases in your description. Apply the most important keywords first because keywords used further along in the description are generally given less weight by the major search engines. If possible, use keywords in combination with other keywords, but make sure your description flows naturally. Round off your description with a call to action. It is amazing how many people do what they are told.

### Pay Careful Attention to All Fields on the Submission Form

When submitting forms to directories, be careful to fill in every field on the form. Some of the directories reject your registration automatically if you have not filled in all the blanks. When you have to choose categories, select them carefully. It would be a shame to have a great golf package, a great destination getaway, and a great vacation site, but be listed in a place where your potential customer would never think about looking for you. I cannot emphasize this enough: read the FAQs or instructions first to ensure that you understand exactly what information is being requested.

Proofread your submission at least twice before you hit the Submit button. It isn't quick or easy to change listings if you make a mistake. Your listing might be wrong for quite a while before it gets corrected. To change a listing you typically have to either contact a category editor directly or fill out a change request form.

### More Directory Submission Tips

It generally takes longer to be indexed in a directory because, often, you have human administrators who review every page submitted before adding it to the database. Make sure your travel page contains quality content, is easy to use, is visually appealing, is free of errors, and is free of performance issues such as a poor load time. It is the administrators who decide if your page is worthwhile before they include it and pages that do not meet the requirements of the administrator will not be added to the directory—whether or not you abide by best practices in Web site development can make or break you when it comes to getting listed in directories.

Consider Yahoo!'s directory. Yahoo! won't add you if you have Under Construction signs on your site. Yahoo! likes sites that are complete, contain good, pertinent information, are aesthetically pleasing and are easy to use. Before you submit, be sure to check if you're already in their directory. You may not want or need to submit your site if you're already where you want to be. If you are in their directory but want to change the information displayed, then you can fill out a form located at *http://add.yahoo.com/fast/change* that is specifically used for changing information already listed in the directory.

The following are some other tips to remember when submitting your site to Yahoo!:

- Remember, your submission counts for almost everything here, so do it right. Yahoo! Directory is a directory, not a search engine. Yahoo! Search is the search engine. Designing your site to be search engine friendly means very little here.

- Make sure that what you submit is actually what your site is about. Yahoo!'s administrators will review your site, and if they feel the description you provided does not match your site, you will not be added to their directory.

- Keep your description to 150 characters or less, and use descriptive keywords that fit naturally within the description. Yahoo! reserves the right to modify your description if they see fit. You're the only one who knows what information is important to include in your description, so you probably do not want Yahoo!'s administrators to modify your description because you might lose an important part of your description, resulting in less traffic. Keep in mind that Yahoo! does not like submissions that sound like an advertisement—they like concise, pertinent information.

- Submit a short, relevant title, but not something like "The Best Vacation Planning Site on the Web." Be sure to use descriptive keyword phrases in your title as well. That way, when searches are performed, your page title will be referenced.

- When you submit your site, develop your page title and descriptions to use keywords in combination with others, as this can also give you a boost. Check out your competitors to see who's on the top and what they're doing right.

- If you're looking for local traffic, then submitting to a regional category might be a good approach for you.

- Don't fill out the submission form using ALL CAPITALS—they hate that. Use proper grammar and spelling. Before you submit, be sure to check and recheck your submission.

- If your domain name contains keywords, you can benefit here. Keywords can help your page stand out when a user performs a search on a keyword that is in your domain name.

- Don't forget to fill out Yahoo!'s submission form exactly as requested! Read the help documentation and FAQs, beginning with "How to Suggest Your Site," which can be found at *http://docs.yahoo.com/info/suggest*.

## Keep a Record of your Submissions

Keep a record of the directories and search engines to which you have submitted. The information recorded should include the following:

1. Date of the submission

2. URL of the page submitted

3. Name of the search engine or directory

4. Description used

5. Keywords used

6. Password used

7. Notes section for any other relevant information, such as the contact person for the search engine or directory

8. Date listed.

This list can come in handy when checking the status of your submissions or if you encounter any problems in the future where you need to contact the search provider or resubmit.

## Effective Use of Submission Tools and Services

There are many search engine submission services available on the Net that will submit your site to varying numbers of indexes, directories, and search engines. They will register your URL, description, and keywords. Use these services only after you have manually submitted to the most important search engines and directories. As I said earlier, many of the major search engines require you to type in a code that is embedded in a graphic on the submission form page. This text is randomly generated, it is different every time a submission is made, and it is embedded in a graphic. Submission software would be unable to read the text embedded in the graphic and, therefore, would be unable to input the required code into the submission form (see Figure 8.4). Be sure to check these submission services to see how comprehensive they are before using them. Here are a couple of sites for you to look at:

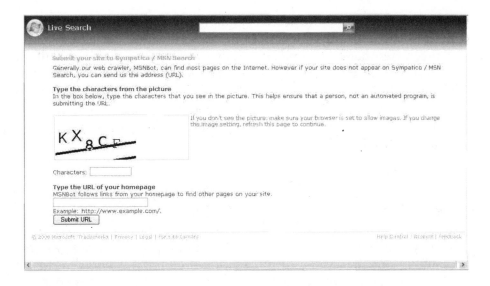

**Figure 8.4.** MSN's submission form with the embedded code in a graphic that must be manually entered in.

## Web Position

*http://www.webposition.com*

This is search engine submission and evaluation software that tells you where your site is positioned in search results of the most popular search engines and directories. It builds traffic by tracking your search engine positions and helping you to improve your rankings.

## Position Pro

*http://www.positionpro.com*

Position Pro is a powerful combination of tools providing you with the ability to analyze your entire Web site like a search engine would. It also offers search engine submission services.

## SubmitPlus

*http://www.submitplus.com*

SubmitPlus has been successfully promoting Web sites around the world since 1998. Its programs and promotion packages were developed with the input of major search engines to assure precise and search engine friendly results.

Although these services save a great deal of time, it is essential that you be registered accurately in search engines and directories. For the best results, register individually in those search engines you have decided to focus on before you resort to multiple-submission sites. There aren't that many search engines or directories that have long submission forms, so submit manually to ensure the best results. If you have taken the time to do the work described earlier, submit to the major engines yourself. This way you can take full advantage of the legwork you have done targeting the differences between the engines.

To summarize, each search engine is different. Know the unique qualities of each before you submit.

## Complete Your Site before You Submit

Before you submit to any of the search engines and directories, take the time to complete your site. Many of the major search engines and directories are not fond of receiving submissions from people who have pages that are not yet complete or that are full of sloppy code. You do not want to spend your time submitting your page only to find out it has not been added because it is still under construction.

Be sure to validate your HTML before submitting. You want your site to be free of errors to ensure your success with submissions. A few of the tools you can use to validate your HTML are:

**W3C HTML Validation Service**
*http://validator.w3.org*

**NetMechanic**
*http://www.netmechanic.com/toolbox/html-code.htm*

**WDG HTML Validator**
*http://www.htmlhelp.com/tools/validator*
See the resources section of my Web site *http://www.TourismInternetMarketingU.com/ max* for other resources.

## Get Multiple Listings

One way to have your travel and tourism site listed many times is to submit many times. Because each page on your site is a potential entry point for search engines and each page has a unique URL, you can submit each URL (each page) in the various search engines, directories, and so on. Each page of your site should be indexed to improve your chances of having your site listed in the top ten search engine results. And because every page on your site is different, each page should have a different title, a different description, and different keywords, all tied in to the keyword phrase you have assigned to that page. That way, you increase your chances of being found by people searching for different criteria and keywords.

It is important to abide by netiquette. In some search sites, the previously discussed practice of submitting multiple times is acceptable and might even be encouraged. In others it is considered abuse and is discouraged. Check each search engine's rules, and use your judgment on this one.

## Some Final Pointers

Here are some important final pointers you should keep in mind. Always read the submission guidelines before submitting. Search engines and directories often provide a number of valuable tips that can help you achieve better rankings.

Periodically review your rankings in the major search engines and directories. To make this manageable, I suggest you make a list of the search engines and directories to which you have submitted. Divide your list into four groups. Every week check your ranking with each of the search engines and directories in one group for your most important keyword phrases. If you have dropped in the ranking or don't appear in the first couple of pages of search results, then you want to tweak your site and resubmit to that particular search engine or directory. The next week, check your ranking with the next group. By doing so you can set a regular schedule for yourself, keep organized, and determine which search engines and directories you need to resubmit to. Sometimes your site may be removed from an index because the search engine has flushed its directory, or maybe it is just one of those things no one can explain—either way, you want to be on top of things. If you make any significant changes to your site, you also might want to resubmit. You want to be sure that your listing reflects your fresh content.

Tools like Web Position (*http://www.webposition.com*) automate the process and can provide reports on demand—you set the keywords that are important to you and the search engines and directories that are important, and then you can run a repot to show you your positions for each keyword phrase with each of the designated search engines and directories.

## Internet Resources for Chapter 8

I have developed a great library of online resources for you to check out regarding search engine and directory submission. This library is available on my Tourism Internet Marketing University Web site *http://www.TourismInternetMarketingU.com/max* in the Resources section where you can find additional tips, tools, techniques, and resources.

I have also developed courses on many of the topics covered in this book. These courses are also available on my Tourism Internet Marketing University Web site *http://www.TourismInternetMarketingU.com/max*. These courses are delivered immediately over the Internet or can be ordered as a CD.

# 9

# Developing Your Pay-to-Play Strategy

It used to be that you could simply optimize your Web site using traditional organic search engine optimization techniques, as described in Chapter 8, which would enable you to place high in the major search engines and create a great deal of exposure for your product or service offerings. This can still be accomplished; however, with thousands of travel and tourism sites competing for the top positions on a given search results page, it is becoming an increasingly more challenging task. This is why many travel and tourism businesses are leaning toward **PPC** online advertising models to generate targeted exposure for their sites, and in turn their travel destinations, packages, services, and related products. So what options are available to enable

> **PPC**
> PPC, or pay-per-click, refers to the advertising model in which advertisers pay for click-throughs to their Web sites. Ads or sponsored listings are served based on keywords or themes.

travel and tourism businesses to create targeted exposure for their Web sites, and how can travel and tourism businesses with minimal advertising budgets utilize these advertising models to increase their visibility on-line? In this chapter, we cover:

- Maximizing exposure through the Google, Yahoo! Search, and MSN advertising networks

- Expanding your reach with contextual advertising

- Geo-targeting ads to better communicate with your target market

- Dayparting and how you can capitalize on increased traffic levels during specific time periods

- Developing effective landing pages for your ads.

## Generating Targeted Traffic Using PPC Advertising

At the end of the day, the success of your search engine positioning strategy boils down to one thing—results! Over the last several years, many search engines have adopted various PPC advertising models that enable advertisers to pay for exposure on their search results pages based on targeted keyword sponsorship. Advertisers pay for click-throughs to their Web site. Ads, or sponsored listings, as they are commonly referred to, appear on the results page of a search based on keywords.

The concept is very straightforward—advertisers bid on specific keywords or keyword phrases to impact the position of their text ads on search results pages. Their ad appears when someone does a search on the chosen keywords or keyword phrases, and if (and only if) someone actually clicks on their ad and is delivered to their site, the advertiser pays. Using PPC, advertisers receive targeted leads delivered to their site, for a fee.

The key is that the lead is "targeted." Using traditional organic search engine optimization techniques can cause your site to appear at the top of search results, generating targeted traffic to your Web site, but even the leading search engines often return results that are not exactly what the searcher desires. What if your travel and tourism Web site always appeared when a searcher conducted a query using a targeted keyword relating to the travel and tourism-related products or services being promoted on your site? What if you could ensure that everyone interested in your destination, packages, products, or services had the opportunity to click on your search engine listing to learn more about what you have to offer?

These are the true benefits of developing your PPC or pay-to-play online promotional strategy. By participating in PPC, you generate targeted traffic to your site and you increase brand awareness for your travel and tourism organization, which ultimately results in increased sales for your business. Over the years some programs have proven successful while others have failed, but at the end of the day, a handful of PPC programs have proven to be extremely successful. These programs include:

- Google AdWords (*http://adwords.google.com*)

- Yahoo! Search Marketing (*http://searchmarketing.yahoo.com*)

- MSN adCenter (*https://adcenter.microsoft.com*).

All of the major PPC programs have in-depth tutorials, case studies, white papers, and tools to help you learn more about their programs and make them easy for you to use. Things are changing rapidly in this area, as the competition for your advertising dollar is fierce. Changes to these programs, whether we're talking about program updates, program features, new pricing, new tools, new offerings, or program enhancements, are being made on a regular basis.

In this chapter I'll provide a very basic overview of Google AdWords and the Yahoo! Search Marketing programs. Other programs you will want to check out include MSN's adCenter, Ask, 7Search and Kanoodle. The information included in this chapter is current as of the date of publication. For the absolute latest information on these programs, I strongly suggest you visit the advertising sections of all the major search engine Web sites.

## Exploring PPC Campaigns in Google and Yahoo!

Google AdWords and Yahoo! Search Marketing have quickly become two of the premier online advertising vehicles for travel and tourism businesses for several reasons. First and foremost, why wouldn't you want to place targeted ads on the Internet's top search engines to generate exposure for your business, your destination, packages, and your related products and services? In addition, by sponsoring keywords and phrases on a cost-per-click basis on such prominent Web portals, you are guaranteed one thing—targeted exposure.

Some PPC programs provide businesses with the opportunity to outbid each other for top placement of their ads. This means that businesses with large advertising budgets can dominate the top placements using these particular programs, which is not exactly fair to those businesses that cannot afford a high CPC.

Google AdWords and Yahoo! Search Marketing help to create a level playing field for all advertisers, meaning that even small travel and tourism businesses with a minimal budget can compete with large enterprises for premium listings. Travel and tourism busi-

**CPC**

CPC, or cost-per-click, refers to the price paid by the advertiser each time a visitor clicks on the advertiser's ad or sponsored listing.

nesses with large advertising budgets can set their CPC for particular keywords well above their competition, but this doesn't mean that their ads will appear above the competition. Google AdWords and Yahoo! Search Marketing rank each ad based on a combination of the ad's CPC and the ad's click-through rate. What this means is that if a travel and tourism business with a high CPC creates an irrelevant ad that does not generate any clicks, that ad slowly moves to the bottom of the listing of ads that appears on Google's search results page and ads on Yahoo!'s search results page and are ultimately removed. This enables travel and tourism businesses with a lower CPC, but more relevant ads, to position higher—at no extra cost!

## How PPC Campaigns Work

Setting up a PPC campaign account in both Google and Yahoo! can be accomplished in 15 to 20 minutes by following a few simple steps. When preparing to launch a campaign, you first determine where you would like your ads to appear on the search engine's network of Web sites, and which languages you plan to target with your ads. You can choose to communicate your ads to the masses, or you can opt to geographically target your ads to specific locations—some even offer advertising to locations within a specific distance from your business's physical location. Now that's targeted advertising!

You then need to design an Ad Group for your PPC campaign in Google or Yahoo!. An Ad Group is a collection of one or more ads that you wish to display on the network of sites. Each ad consists of a headline and description that, if designed correctly, relates specifically to the keywords that are associated with the overall Ad Group. Once each ad in a given Ad Group is designed, you select targeted keywords that you wish to be associated with the Ad Group.

Why does an Ad Group contain one or more ads? Google's AdWords program and Yahoo!'s Search Marketing program are both designed to work effectively for advertisers, weeding out ads that are not generating targeted traffic for them. To illustrate, assume that a given Ad Group consists of five different ads relating to a specific topic, each with a unique headline and description. When an advertiser launches a campaign, Google AdWords and Yahoo! Search Marketing randomly display each ad in the Ad Group to the advertiser's target market. Eventually, certain ads in the Ad Group perform better than others, generating more click-throughs. When this happens, Google AdWords and Yahoo! Search Marketing then display only ads within the Ad Group that are generating results for the client, and slowly remove the others from the rotation. This helps to maximize the effectiveness of the overall ad campaign.

When launching an ad campaign, you are given the opportunity to set a budget for your campaign. You can set a maximum CPC for each Ad Group along with a maximum daily budget for your campaigns.

If you are unsure of what your maximum CPC should be, or if you simply do not have the time to spend on such decisions, Google AdWords provides the Budget Optimizer feature. With the Budget Optimizer you simply set your target budget, and the Adwords system does the rest, seeking out and delivering the most clicks possible within that budget. The Budget Optimizer considers keywords, competitive bids' ad positions, time of day, and many other factors to give you the most possible clicks for your money—automatically.

Both Google Adwords and Yahoo! Search Marketing offer excellent traffic-estimation tools that can help you estimate daily traffic for selected keywords and phrases. The traffic-estimation tool helps you fine-tune what your maximum CPC should be, based on your overall online advertising budget and campaign objectives. By manipulating the maximum CPC, you are able to determine what your daily expenditures would be based on traffic patterns associated with the keywords that you have selected, along with where your ads will be positioned during the campaign.

### Where Do Your Ads Appear?

These paid listings usually appear separately from the organic results—sometimes these sponsored listings appear at the top of the page, sometimes they appear as a sidebar to the right of the page, and sometimes they appear at the bottom of the page.

When you implement a campaign on the Google AdWords network, your ads appear in more places than just within Google's search results. Through building relationships with some of today's top industry-specific Web sites and search portals, Google expands the reach of your ads to the masses. Popular Web sites such as the New York Times, AOL, Ask.com, and Netscape all display AdWords' advertisements when a Web surfer conducts a search using those sites' search tools. Figure 9.1 shows some of AdWords' more prominent advertising partners.

Similarly, when you implement a campaign on the Yahoo! Search Marketing network, your ads appear in more places than just within the Yahoo! search results. Yahoo! Search Marketing displays its pay-for-performance sponsored search results on prominent Web sites such as Yahoo!, NBC, All The Web, and AltaVista. Figure 9.2 shows some of Yahoo!'s more prominent advertising partners.

**Figure 9.1.**   Google Adwords' strategic advertising network.

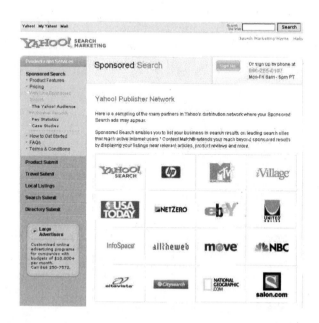

**Figure 9.2.**   Yahoo! Search Marketing's strategic advertising network.

The network sites change from time to time. At the time of this book's publication, the above is the most current listing of Web sites that display Google Adwords' and Yahoo! Search Marketing's PPC listings in their search results.

## Maximize Exposure with Contextual Advertising

Imagine that a consumer is currently in the market for a weekend golf retreat and is viewing a recognized informational travel Web site to learn more about the latest in all-inclusive golf resorts. If you were a salesperson in a traditional brick-and-mortar store and a consumer wandered into your department, you would approach the consumer as if he or she were already semi-engaged in the sale, just trying to figure out what to buy. In a similar way, the latest advancement in contextual advertising enables you to reach those same consumers, but in the online marketplace.

To further illustrate the example, assume that you are that same consumer on the informational travel Web site and you are viewing a page of content that only provides information on golf resorts. Accompanying the content on this page is a listing of ads for online retailers who are promoting golf resort packages for sale online. Because the ads relate directly to your area of interest, you click on a link, are directed to a Web site, and ultimately book your weekend golf retreat with the online retailer.

Similar to the way a Web surfer searches for information using a major search engine and is presented with PPC ads, contextual ads enable advertisers to promote their ad listings on content sites that relate to specific information (for example, golf courses). Contextual advertising provides advertisers with yet another opportunity to target specific customer segments with targeted advertisements. Both AdWords and Yahoo! Search Marketing currently offer advertisers the ability to take advantage of contextual advertising opportunities by promoting their ad listings on related content sites within their respective advertising networks.

## Geo-Targeting Your Campaigns

Implementing a PPC strategy enables you to advertise to a mass audience, or to target Internet users in a specific geographic location. Both Google AdWords and Yahoo! Search Marketing PPC campaigns provide you with the opportunity to target customers not only on a state or provincial level, but also on a local level, by displaying advertisements only to potential customers conducting searches in your business's local area or in the area of your destination.

With AdWords alone, you can choose to target over 250 different countries in up to 14 different languages. You can also choose to advertise within over 200 different regions throughout the United States. Geo-targeting provides you with an increased level of control over where your ads are displayed and how they figure into your advertising budget. By targeting only those locations where you wish your ads to appear, you can maximize your online advertising dollars whether you are working with a small or a large budget.

## Dayparting

When you are analyzing your Web traffic logs, you will most likely notice that your traffic levels spike on a particular day of the week or during a specific time period throughout the day. When monitoring the performance of your PPC strategy, you can also note when searchers are more apt to click on one of your ads to visit your site and learn more about what you have to offer. If you notice a significant increase in your click-through rates at a specific time, you can capitalize on this increased visibility.

Adjusting your PPC advertising strategy to capitalize on traffic during a particular point of the day is what is referred to as "dayparting." Reports reveal that when you capture your target market when they are more apt to visit your Web site (for instance, during a particular time of the day, or on a particular day of the week), they will be more apt to click on your ad and ultimately convert to a customer. This strategy requires in-depth analysis of conversion rates, click-through rates, and general traffic levels (these are discussed more in Chapter 28). The basic premise behind dayparting is that advertisers increase their CPC during the time of the day when searchers will be most apt to view information on their destination, packages, products, and services. By increasing your CPC during this timeframe, you maximize the exposure for your destination, services and travel and tourism related products—provided that you are presenting the searcher with optimized ads.

## Maximizing Your Exposure

Developing ads for your PPC strategy is not just a matter of throwing together a headline and description in the hopes that a customer will click on one of your ads. Well, it could be, but this strategy will not result in your meeting your campaign objectives of click-throughs and conversions. Your ads should be designed to entice the searcher, but be wary that if you create ads that are too inviting, you can rack up your click-through rate quickly without converting any visitors at all. The bottom line is that you do not want to entice uninterested searchers to your Web site, as you would be wasting your online advertising budget.

To avoid this issue, make sure that your ads relate specifically to the keywords they are associated with and make sure your message is clear. When a true potential customer views one of your ads, you want that person to say, "Wow, that's exactly what I am looking for." This ensures that your click-throughs are more targeted.

In addition to developing targeted ads for your campaigns, you also want to be sure that when searchers click on your ad, the page they are directed to provides them with information about what you are promoting. Too often, travel and tourism businesses simply point click-throughs to their Web site's homepage, which requires the potential customer to navigate further through the Web site to find more information about the company, destination, packages, services, and related products. This often results in wasted clicks and fewer conversions.

Instead, try pointing Web surfers to landing pages that are tailored to specific advertisements. You have to remember that people are not going to initiate contact or sign up for your mailing list, or even buy, simply by clicking on your ads—they want information. That's why you would never simply point a new customer to your online order form. However, if you develop a landing page that communicates the features and benefits of your travel packages, your services and/or products, and provides the visitor with a clear "Book Now" call to action, you can increase the likelihood that the visitor will convert to a customer.

When developing landing pages for your PPC strategy, you should design various pages and test their effectiveness (for more on landing pages see Chapter 7). The key thing to remember is that if someone is searching for "New York hotels," you do not want your landing page to say something unrelated, but rather to include a call to action that says "Click here for New York hotels." You want to make sure that you provide the viewer with the information that she or he is looking for. In addition, make sure that you do not overwhelm visitors with navigation options that would distract them from understanding the message you are trying to communicate. Clear communication of your value proposition is the key.

## Maximizing Your Budget

One of the biggest mistakes that many travel and tourism organizations make is assuming that they have to bid into the number one position to make their PPC strategy work. Being number one is associated with being the best; thus it is very easy to let your ego get in the way of your marketing objectives. Bidding into the top positions for more competitive keywords generates optimal exposure, but it also blows through your budget more quickly than if your ads were appearing in the lower ranks. When creating the strategy for your PPC campaigns, you should develop a strategy to maximize both your daily budget and the exposure for your travel and tourism business. Constantly bidding into top positions can result in having to start and stop your campaigns if the budget is not available to constantly maintain them.

To maximize the effectiveness of your budget, try bidding into the lower ranks to minimize your average CPC. This helps you to stay under your daily budget and lets you implement longer campaigns with your advertising dollars. Also, bidding on the most competitive keywords is not always the best strategy. Use the tools that are available with your PPC program to identify keywords that are proven to be effective but are not being capitalized on by your competitors. These are the words that can help you to drive targeted traffic to your Web site, but will have a minimal CPC as nobody else is sponsoring these words. Advertisers typically focus their efforts on the keywords that are most utilized by their target market and avoid keywords that are less popular.

There have been many books written on pay-per-click advertising (PPC), or pay-to-play as some like to call it, and many, if not all, are outdated as soon as they get to market due to the overwhelming rate of enhancements and changes that are occurring with the companies that offer PPC advertising. For the absolute latest information on these programs, I strongly suggest you visit the advertising sections of all the major search engine Web sites to get the more intricate details.

## Internet Resources for Chapter 9

I have developed a great library of online resources for you to check out regarding PPC. This library is available on my Tourism Internet Marketing University Web site *http://www.TourismInternetMarketingU.com/max* in the Resources section where you can find additional tips, tools, techniques, and resources.

I have also developed courses on many of the topics covered in this book. These courses are also available on my Tourism Internet Marketing University Web site *http://www.TourismInternetMarketingU.com/max*. These courses are delivered immediately over the Internet or can be ordered as a CD.

# 10

---

# The E-mail Advantage

E-mail is one of the most crucial forms of communication you have with your clients, potential customers, suppliers, and colleagues. E-mail is a widely accessible and generally accepted form of business communication. We are seeing a huge increase in commercial e-mail volume. The reason for this significant increase is understandable given that e-mail is a very cost-effective, time-efficient tool that has a high response rate. E-mail is used to build your community online, sell your destination, and provide customer service, reinforce brand awareness, and encourage customer loyalty.

In the online community, e-mail is an extremely efficient way to build and maintain relationships. As a marketing tool, e-mail is one of the most cost-effective ways to maintain an ongoing dialogue with your customers and potential customers.

However, with the overabundance of spam, spam-detection software, filtering of e-mail, and anti-spam legislation, things are changing rapidly in the e-mail world. It is becoming a challenge to make sure that your e-mail is received, opened, and responded to.

This chapter focuses on individual e-mails that you send. Mass-marketing e-mails you send to your target market are more fully discussed in Chapter 14 on private mail list marketing.

In this chapter, we cover:

- Strategies for creating effective e-mail messages

- E-mail netiquette

- E-mail marketing tips.

## Making the Connection

E-mail is a communication medium, and, as with all forms of communication, you do not get a second chance to leave a first impression. E-mail must be used appropriately. People receive large amounts of e-mail each day, and the tips in this chapter will help to ensure that your e-mail is taken seriously.

One of the greatest benefits of e-mail is the speed with which you can communicate. E-mail takes seconds rather than weeks to send a message around the world. The cost of this form of communication is negligible, compared to making a long-distance phone call or sending a fax. The economies of scale are significant. One e-mail message can be sent to millions of people across the globe simultaneously. This type of mass mailing is done at a fraction of the cost and a fraction of the time (and internal resources) it would take with **snail mail**.

### Snail Mail
Slang term for the regular postal service.

All kinds of files can be sent via e-mail, including audio, video, data, pictures, and text. With an autoresponder, information can immediately be sent automatically to customers and potential customers 24 hours a day, 7 days a week, 365 days a year in response to their online requests. We discuss autoresponders in Chapter 12.

E-mail is interactive. Your current and potential customers can immediately respond to you and carry on an ongoing dialogue with you. E-mail is seen much more like a conversation than a text document. It is perceived as being more personal than snail mail and can go quite a long way in building relationships.

## E-mail Program versus Mail List Software

The time has come where mail list software is essential for sending mass, permission-based, marketing e-mail. In this chapter we'll talk about regular, day-to-day e-mail. See Chapter 14 for the discussion on marketing e-mail sent to a group or private mail list marketing.

## Effective E-mail Messages

Most people who use this medium get tons of e-mail, including their share of junk e-mail. Many use organization tools, filters, and blockers to screen incoming e-mails. The following tips will increase the effectiveness of your e-mail communication to ensure that you have the best opportunity for your e-mail to be opened, read, and responded to.

### The Importance of Your E-mail Subject Line

The first thing most people do when they open their e-mail program is start hitting the delete key. They have an abundance of mail in their inbox and they want to get rid of the clutter, so they delete anything that looks like spam or an ad. How do they determine what is junk? The subject line is usually the deciding factor. It is essential that your e-mail subject line not look like ad copy.

Never send an e-mail message without a subject line. Subject lines should be brief, with the keywords appearing first. The longer the subject line is, the more likely it will not be viewed in its entirety because different people set the viewable subject line space at various widths.

The subject line is equivalent to a headline in a newspaper in terms of attracting reader attention. When you read a newspaper, you don't really read it; generally you skim the headlines and read the articles whose headlines grabbed your attention. The same is true with e-mail. Many recipients, especially those who receive a significant number of e-mails daily, skim the subject lines and read only the e-mails whose subject line grabs their attention. The subject line is the most important part of your e-mail message because this phrase alone determines whether or not the reader will decide to open your e-mail or delete it.

Effective subject lines:

- Are brief, yet capture the reader's interest

- Don't look like ad copy

- Build business credibility

- Attract attention with action words

- Highlight the most important benefits

- Are always positive

- Put the most important words first.

Effective subject lines should grab the reader's attention, isolate and qualify your best prospects, and draw your reader into the subheads and the text itself. Avoid SHOUTING! Using CAPITALS in your subject line is the same as SHOUTING AT THE READER! DON'T DO IT! Stay away from ad copy in your subject lines—it is the kiss of death for an e-mail. When most people open their e-mail, they delete all the ads as the first step.

### E-mail "To" and "From" Headings Allow You to Personalize

Use personal names in the "To" and "From" headings whenever possible to create a more personal feeling. People open e-mail from people they know and trust. If your message is coming from 257046@aol.com rather than Jane Doe, will your friends know it is coming from you? Most e-mail programs allow you to attach your own name to your e-mail address.

If you are using Microsoft Outlook, the following are the steps to set up your name in the "From" heading:

1. On the menu bar, click "Tools."

2. On the drop-down menu, click "E-mail Accounts."

3. In the E-mail section make sure that "View or change existing e-mail accounts" is checked. Then click Next.

4. Highlight the e-mail account you want to edit and click Change.

5. In the User Information section, put your name as you want it to appear in your recipient's From field in the Your Name area. Then click Next.

6. Click Finish and you're done.

For all other e-mail programs, consult the Help file included in the program.

### Blind Carbon Copy (BCC)

Have you ever received an e-mail message in which the first screen or first several screens were a string of other people's e-mail addresses to which the message had been sent? Didn't you feel special? Didn't you feel the message was meant just for you? This sort of bulk mailing is very impersonal, and often recipients will delete the message without looking at it.

A few years ago I would have suggested using the BCC feature when sending bulk or group e-mails. Today, a number of Internet service providers look for multiple addresses in the BCC area to determine if an incoming message is spam. If your message is deemed to be spam, it will probably not get through to your intended recipient. This is one of the reasons I recommend moving to private mail list software for marketing messages that are going out to a group. See Chapter 14 on private mail list marketing.

---

**BCC**
When blind carbon copy is used in an e-mail message, all recipients' names are hidden so that no one sees who else has received the e-mail.

---

## Effective E-mail Message Formatting

The content of the message should be focused on one topic. If you need to change the subject in the middle of a message, it is better to send a separate e-mail. Alternatively, if you wish to discuss more than one topic, make sure you begin your message with "I have three questions" or "There are four issues I would like to discuss." People are busy; they read or scan their e-mail quickly and they assume you will cover your main points within the first few sentences of your message.

E-mail is similar to writing a business letter in that the spelling and grammar should be correct. This includes the proper use of upper- and lowercase lettering, which many people seem to ignore when sending e-mail. However, e-mail is unlike a business letter in that the tone is completely different. E-mail correspondence is not as formal as business writing. The tone of e-mail is more similar to a polite conversation than a formal letter, which makes it conducive to relationship building.

In general, you should:

- Keep your paragraphs relatively short—no more than seven lines.

- Make your e-mail scannable.

- Make your point in the first paragraph.

- Make sure that what is likely to be in the preview screen will encourage the recipient to open your e-mail.

- Be clear and concise.

- Use *http://* at the beginning of any Web address to ensure that you make it "live." When you provide the URL starting with the *www,* the reader sometimes has to copy and paste the Web address into the address field in the browser if he or she wants to visit your site. When you place *http://* before the *www,* the link is always "live" and the reader just has to click on the address to be taken directly to your site. Make it as easy as possible for your reader to visit your Web site.

- Give your reader a call to action.

- Avoid using fancy formatting such as stationery, graphics, different fonts, italics, and bold, because many e-mail programs cannot display those features. Your message that reads: "Play golf today on the best course" could be viewed as "Play <I>golf<I> today on the <B>best course<B>" if the recipient's e-mail software can't handle formatting. That kind of loses the impact!

- If your e-mail software doesn't have a spell-check feature, you might want to consider composing your message first in your word-processing program. Spell-check it there, then cut and paste it into your e-mail package. If your e-mail software does have the spell check option, turn it on!

- Choose your words carefully. E-mail is a permanent record of your thoughts, and it can easily be forwarded to others. Whenever you have the urge to send a nasty response, give yourself an hour or two (maybe even 24) to reconsider. Those words can come back to haunt you—and they usually do.

## A Call to Action

When you give your readers a call to action, it's amazing how often people will do as they're told. I'll give you an example of something we did. We ran a series of ten Internet marketing workshops for a large organization. Their staff and selected clients were invited to participate in any, some, or all of the workshops. Their clients could include up to three employees. Because the workshops extended beyond noon, lunch was provided.

Because we were responsible for organizing and managing the project, we needed to know the approximate number of people who would be attending each of the workshops to organize the luncheons. When we contacted each company's representatives by e-mail looking for participation RSVPs, we conducted an experiment. We sent half the representatives one version of the message and the other half a slightly different version. The only difference between the two messages was that in one we included a call to action. In that message we asked: "RSVP before Wednesday at noon indicating if you will be attending as we must make arrangements for lunch," and in the other, this same line read: "Please let us know if you are planning to attend as we must make arrangements for lunch."

There was a 95 percent response rate from the group who received the first message. This is because we gave people a call to action and a deadline and they felt obligated to respond more promptly. Meanwhile, fewer than 50 percent of the people in the second group responded to our message. What does this tell us? To improve your response rate, give your readers a call to action when you send them e-mail. People respond when told to do something; they act with more urgency when there is a deadline.

### Appropriate E-mail Reply Tips

Do not include the entire original message in your replies. This is unnecessary and is aggravating to the original sender of the message. However, use enough of the original message to refresh the recipient's memory. Remember to check the "To" and "CC" before you reply. You would not want an entire mail list to receive your response intended only for the sender. The same applies for selecting "Reply to All" instead of "Reply."

### Always Use Your Signature Files

As discussed previously, signature files are a great marketing tool. Always attach your signature file to your online communication. See Chapter 11 for information on signature files. Remember to be sure that the signature files are right for the intended audience.

### Discerning Use of Attachments

If you are sending a fairly large amount of data, you might want to send it as an attached file to your e-mail message. However, only include an e-mail attachment if the recipient is expecting it. You would never consider going to someone's home, letting yourself in, finding your way into their living room, and then leaving your brochure on the coffee table. However, people do the online equivalent of this when they send an unsolicited attachment. The attachment is sent across the Internet to the recipient's computer and is downloaded and stored on the computer's hard drive. This is considered quite rude and, in most cases, unwanted.

Also, unless the recipient of your e-mail is aware of the file size and is expecting it, don't send an attachment that is larger than 50K. Although your Internet connection might be a cable modem or a T1 line, and a 3 MB file is sent in seconds, the person who is receiving your message and attachment might be using an old 14.4 Kbps modem and a slow machine. If you send a 3 MB file, it might take the person with the 14.4 Kbps modem two hours to download the file. Needless to say, he or she won't be too pleased. Yes, there are still people on dial-up.

Another factor to consider when sending an unsolicited attachment is that the attachment you are sending might be incompatible with the operating system or the software on the recipient's system. You might be using a different platform (Mac/PC) or different operating system, and the recipient might not be able to open and read your file. Even PC to PC or Mac to Mac, the recipient might not be able to open and view the attachment if that particular program is not installed on his or her machine. Someone using an old version of Corel WordPerfect might not be able to read a Microsoft Word 2007 document sent as an attachment. Thus, you have wasted your time sending the file and the recipient's time downloading the file.

Finally, it is a well-known fact that e-mail attachments can act as carriers for computer **viruses**. Many people will not open anything with an attachment, even if it is from someone they know, unless they have specifically requested a file. You might unknowingly send someone an attachment with a virus, and even if the file you send is virus-free, you could still take the blame if recipients

**Viruses**
Programs that contaminate a user's hard drive, often with unwanted results.

find a virus on their system, just because you sent them an attachment. Basically, avoid sending e-mail attachments of any type unless you have the recipient's permission. Be mindful of the size of the file you intend to send, compatibility with other platforms, and computer viruses. One alternative to sending a large attachment is to post the file on a Web server, and in your e-mail message direct users to a URL from which they can download the file.

## Expressing Yourself with Emoticons and Shorthand

In verbal communication, you provide details on your mood, meaning, and intention through voice inflections, tone, and volume. You also give clues about your meaning and intention through facial expression and body language. E-mail does not allow for the same expression of feeling. The closest thing we have to this online is the use of **emoticons**.

*Emoticon* is a combination of "emotion" and "icon." Emoticons are combinations of keyboard characters that give the appearance of a stick figure's emotions. They have to be viewed sideways and are meant to be smiling, frowning, laughing, and so on. Emoticons let

---
**Emoticons**
Symbols made from punctuation marks and letters that look like facial expressions.

---

you communicate your meaning and intentions to your reader. For example, if your boss gives you an assignment via e-mail and your response is, "Thanks a lot for unloading your dirty work on me," your boss might become upset at your obvious defiance. But if you replied with this: "Thanks a million for unloading your dirty work on me :-)," your boss would understand that you were jokingly accepting the assignment.

Emoticons enable you to add a little personality and life to your text messages. However, their use is not universal and generally should not be used in business correspondence. Some of the more commonly used emoticons include:

| | |
|---|---|
| :-) | Smiling |
| :-@ | Screaming |
| :-0 or :-o | Wow! |
| :-p | Tongue wagging |
| ;-) | Wink |
| (-: | I'm left-handed |
| :-V | Shout |
| :-& | Tongue-tied |
| :-r | Tongue hanging out |
| ;-( or ;-< | Crying |
| :-# | My lips are sealed! |
| :-* | Oops! |
| :-S | I'm totally confused. |

| | |
|---|---|
| 8-0 | No way! |
| :- | Skeptical |
| :-< | Sad or frown |
| ~~:-( | I just got flamed! |
| %-0 | Bug-eyed |
| :\ | Befuddled |
| :-D | Laughing, big smile |
| }:-> | Devilish, devious |

E-mail shorthand is used in newsgroups and other e-mail to represent commonly used phrases. Some common abbreviations are:

- BTW          By the way
- IMHO        In my humble opinion
- IMO          In my opinion
- IOW          In other words
- JFYI          Just for your information
- NBD          No big deal
- NOYB        None of your business
- TIA           Thanks in advance
- PMFJI       Pardon me for jumping in
- OIC           Oh, I see . . .
- OTL           Out to lunch

- OTOH            On the other hand

- LOL             Laughing out loud

- LMHO            Laughing my head off

- ROFL            Rolling on the floor laughing

- BFN             Bye for now

- CYA             See ya!

- FWIW            For what it's worth

- IAE             In any event

- BBL             Be back later

- BRB             Be right back

- RS              Real soon

- WYSIWYG         What you see is what you get

- <g>             Adding a grin

Because e-mail shorthand is most commonly used in newsgroups, text messaging, instant messaging, and chat rooms, you will be most successful when using these acronyms with others who are familiar with them.

## E-mail Marketing Tips

Be prepared. You will receive a number of e-mails requesting information on your company, your products, your locations, and so on, from people who have seen your e-mail address on letterhead, ads, business cards, and sig files. Don't wait for the first inquiry before you begin to develop your company materials. Here are some tips. Following them will make you more prepared to respond.

## Include a Brochure and Personal Note

Have an electronic brochure or corporate information available that you can easily access and send via e-mail. Try to send a personal note in your e-mail along with any material requested.

## Provide Customer Service

Treat your customers right and they will treat you right. Your best referrals come from satisfied customers. If your new customers are taking a cruise, provide them with a list of details on such things as the boarding procedure, what to wear, and what they cannot bring on board.

## Gather a Library of Responses

Different people will ask a number of the same questions, and over time you should develop a library of responses to these frequently asked questions. When responding to an e-mail, ask yourself if you are likely to get the question again. If your answer is yes, then consider developing a document called "Frequently Asked Questions," or "FAQs" and save it. In the future, when you get a question that you have answered before, simply cut and paste your response from your FAQs file into your e-mail message. Always make sure to appropriately edit and personalize your responses.

## Following Formalities with E-mail Netiquette

When writing e-mails, remember these points:

- Be courteous. Remember to use please and thank you.

- Reply promptly—within 24 hours at the very latest.

- Be brief.

- Use upper- and lowercase characters appropriately. ALL CAPITALS indicates SHOUTING!

- Use emoticons only where appropriate—that is, if the person you are sending the e-mail to is a personal friend or colleague.

- Check your grammar and spelling.

- Use attachments sparingly.

- Do not send unsolicited bulk e-mail.

## Graphic Headers and HTML

For a long time, text e-mails were the main form of Internet communication. However, the surge in popularity of HTML e-mails has raised the bar in Internet marketing and communication with its informative imagery and easily accessible links. HTML e-mail, or even using HTML and graphics in your e-mail messages, is definitely something that should be taken into consideration by any travel or tourism professional. If you are considering using HTML e-mails you want to make sure it is done right. Otherwise people will not be able to read your message or it may appear as if you are trying to send them an attachment —as we have said, people tend not to download attachments from people they don't know or are not expecting. HTML e-mails are covered in more depth in Chapter 14 and HTML signature files are covered more in Chapter 11.

## Reply Promptly

Replying to e-mail inquiries as promptly as possible is very important in the travel and tourism industry. The fact of the matter is people are pressed for time. If someone has decided that on Tuesday night they are going to research, plan, book, and finalize their vacation, they want their questions answered as soon as possible. If they have to wait 15 or 24 hours for a response from you, you may have already lost their business.

## Leverage with Viral Marketing

Vacationers want to share their experiences with their family and friends. Make it easy for them to do this by providing a personal blog or a personal photo album on your Web site. Set it up so that all they have to do is fill in their family and friends' e-mail addresses, names, and a brief message (if they want) along with a link to the page on your Web site that contains their photo album.

## Internet Resources for Chapter 10

I have developed a great library of online resources for you to check out regarding e-mail. This library is available on my Tourism Internet Marketing University Web site *http://www.TourismInternetMarketingU.com/max* in the Resources section where you can find additional tips, tools, techniques, and resources.

I have also developed courses on many of the topics covered in this book. These courses are also available on my Tourism Internet Marketing University Web site *http://www.TourismInternetMarketingU.com/max*. These courses are delivered immediately over the Internet or can be ordered as a CD.

# 11

## Utilizing Signature Files to Increase Web Site Traffic

**A** signature file is your electronic business card. Signature files are commonly referred to as a sig file and take the form of a short memo that is attached to the end of all of your e-mail messages. Tourism related businesses and organizations can use signature files in a number of clever ways, from just giving out phone numbers and addresses, to offering more substantial information such as the promotion of your e-club, or to inform people about new packages or specials on your Web site. Signature files can also be used to show off an award or honor your company has received. In this chapter, we cover:

- The appropriate size of sig files

- The content and design of sig files

- Creating sig files to add statements to your messages

- The benefits of sig files.

### Presenting Your e-Business Card

A signature file is your e-business card and should be attached to the end of all of your e-mails including e-mails that are sent to individuals, forums, discussion groups, newsgroups, and mail lists. If your e-mail program doesn't allow for the use of a signature file you should consider switching e-mail programs. Sig files are readily accepted online and, when designed properly, comply with netiquette. Sig files can also be quite effective in drawing traffic to your Web site when used appropriately.

Your sig file should always include all basic contact information: your name, organization name, snail mail address, phone, fax, e-mail, and **URL**. You should provide every way possible for recipients to reach you. The customer is king and it is the recipients' choice if they would rather call than e-mail you.

Some tourism-related businesses also include a line that reads "Click here to go to our Web site" on their sig file, and when you "click here" you go directly to their Web site. This is a nice idea, but you must also remember to include your actual URL so that the recipients can see it, read it, and have it. Some people print their e-mail to take home at night. If your full URL is printed, then they can read it and access your Web site wherever they are. They can't get to your Web site by trying to click on a piece of paper.

**URL**
The unique address for a file that is accessible on the Internet.

It is also a good idea to include a **tag line** in your sig file. Many tourism-related businesses use tag lines to offer information about their operation, their destination, their e-club, their packages or specials, an award their company has received, or other marketing-focused information.

**Tag Line**
A variant of a branding slogan typically used in marketing materials and advertising.

When creating your sig file it is important to always remember to make URLs and e-mail addresses hypertext linked. This allows readers to click on the URL to take them directly to your Web site or to click on the e-mail address and e-mail you without having to copy and paste the address in their browser or e-mail program. To make your URLs and e-mail address hypertext links, place *http://* before Web site URLs and *mailto:* before e-mail addresses. Without the *http://* before the *www*, some older e-mail programs don't recognize it as a link, meaning that to get to your site recipients have to copy the address, open their browser, and paste the address in the address field to get to the page you are recommending.

## How to Develop Your Signature File

Again, if your e-mail program doesn't allow for the use of a signature file, you should consider switching e-mail programs. When preparing the design of your sig file, first you should decide what information you want to include. Once that is done, then you can decide what you want your e-business card to look like. Depending on which e-mail program you are using, you can either create your sig file using a word processor such as Windows Notepad or Microsoft Word, and save it as a text file (with a .txt extension), or you can create your sig file within the e-mail program itself.

All e-mail programs have instructions on how to set up your signature file in their "Help" file. If you are using Microsoft Outlook, take the following steps to develop your sig file:

1. On the menu bar, click "Tools."

2. In the drop-down menu, click "Options."

3. Click the "Mail Format" tab.

4. Click the "Signatures" button.

5. Then click the "New" button to add your new signature.

6. Enter a name for your signature, select the appropriate "radio" button and click "Next."

7. Enter your signature and click "Finish."

8. If you have more than one signature, pick one that will be used as a default.

9. Click "OK," then "OK" again.

## Graphic Headers and HTML

Using graphics or HTML in your signature file could result in higher brand awareness and more visitors to your Web site. To increase brand power, make sure to match up your logo and colors with what can be found on your Web site and other online and offline promotional material.

If incorporating an HTML header or footer into your sig file is something you are thinking of, it is very important that it is done correctly. You may even want to look into getting your header professionally developed because if this is done wrong it could have a negative impact on your business. You should include your telephone number and your Web address. See Figure 11.1 to see how we use an HTML header and footer in my office.

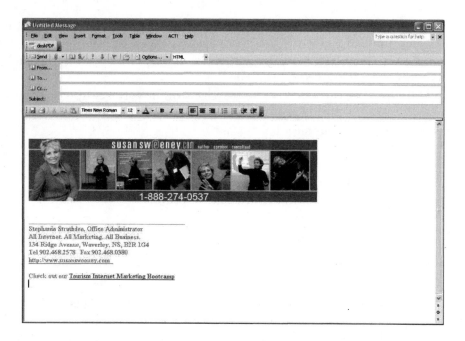

**Figure 11.1.**   We use an HTML header and footer in all e-mails that are sent from my office.

Once you have your header image designed, make sure that the image is saved as an HTML file with an extension of .htm or .html and make sure it is uploaded to a Web server. You do not want to link to an image that is saved on your computer, if you do it will appear as an attachment—people tend not to download attachments from people they don't know or are not expecting.

## The Do's and Don'ts of Signature Files

Some travel-related companies and organizations develop different signature files to use with different groups of recipients. It is a good idea to use a different sig file for each different group you are targeting, one that is appropriate for that group. It is also important to update the tag line in your sig file often to reflect current marketing-related information.

Some e-mail programs allow sig files a maximum of 80 characters per line. No matter what program you are using, you should design your sig file to fit well within the limits of all programs. To be assured that your sig file will be viewed just as you have designed it, a good rule of thumb is to use no more than 65 characters per line. Sometimes people open and view their e-mail in a small window and not the full screen. To help ensure that what you have on one line in your sig file appears on one line (and not two) in your viewer's browser, the fewer characters used the better.

Some travel-related businesses and organizations get really innovative in the design of their sig files by including sketches, designs, or logos developed by combining keyboard numbers and punctuation. Including graphics, icons or sketches in your sig file that are developed with numbers and punctuation is not a good idea. It might look quite nice on your screen, but when you send it to another person who has a different e-mail program or is using a different screen resolution, it could look quite different on their monitor.

On the other hand, professionally designed graphics can really reinforce your brand and your identity—people do business with people they know and trust.

The use of sig files offers a number of benefits to your company. If you use sig files appropriately, you promote your company and your online presence in the following ways:

- The use of sig files increases your company's online exposure. By merely placing a sig file at the end of a posting to a newsgroup, you ensure that your company name will be seen by thousands of people. A great tag line with a call to action can encourage people to visit your site.

- As with any advertisement, the design and content of your sig file can be used to position your business and create or complement a corporate image.

- Using your sig file can enhance the reputation of your company based upon the e-mail that it is attached to. If your postings to newsgroups and mailing lists are helpful and continually appreciated, this will become associated with your company name.

- Using appropriate sig files signals to the online community that you are a member who respects proper netiquette.

| Sig File Do's | Sig File Don'ts |
| --- | --- |
| Do list all appropriate contact information. | Don't list prices of any kind. |
| Keep it short, say four to eight lines. | Don't use a sales pitch. |
| Keep it simple. | Don't use too many symbols. |
| Provide an appropriate and professional tag line. | Don't list the company's products or services. |

## Creating Sig Files to Bring Traffic to Your Web Site

For travel-related businesses and organizations the major benefit of sig files is that they can attract visitors to your Web site. Sigvertising is when you use your signature file as a mini-advertisement for your company and its products and services. With sigvertising you can go beyond offering the basic contact information—you can use your sig file as a tool to bring traffic to your Web site. Do this by using your sig file to give the reader some insight into your business or destination and a reason to visit your site—not just to provide your company's phone number and URL.

One of the most important elements of your signature file from a marketing perspective is the tag line. A tag line is a small sentence that is used in branding and is often recognizable without even the mention of the company name.

Do you recognize any of these tag lines?

- "We try harder."

- "It's the real thing."

- "Like a rock."

- "Just do it."

- "Kills bugs dead."

Your signature file should always include a one-line tag line or catch phrase. A catch phrase is simply something that catches the reader's attention and intrigues him or her to find out more. It's a good idea to include a call to action in the catch phrase, wherever possible, to get your reader to take action. I often include the catch phrase "Check out our Internet Marketing Bootcamp" in my signature file with a hypertext link to my Web site. I get positive results with this, as recipients often do check out our Internet Marketing Bootcamp, ask for additional information on the Bootcamp, and often attend. It works!

Your catch phrase has to be relevant to your objectives and your target market. For example, if your objective is to get more people to your Web site and your target market is vacation home rentals, your catch phrase could be something like this: "We've got the largest selection of Idaho vacation homes—check them out!" with a hypertext link to your Web site. Or perhaps your objective is to get more people to sign up to your e-club and your target audience is amusement park enthusiasts. Your catch phrase could be something like this: "Join my e-club and receive great tips and coupons for the best amusement parks in the world," with a hypertext link to your e-club sign up.

Consider some of the following tag line or catch phrase possibilities to help increase the traffic to your tourism Web site:

- Tell people about your e-Club. Provide a call to action to get people to join.

- Let people know about your e-specials and invite them to your site for more information.

- Let people know about the great content on your site, for instance, your podcasts, videocasts, or articles.

- Announce a contest. If your site is holding a contest, tell readers that they can enter by visiting your site.

- Announce an award or honor. If your company or your Web site has received special recognition, tell people about it through your sig file.

Generally, sig files are accepted everywhere online in e-mail, newsgroups, mail lists, discussion groups, and many consumer generated media sites (consumer generated media is covered more in depth in Chapter 13). However, be cautious when developing your sig files to ensure that they will be well received. Sig files that are billboards, or sig files that are longer than most of your text messages, are to be avoided. Sig files that are blatant advertisements definitely are not appreciated. The online community reacts unfavorably to hard-sell advertising unless it is done in the proper forum. Here is an example of a sig file that might offend Internet users:

```
xxxxxxxxxxxxxxxxxxxxxxxxxxxxxxxxxxxxxxxxxxxxxxxxxxxxxxxxxxxxxxxxxxxxxxxx
LIMITED OFFER – 75% OFF
Availability is limited, so call today!
Florida & Bahamas Cruise Vacations!
Complimentary BONUS vacations for ordering today!
Talk to Jane Doe about your options!
101 Main Street, Woodstock, New York 10010
Tel: (800) 555-0000
Cell: (800) 555-1010
Fax: (800) 555-1020
www.svtravel.com
xxxxxxxxxxxxxxxxxxxxxxxxxxxxxxxxxxxxxxxxxxxxxxxxxxxxxxxxxxxxxxxxxxxxxxxx
```

Another mistake that travel companies make is that they try to make their sig files too flashy or eye-catching. Using a lot of large symbols might catch people's eyes, but the impression it leaves will not be memorable. Here is an example of what not to do:

```
??        :):):):)?:):):):)?:):):):)?:):):):)?:):):):)?:):):):)?:):):)    ??
??        ! Sunnyvale Travel !                                            ??
??        !Jane Doe, Sales Representative!                                ??
??        ! jdoe@svtravel.com !                                          ??
??        232 Main Street ?     ?800) 555-0000                           ??
??        Woodstock, New York ?       ? (800) 555-0002                   ??
??        30210                                                          ??
??        "Find Special Travel Packages @ www.svtravel.com" ??
??        :):):):)?:):):):)?:):):):)?:):):):)?:):):):)?:):):):)?:):):)    ??
```

Here are some examples of what sig files should look like:

```
========================================================
Ridgevale Travel Agency
Jane Doe, Travel Agent
mailto:jdoe@rvtravel.com
101 Main Street, Woodstock, New York, 10010
Tel: (800) 555-0000 Fax:(800) 555-0002
"Our Spring Break event is on now @ http://www. rvtravel.com"
========================================================
```

```
_____

Jane Doe, Travel Representative
Ridgevale Travel
jdoe@rvtravel.com
101 Main Street                    Tel: (800) 555-0000
Woodstock, New York, 10010         Fax: (800) 555-0001
Check out our online contest http://www.rvtravel.com today and WIN!

_____
```

```
>>>>>>>>>>>>>>>>>>>>>>>>>>>>>>>>>>>>>>>>>>>>>>>>>>>>
Jane Doe, Travel Representative
Sunnyvale Travel
101 Main Street                    jdoe@svtravel.com
P.O. Box 101                       Tel: (800) 555-0000
Woodstock, New York 10010          URL: www.svtravel.com
"2007 Winner of the Distinguished Service Award"
>>>>>>>>>>>>>>>>>>>>>>>>>>>>>>>>>>>>>>>>>>>>>>>>>>>>>
```

## Using Signature Files as an E-mail Template

When replying to routine e-mail inquiries, you can set up signature files as pre-written responses. When a routine question comes in, simply click the reply button and choose the appropriate signature with the pre-written response. To accomplish this in Microsoft Outlook:

1. On the menu bar, click "Tools."

2. In the drop-down menu, click "Options."

3. Click the "Mail Format" tab.

4. Choose the appropriate signature.

5. Click "OK."

Always personalize any e-mail you send. In the case of a pre-written response simply highlight the areas that should be personalized with upper case font and brackets. For example, [FIRST NAME], [COMPANY NAME] or, if you want to add a full sentence or two, [ADD PERSONALIZED SENTENCE(s) HERE]. This will not only save you time, it will also give you the opportunity to tailor a better response or set up an automated drip campaign.

## Internet Resources for Chapter 11

I have developed a great library of online resources for you to check out regarding signature files. This library is available on my Tourism Internet Marketing University Web site *http://www.TourismInternetMarketingU.com/max* in the Resources section where you can find additional tips, tools, techniques, and resources.

I have also developed courses on many of the topics covered in this book. These courses are also available on my Tourism Internet Marketing University Web site *http://www.TourismInternetMarketingU.com/max*. These courses are delivered immediately over the Internet or can be ordered as a CD.

# 12

---

# Autoresponders

**A**utoresponders, as the name suggests, provide a designated automatic response to an incoming e-mail. You send an e-mail to an autoresponder e-mail address and you get back the requested information via e-mail. In this chapter, you will learn:

- What autoresponders are

- Why you should use autoresponders

- What types of travel and tourism information to send via autoresponders

- Autoresponder features

- Tips on successful tourism marketing through autoresponders.

## What Are Autoresponders?

An autoresponder is a utility created to work with e-mail programs. They are set up automatically to return a prewritten message to anyone who submits e-mail to a particular Internet address. The autoresponder reply can be a single e-mail message or a series of preprogrammed messages. Autoresponders are known by many names, such as infobots, responders, mailbots, autobots, automailers, or e-mail-on-demand. They enable you to do drip marketing quickly and easily. Drip marketing is a strategy that involves sending out a number of promotional pieces over a period of time to a subset of your database.

> **Autoresponder**
> A computer program that automatically returns a prewritten message to anyone who submits e-mail to a particular Internet address.

Autoresponders have been around for many years. The first generation of autoresponders were basically used to send "Out of Office" notifications. If you were going to be out of the office for a period of time, you would turn on your autoresponder to let people know this in case they were expecting an immediate response to their e-mail.

The second generation of autoresponders, while still using very simple technology, were used to send things like price lists and e-brochures.

Today's autoresponder works much the same way—you send an e-mail to a specified e-mail address and you get back the requested information via e-mail. However, over the last few years, we have seen major changes in the technology being used. Today autoresponders are more sophisticated and the enhanced features have provided many opportunities for marketers and merchants alike, as outlined in the next section.

## Why Use Autoresponders?

One of the major benefits of using an autoresponder is the immediate response—24 hours a day, 7 days a week, 365 days a year—providing immediate gratification for the recipient. This is particularly valuable in the travel and tourism industry where the faster the response, the better the chance you have of getting the business.

Autoresponders are a real time saver, eliminating the need for manual responses for many mundane and routine requests. They also enable you to track responses to various offers to assist you in your ongoing marketing efforts.

One big advantage with today's autoresponders is the ability to schedule multiple messages at predetermined intervals. The first response can go immediately, with a second message timed to go two days after the first, a third message to go five days after the second, and so on. Market research shows that a prospect needs to be exposed to your message multiple times to become a motivated buyer.

Today's autoresponders are getting even more sophisticated in terms of mail list administration. These programs gather the e-mail addresses of people requesting information, and store them in a database. The program adds new names to the database and eliminates e-mail addresses that no longer work. Today's autoresponder programs also provide reports about site visitors requesting information. This technology is very cost-effective when compared to manual responses by a human, not to mention the associated telephone and fax costs.

Personalization is a standard feature of today's autoresponder programs. Autoresponders are used to send all kinds of information:

- Articles on your destination

- Trivia about your destination

- Weekly golf tips, ski tips, or other tips of interest to your target markets

- Destination of the week or featured destination series

- Checklists appropriate for your target market

    - cruise checklists

    - golf trip checklists

- Wedding planning information, where you send a list of items that need to be taken care of, in the month they need to be taken care of.

You can provide a copy of your newsletter so people can read a copy before subscribing, or anything else in which your target market might be interested.

Why use an autoresponder when you could just provide the information on your Web site? There are many reasons. With the autoresponder you have the interested party's name and e-mail address; you don't get that from a visitor to your site. The autoresponder also provides you with the opportunity to send multiple or sequential messages to your potential customer.

You can incorporate viral marketing tactics into your autoresponder messages as well. Use this opportunity to encourage recipients to tell others about the information they are receiving, or present a way for them to provide a copy of the information to their friends. It's important when using viral marketing to provide the recipient with the opportunity to subscribe to receive your information. See Chapter 5 for more on viral marketing.

## Types of Autoresponders

There are three different types of autoresponders:

- Free

- Web host

- Other autoresponder providers.

There are many free or minimal-fee autoresponders available that come with an ad on your responder page. Some Web hosting companies provide autoresponders in their Web hosting packages. Some storefront providers are including autoresponders in their product offerings. There also are many autoresponder service providers that offer packages for a fee if you don't want to have ads placed on your responder page.

The important thing is to get the autoresponder that has the features you are looking for. See the Resources section of my Web site (*http://www.TourismInternetMarketingU.com*) for appropriate autoresponder resources.

## Autoresponder Features

When you are looking for an autoresponder, you want to make sure it has all the features to enable you to make the most of this marketing activity. Today's autoresponders keep getting better—new features are being added all the time. Some of the things you want to look for are discussed below.

### Personalization

Today's autoresponders capture the requester's name as well as e-mail address, allowing personalized responses.

### Multiple Responses/Sequential Autoresponders

Studies have shown that a potential customer has to be exposed to your message multiple times before he or she is ready to buy. Many autoresponders allow multiple messages on a scheduled time line.

## Size of Message

Some autoresponders have a limit on the size of the message that can be sent. Ensure that your autoresponder can handle any message you would want to send to prospective customers.

## Tracking

You must have access to tracking reports that provide you with information to enable you to track the results of your marketing efforts. You need to be able to determine what is working and what is not.

## HTML Messaging

Choose an autoresponder that can handle HTML and plain text e-mails. Studies have shown that HTML marketing e-mails get a higher click-through rate. Autoresponders are constantly being enhanced. Stay current.

# Successful Marketing through Autoresponders

The technology itself is only one piece of this marketing technique. The content of the messages sent out by the autoresponder is the determining factor in converting recipients of your message to customers. The following tips will help you produce effective messages:

- Personalize. Personalize your messages using the recipient's name throughout the message and in the subject line.

- Tone. Selling is all about relationships. Give your messages a tone that builds relationships.

- Focus on the reader's needs and how your travel-related product or service provides the solution. Focus on the benefits.

- Subject line. Have a catchy subject line, but don't use ad copy. Ad copy in a subject line is a sure way to get your message deleted before it is read.

- Include a call to action. It is amazing how often people do what they are told to do.

- Use correct spelling, upper- and lowercase letters, grammar, and punctuation. This correspondence is business correspondence and is a reflection of everything related to how you do business.

- Get to the point quickly. Online readers have little patience with verbose messages.

- Write for scanability. Have a maximum of six or seven lines per paragraph.

## Internet Resources for Chapter 12

I have developed a great library of online resources for you to check out regarding autoresponders. This library is available on my Tourism Internet Marketing University Web site *http://www.TourismInternetMarketingU.com/max* in the Resources section where you can find additional tips, tools, techniques, and resources.

I have also developed courses on many of the topics covered in this book. These courses are also available on my Tourism Internet Marketing University Web site *http://www.TourismInternetMarketingU.com/max*. These courses are delivered immediately over the Internet or can be ordered as a CD.

# 13

## Consumer Generated Media

The Internet has given consumers a voice like no other form of media. It has provided consumers with a platform where they can publish their opinions for others to read, research, listen to, and share. Consumer generated media (CGM) encompasses these opinions along with consumers' comments, reviews, critiques and complaints. It also includes consumer blogs, wikis, videos on YouTube, and the like. CGM is nothing more than the online version of word-of-mouth behavior, but it is quickly becoming an important part in marketing effectively for the travel and tourism industry.

Consumer generated media is the fastest growing media online and it is one where consumers are in control—in control of what information they want to see on the Web, in control of when they want to see that information, and in control of what information they want to generate on the Web.

The Web has given consumers a voice that simply cannot be ignored. With a massive amount of media being generated across the Internet on a daily basis, they could be talking about your travel and tourism business, products, packages, or destination in their blog, or showing your destination in their online photo album or through their video on YouTube. In this chapter you will learn:

- What is consumer generated media?

- Why is it important?

- The effects of CGM on your corporate reputation.

- Where do you find consumer generated media?

## What is Consumer Generated Media?

Unlike paid media, such as print or banner ads, consumer generated media is created solely by consumers, not professional writers, journalists, or publishers. It is created by consumers, for consumers. It can include anything from facts, opinions, impressions, experiences, rumors, reviews, complaints, praises—anything. CGM is made available to other Internet users through discussion boards, blogs, and other social media networks. CGM encompasses opinions, experiences, advice, and commentary about products, brands, companies and services, and is usually informed by personal experience.

According to *Pew Internet & American Life Project*, 90 percent of consumers have used the Internet to research a product or a service. Consumers are using the Internet to consult with other consumers. They are reading sites dedicated to consumer opinions, consumer reviews, and personal experiences. They are frequenting discussion boards where they share information, give feedback, ask questions, or simply read what others are saying.

CGM is viewed by consumers as trusted third-party advice and information and they are using this information to form their own opinions on your travel destination, travel products, services, and packages and are using this information to help them in their purchasing decision.

## Why Consumer Generated Media is Important

The World Wide Web is host to more than 100 million comments from consumers alone. Consumer generated media is the fastest growing media online and should be as important to travel and tourism-related businesses as it is to other consumers. Listening to and leveraging consumer generated media may well be the most important source of competitive advantage for any travel and tourism company. Studies have shown that when it comes to product information, consumers place far more trust in other consumers than they do in manufacturers, marketers, and advertisers. By listening to CGM and to what your customers are saying, you can gain truthful insights as to how they view your business, products, services, and destination.

Consumers consistently rank word-of-mouth as one of the top sources for making purchasing decisions. An eMarketer study found that 65 percent of consumers trust their friends the most for product recommendations, while 27 percent trust experts and 8 percent trust celebrities. It is for this reason and the rapid growth of this trend that it poses both challenges and opportunities for marketing, advertising, and public relations teams.

Merrill Lynch estimates that in 2007 one-third of all travel reservations in the U.S. will be done online, and that by 2010 online reservations will account for 45 percent of all reservations in the travel and tourism industry. With such an increase in online usage, the likelihood of more and more consumer comments being generated online also increases. With more consumers incorporating some form of multi-media, such as photos or videos in their comments, they are becoming even more persuasive.

## The Effect of CGM on Corporate Reputation

Because consumer generated media is easy to find through search engines, traditional travel and tourism marketers and advertisers no longer have control over the messages being circulated about their company, packages, or destination. Nor do they have control over the medium in which those messages are being presented. When a consumer uses a search engine to search for a particular company, brand or product, it's almost certain that postings created by other consumers will be among the top results.

Understanding and monitoring the impact CGM has on consumers' decision making process is extremely important for online success. According to *Pew Internet & American Life Project*, over 40 percent of online consumers have created some form of online content. CGM comments are online forever, archived, until the person who posted them removes them. It is estimated that the number of comments will grow by about 30 percent each year.

CGM leaves a digital trail, which means it is a highly measurable form of media. It can be converted into market research. It allows travel and tourism companies to gauge their brand equity, reputation, and message effectiveness. It is important for travel and tourism companies to take into account the scope and effect of CGM and use it to help them make more informed decisions.

There are any number of message boards and forums where people can post what's on their mind, whether it be to tell of their harrowing experience or the exceptional customer service they received. Any one of these can affect your travel and tourism operation. You need to pay close attention to what is being said in both traditional media and consumer generated media.

You could lose the chance to demonstrate a commitment to customer service by not addressing complaints. The news cycle has accelerated tremendously and consumers' expectations that companies will frequently and directly communicate with them has been raised, thanks to the Internet. If there is no response from your company on a given issue, consumers are likely to spread the news and further speculate about the issue. Along with other traditional forms, blogging and engaging in social media should now be part of any travel and tourism company's media outreach.

## CGM—Opportunity or Threat?

Consumers actively gather to review, rate products and services, and participate in online discussions. There are approximately 20 million blogs online right now, with about 80,000 new ones being created each day.

Blogs are typically updated once a day, or no less than three times per week, with news, information, or views on a particular subject or product. Because blogs are updated so frequently, and on a regular basis, they get very good rankings from the search engines and can be very visible on the Web—whether they are being used to express positive or negative views or opinions. For more on blogs see Chapter 21.

CGM comments have the power to influence anyone who sees them and are a very valuable research tool for travel and tourism businesses. It creates a competitive advantage as it allows you (and everyone else online) to find out how your consumers really feel about your destination, travel packages, and travel-related products and services.

CGM comments give travel and tourism businesses the opportunity to listen to what consumers are saying, to learn what it was about their destination, packages, or services that encouraged (or discouraged) the purchasing decision; and it gives them the opportunity to act accordingly. For example, amusement park marketers can gain unfiltered insights into customer experiences that they could only have gotten through surveys and comment cards in the past.

Travel and tourism companies can create interactive relationships with their customers through these social media outlets since corporate-sponsored CGM initiatives are becoming more and more popular. For example, at Sheraton Hotels and Resorts Belong (pictured in Figure 13.1), consumers are invited to share their stories with others.

Travel and tourism companies can now use these social media outlets to promote their packages, destination, services, and products as many social media outlets now allow sponsorships and paid advertising. For example, HotelChatter.com (*http://www.hotelchatter.com*) and TripAdvisor (*http://www.tripadvisor.com*) accept display advertising.

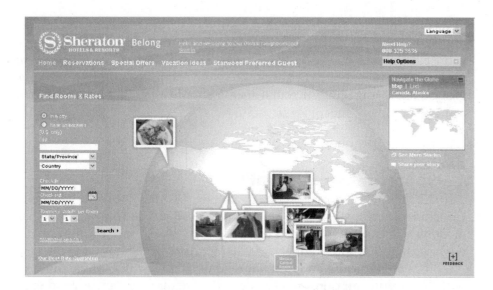

**Figure 13.1.** Sheraton Hotels and Resorts Belong encourages consumers to share their stories with others.

Measuring the impact of CGM along with Web traffic analysis (see Chapter 26), and other more traditional media, will give travel and tourism organizations insight into the effectiveness of their marketing strategies, along with any threats to their corporate reputation. CGM gives travel and tourism companies the opportunity to create strategies for brand management and corporate reputation that tie into their business objectives and also drive their competitive analysis.

## Developing a Social Media Strategy

Consumer generated media is a great tool that can give travel and tourism businesses firsthand insights into their customers' experience, it can help travel and tourism businesses establish interactive relationships with their customers, and it can also provide them with a new medium to promote their destinations, packages, and travel and tourism-related services and products.

A social media strategy should only be created once you have launched a successful online marketing and distribution strategy, including an optimized, user-friendly Web site, successful e-mail marketing and strategic linking and link popularity strategies, and successful online advertising initiatives. And as with everything related to your business and your Internet marketing, your social media strategy must take into account your objectives and your target market.

You first must determine what your situation is in terms of CGM. If you find that there is a lot of chatter about your travel and tourism organization, then perhaps it is time to come up with a social media strategy that allows you to communicate more openly. Determine which CGM sites are talking about you, monitor postings, address criticisms, and implement any suggestions for improvement.

If, however, you find that your goal is simply to leverage your expertise, then perhaps a corporate sponsored blog or wiki would be best. Post articles from the different areas of your organization or destination. For example, the golf pro could post an article one week, the spa manager the next week, and so on.

There is also the option of simply advertising on relevant CGM sites that have high volumes of targeted traffic.

According to *Harris Interactive Survey*, 85 percent of respondents said word-of-mouth communication is credible, compared with 70 percent for PR and advertising. This is why it is important for those in the travel and tourism industry to understand and try to manage CGM's impact on their success.

## Where Do You Find Consumer Generated Media?

Discussion forums, message boards, and Usenet newsgroups were among the first generation of CGM, while blogs, wikis, podcasts, and videocasts represent the second generation—all still very easy and inexpensive to create.

Consumer-created postings can typically be found on Internet discussion boards, forums, newsgroups, blogs and wikis (see Chapter 21), podcastings and videocastings (see Chapter 22). CGM can include text, images, photos, videos, and other forms of media.

There are all kinds of Web sites dedicated to all kinds of CGM that allow consumers to communicate with their network, post their videos for the world to see, post complaints, rate products and services, or give feedback. A few such Web sites include:

- Complaints.com - *http://www.complaints.com*

- Trip Advisor - *http://www.tripadvisor.com*

- Epinions.com - *http://www.epinions.com*

- PlanetFeedback - *http://www.planetfeedback.com*

- Facebook - *http://wwwfacebook.com*

- MySpace - *http://www.myspace.com*

- Flickr - *http://www.flickr.com*

- YouTube – *http://www.youtube.com*

- Outloud.TV - *http://www.outloud.tv*

- Revver - *http://one.revver.com/revver*

- Wikipedia - *http://wikipedia.org.*

Consumer generated media can give travel and tourism organizations unfiltered insights into their customers' experiences. It can create interactive relationships with consumers and also provide a new way of advertising and promoting travel and tourism-related products, services, destinations, and packages. However, your travel and tourism Internet marketing strategy must be comprised of many tactics designed to grow your online success—Web site optimization, customer segmentation, strategic linking, keyword rich copy, e-mail marketing, online advertising, and sponsorship. Your social media strategy is just one piece of your Internet marketing strategy.

## How Do You Use Consumer Generated Media?

Travel and tourism organizations should be taking advantage of CGM and adapting their online marketing so that it is interactive with their consumers. To begin adapting to the new CGM you simply need to:

- Observe, listen to and engage customers and potential customers in your target market

- Provide your customers and potential customers with a convenient way to communicate with you and participate in your marketing.

Understanding the trends in CGM is what will give you the competitive advantage. Listening to and leveraging such media may be the most important source of competitive advantage for travel and tourism companies.

Leverage CGM by having systems in place to help you listen to and understand what your customers are saying about your company, your destination, your products and services, and even your competitors. Pay as much attention to unsolicited commentary as possible. Invite active consumers into a discussion to help gain more control over the buzz that is being generated about your travel and tourism operation.

Different companies use CGM for different reasons. The most important uses of CGM for the travel and tourism industry are to:

- Get in sync with consumers—Use CGM to find out what consumers are looking for from travel and tourism sites and use that information as a way to come up with new content for your site or your corporate blog.

- Track your online ads—Use CGM to identify what buzz words people are using to describe your travel and tourism operation or destination and use this information to help you decide what keywords you want to use in your ads and where the best place is to advertise.

- Track your competitors—Use CGM to find out what is being said about your competition. Implement any positive elements from what they are doing and avoid any negative elements.

Consumer generated media is a great tool in helping travel and tourism operators understand their target markets, what they want and what they need.


## Internet Resources for Chapter 13

I have developed a great library of online resources for you to check out regarding consumer generated media. This library is available on my Tourism Internet Marketing University Web site *http://www.TourismInternetMarketingU.com/max* in the Resources section where you can find additional tips, tools, techniques, and resources.

I have also developed courses on many of the topics covered in this book. These courses are also available on my Tourism Internet Marketing University Web site *http://www.TourismInternetMarketingU.com/max*. These courses are delivered immediately over the Internet or can be ordered as a CD.

# 14

## Establishing Your Private Mailing List

Having your own private mailing list enables you to create one-way communication to your target market. Private mailing lists are also a tremendous vehicle for building relationships and a sense of community. Generating your own private mailing list is highly recommended in the travel and tourism industry because a targeted opt-in list has many marketing uses. The list can be used to maintain communication with customers and potential customers regarding your destination, your packages, your vacation specials, and so on. It can also be used to distribute corporate newsletters, last minute getaways, new vacation packages, e-specials, and upcoming events. In this chapter, we cover:

- Why have your own mailing list?

- The issue of privacy

- Managing your mail list

- Building your mail list

- Promoting your mail list

- Tips to stay under the spam radars

- Recent legislation

- Why e-mail is not dead—the latest.

## Why Have Your Own Mailing List?

There are numerous reasons to own and use your own mail list. They include some of the same reasons that make it imperative to join someone else's list. Running a permission-based private mailing list can be beneficial in many ways, including:

- Gets you in front of your customers and potential customers on a regular basis

- Conserves contacts

- Builds repeat traffic to your Web site (as discussed in Chapter 3)

- Branding

- Promotion of your destination, packages, specials, and events

- First of mind marketing

- Potential source of revenue.

### Permission-Based Marketing

Permission and privacy are critical to the success of any e-mail marketing campaign. Although unsolicited direct "snail mail" might be generally accepted or at least tolerated by many consumers, the rules are completely different on-line. Unsolicited e-mail (known as spam) runs the risk of damaging your company's reputation, not to mention the very real possibilities of flames, public blacklisting, hack attacks, or having your Internet services revoked. For serious spammers, recent legislation adds heavy fines and the possibility of prison. Online consumers are quick to let you know when you have crossed the line, and unsolicited e-mail definitely crosses the line. Because of this, online marketers are using many techniques to get their customers, potential customers, and Web site visitors to give them "permission" to send e-mail on a regular basis.

Permission marketing is really a win-win situation. Recipients receive information that they asked to receive, and the marketer is communicating with an audience that has expressed interest in what is being marketed. Online market-ers claim that permission e-mail marketing is one of the best ways to improve customer retention and boost sales.

So how do you get this coveted permission? Generally you have to provide something of value and of interest to your target market. There are many op-portunities on your Web site to ask for permission. Make sure you take advan-tage of them. Make sure your permission marketing is above the fold and grabs the readers' attention.

The more repeat-traffic generators on your site, the more opportunities you can provide for visitors to give you their permission. (See Chapter 3 for discus-sion of repeat-traffic generators.) You should leverage repeat-traffic generators with permission marketing that "sells the sizzle" and accelerates responses with a call to action. On my Web site I have a call to action that says, "Sign Up Now for Susan's biweekly newsletter filled with tips, tools, techniques and resources to assist you in achieving your Internet marketing goals." Here are some typical examples:

- "We change our coupons every week! Click here to join our e-club to be notified as soon as we update."

- "Click here to join our e-club and receive our biweekly newsletter filled with industry news, updates, and special offers."

- "We have new specials on a regular basis. Click here to be notified by e-mail when we post our new specials."

- "We have a new contest every three weeks. Keep checking back or click here if you'd like to be notified by e-mail every time we begin a new contest."

- "We constantly update our calendar of events. Keep checking back or click here if you'd like to be notified by e-mail every time we update."

- "Join our e-club to receive our e-specials, coupons, our great newsletter, and other great offers available only to our e-club members!"

You get the picture. Almost every page on your Web site provides an oppor-tunity for you to offer permission marketing. Of course, when site visitors click, they are taken to a screen where they add themselves to your e-mail list. It is important not to ask for too much too soon. If your visitors have to fill out a lengthy form to be added to your mailing list, they probably won't. The two most important things to ask for are the e-mail address and the visitor's first name. You want their first name so that you can personalize any correspondence with them. If you have more than one permission-based offer, your mail list program should keep track of the element the visitor has given you permission to send. If someone signed up to receive your newsletter, you cannot send them information on your newest golf packages. The best thing to do is to get umbrella permission. When you get umbrella permission you can send out all of your permission based marketing materials to all the people who signed up. One way of getting umbrella permission is to offer an e-club. When someone signs up for your e-club tell them that they will receive advanced notice of package specials and promotions, destination information, and updates of events. San Antonio's Menger Hotel, pictured in Figure 14.1, for example, invites its Web site visitors to join its e-club.

Your mail list software should be integrated with the Web site so when someone gives you permission, his or her name is automatically added to your database.

Permission marketing enjoys its success because it is personal, relevant, and anticipated. Your messages should be personalized, enhancing the one-to-one relationship marketing element.

Privacy is a very big issue when a Web site visitor is deciding whether to give you an e-mail address or not. It is very important to assure your visitors that you will not pass on their e-mail address to others or use it for anything but the purpose intended. Your privacy policy should be clearly evident on your Web

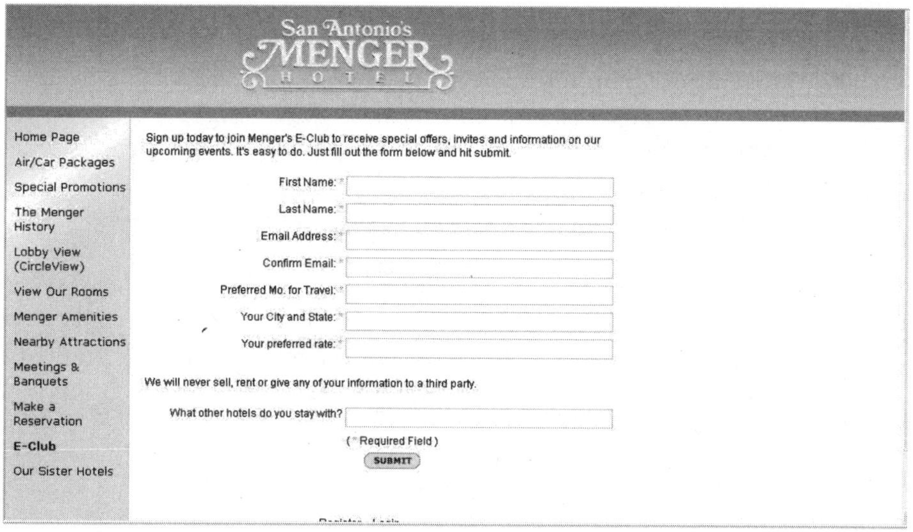

**Figure 14.1.** San Antonio's Menger Hotel invites its Web site visitors to join its e-club.

site on every page that asks for permission. The privacy policy can read like a legal document or be short and to the point.

## The Issue of Privacy

Privacy is a growing concern among many online users. You can boost your mailing list's sign-up rate by guaranteeing that subscribers' e-mail addresses are kept confidential and are not sold to or shared with anyone else. If you cannot assure them that your company will use their e-mail address solely for your correspondence with them, they will not feel comfortable giving their e-mail address to you. Provide people with your privacy policy statement. Make them feel comfortable about divulging their e-mail address to your business. To do this, you should have your privacy policy everywhere you ask permission or, alternatively, place a link to your business's privacy policy in a prominent location on your Web site, especially on your e-mail list sign-up page.

You should never add someone's name to your mailing list without his or her permission. People really resent receiving unsolicited mail, even if you give them the option to unsubscribe.

## Where We Need To Be

There are only two ways to do more business online:

- Have more people receive your offer.

- Improve your conversion rate of Web site visitors to Web site customers.

There are only a few ways to have more people get your offer:

- Increase the number of visitors to your Web site.

- Increase the number of people whom you reach with your online marketing in newsgroups, public mail lists, affiliate marketing, or any of the 101 ways in this book.

- Increase the number of people in your e-mail list who have given you permission to send them e-mail on an ongoing basis.

Ideally, where we'd like to be in terms of mail list marketing is:

- Have the right mail list technology.

- Grow your mail list through permission-based marketing as big as you can as fast as you can.

- Provide consistently valuable content to your list on an ongoing basis.

- Learn as much as you can about everyone on your list, building a profile on each person, so that you can send more targeted communication.

## The Right Mail List Technology

There are several ways that you can manage your mail list:

- Use your e-mail program (not recommended).

- Use mail list software.

- Outsource your mail list management.

## Using Your E-mail Program

Although managing your mail list through your e-mail program might look like a great option in that it doesn't cost you anything and is run from your desktop, giving you ultimate control, there are limitations.

Your e-mail program doesn't easily afford you the opportunity to segment your mail list—those who asked to receive your newsletter versus those who asked to receive notification when you update your What's New section, for example.

Your e-mail program doesn't generally provide the technology to quickly and easily personalize your communication—that is, insert the recipient's first name in designated areas within the e-mail. E-mail programs do not provide much in the way of tracking information, either.

It would be nice to be able to track such things as how many people opened your e-mail, how many sent a copy to a friend, and how many clicked through and visited your Web site. The tracking technology is generally available only through mail list software or from the third party that manages your mail list marketing if you choose to outsource this activity.

Another drawback is the administrative headache of manually managing all the "Subscribes," "Unsubscribes," and "Changes of E-mail Address," particularly when you have multiple sign-up opportunities on your Web site—for example, someone wants to unsubscribe from your e-specials but still wants to receive your newsletter and coupons. The time really has come when you need to invest in mail list software or outsource if you want to take this element of online marketing seriously.

## Using Mail List Software

There are numerous mail list management software programs available to help you organize your list distribution (see the Internet Resources at *http://www.TourismInternetMarketingU.com/max* for links to mail list software programs). This software enables you to easily add or remove subscribers. Mail list management software enables you to draft and send properly formatted html and text messages directly from within the software and it generally allows you to personalize your e-mails quickly and easily. Most of these programs can be integrated with your Web site so that people can add themselves to your list right from the site. You can also use this software to set up notification mechanisms to reply to subscribers, confirming that they have been added to the list. This makes running your mail list less time-consuming, as the software does most of the work for you.

Using your own mail list software requires an initial investment to purchase the program or an ongoing cost if you use an Application Service Provider (ASP)—a company that develops the mail list software and provides it to you as a monthly or annual service rather than as a product. The major advantage to this model is that as new bells and whistles are introduced, they are immediately available to all users of the software.

The cost to purchase software can range from an entry-level program at $99 to a robust, full-featured program at $2,500. The ASP model could cost you from $30 a month to several thousand dollars if you use an application that charges you per e-mail sent and you have a very large database.

Some of these programs run from your desktop; others have to be run from your server or through your Internet service provider. Many of the ASP model programs are run from the ASP's server. Most of these programs are sophisticated enough to allow you to segment the e-mail addresses in your database so you know who has asked to receive what from your Web site.

Most of these programs today have the personalization capability to allow you to insert a recipient's first name throughout the correspondence and in the subject line of the message as well. For this to work you have to capture the first names for each e-mail address in your database. Keep this in mind when asking people if they'd like to give you permission to send them e-mail for whatever reason—in addition to their e-mail address, have a mandatory field for their first name.

More and more of these programs are incorporating tracking features to let you know what's working and what's not. From an administrative perspective, many of these programs do a great job of adding new "Subscribes," deleting "Unsubscribes," and managing undeliverable addresses. This feature alone is worth its weight in gold.

Features to look for in mail list software include:

- Personalization capability—You want to be able to personalize each e-mail by inserting the recipient's first name in the subject line, in the salutation, and throughout the body of your message.

- HTML capability—You want to be able to send HTML e-mail (e-mail that looks like a Web page rather than text), which gets much higher readership than text e-mail.

- Message editor—You want to be able to bring up a past e-mail, edit it, and re-send it to a group.

- Previews—You want to be able to preview your message before you send it to make sure the formatting is correct, the personalization is working and the message looks great.

- Spam checker—The spam checker is a valuable tool to ensure that your message has the best chance of being received and not being rejected as spam. You want to be able to run your message through the spam checker to see how you score before you send any message. Today, if you score 5.0 or higher in the spam checker, you will want to edit your message to reduce your score before you send.

- Multi-threaded sending—This feature is important for large lists. It divides a list and sends multiple messages at one time through different streams.

- Filtering—This feature allows you to send specific messages to parts of your list. You could send a message only to those individuals in a specific state by filtering on the name of the state. You could send a message only to those interested in golf if you have that information in a field in your database.

- Scheduling—This allows you to prearrange to send your e-mail at a specific future time and date. Great if you want to set up all of your "Tips of the Week" in advance, or if you are going to be traveling when you want your newsletter to be sent out.

- Autoresponders—Some mail list software applications have autoresponders built in. See Chapter 12 for details on their uses.

- Web site integration—You want your mail list software to work with your Web site so when someone subscribes from your site, his or her contact information is automatically included in your mail list software. If someone wants to unsubscribe or change contact information, this can be taken care of through your site or through the e-mails you have sent. This really cuts down on the administration you have to deal with.

- Reporting and tracking—Some mail list software provides reports on messages sent (audience selected, date sent, clicks, total sent, number of bounces), subscriber activity (subscribes, unsubscribes, e-mails opened), link tracking, and bounce activity (number of undeliverables, hard bounces, soft bounces).

## Outsourcing Your Mail List

A third option is to outsource your mail list management to a third party. There are companies that specialize in this service that have a great depth of experience. One such company that we have had the pleasure to work with is Inbox360.com (*http://www.inbox360.com*).

When you outsource this activity, of course you have a monthly service fee. The software is run from the outsource company's server or its ISP's server.

Virtually all of the mail list service providers have the latest software, allowing you to personalize your messages, segment your lists, and get great tracking reports. Generally, administrative issues like adding the "Subscribes," deleting "Unsubscribes," and managing the undeliverables are handled by software used by the outsource company.

On the down side, you might lose some control—over content, over your customer, and over timing of your message release. It is imperative to have a clearly laid-out contract with the outsource company, addressing:

- Ownership of e-mail addresses

- Use of e-mail addresses

- Timing of correspondence

- Final approval of content

- Responsibility and timelines for replies to subscribers.

It is important that you retain ownership of all e-mail addresses and that the contract clearly states that all subscribers' names and e-mail addresses are the property of your company. Also include in the contract that you are provided with the current list in digital format every month. This way, if you decide to change service providers, your list goes with you. It takes a lot of effort to build your list, and it is a very valuable asset. Make sure you protect it.

Make sure that your contract clearly states that your e-mail addresses are not to be used by anyone else or provided to anyone else for any purpose whatsoever. People on your list have given you their e-mail addresses in confidence. They trust that you will not abuse the relationship. Make sure it is in your power to live up to that expectation.

Make sure that you have final control over the timing of your communications. It is important that your messages be delivered when you want them delivered. Timing is everything. We discuss timing later in this chapter.

Make sure that your contract has a clause that permits you to approve the final content going out to your list. You want to see and approve everything. You want to make sure the formatting is the way you want it; you want to be sure the personalization is working as it should; and you want to make sure there is no problem with graphics or word wrap.

You want to have a clear understanding with the outsource company regarding replies from messages going out to your list. Often the "From" field, although it looks like it is coming from you, is actually an address that resides with the outsource company. Discuss and agree on what happens when a recipient replies to your communication. Where does it go? When does it go? To receive a batch of replies three weeks after your communication went out is not acceptable.

There are certain benefits to outsourcing this activity to a third party that specializes in mail list marketing. This is their core responsibility. Often the outsource company has been involved in many campaigns—gaining expertise in what works and what doesn't. Often they can help you tweak your content or format to help achieve your objectives. Also, outsourcing this activity to a competent third party frees up your time and allows you to focus on other priorities.

## Building Your Database or Mail List

Once you are committed to private mail list marketing, you want to focus on building your database of e-mail addresses. The more people you can reach in your target market with your message, the better.

There are many ways to grow your list:

- Depending on where your database resides and current legislation, you may be able to import from your existing database. You probably already have a customer or prospective customer list that you can import into your mail list. You may be able to send a one-time message asking them if they'd like to be on your list or join your e-club. Tell them what they'll be receiving and how often, and stress the benefits. Provide them with a link to the sign-up page on your Web site. You need to be careful here with current legislation and where your database members are located (particularly if they reside in Canada).

- Use permission marketing techniques to ask if site visitors would like to be included in your list to receive your newsletter, your e-specials, your coupons, or anything else you want to use to entice them to join your list. See Chapter 4 for more information on permission marketing.

- Collect names and e-mail addresses at all points of contact—registration desk at a hotel, welcome centers for state tourism offices or destination marketing organizations, trade shows if you participate, member renewal, or registration forms for membership associations or organizations. Ask permission to add them to your e-club—remember to "sell the sizzle."

- Have employee contests and reward the employee who collects the most sign-ups for your e-club.

- Have posters in your bricks-and-mortar location promoting your e-club and letting people know how to join. Think about providing an incentive: "Join our e-club and get a 10 percent off coupon for your next purchase or a free gift."

- Promote your e-club in all of your direct-mail pieces and ads.

- Use direct e-mail rental lists to ask for sign-ups.

- Use brokers to run campaigns on complementary sites to get targeted sign-ups.

- Promote your e-club in your signature file.

- Encourage viral marketing via existing list members: "Send a copy to a friend" works for a number of repeat-traffic generators such as coupons, newsletters, e-specials, contest information, special offers, and promotions and packages. Make sure that every viral marketing communication includes sign-up information so recipients can add their names and e-mail addresses to your list as well: "If you've received a copy of this newsletter . . . or coupon . . . or e-special from a friend and would like to join our e-club to receive your own in the future, click here." The link should take them to a sign-up page on your Web site or open a new message in their e-mail program with "Subscribe" in the subject line and details of what exactly they would like to subscribe to in the body of the e-mail message.

- If you use tele-sales, add to the script a line that promotes your e-club and asks if the person would like to join.

- Partner with other, non-competing Web sites that have the same target market as you. Choose sites that have lots of traffic and a big database.

## Promoting Your Private Mail List

Promote your private mail list wherever you can reach your target market: on your site, online through various online marketing techniques, and offline. You will:

- Encourage your Web site visitors to join your list by making sure you have "Join our e-club—click here" calls to action throughout your site. You might enhance this with an incentive "Join our e-club to receive our biweekly tips, tools, and techniques and to be included in our drawing for a weekend stay—click here."

- Include a viral marketing element as previously described to encourage your subscribers to recommend your mail list to others.

- Invite your friends, colleagues, current clients, and potential clients to join your list.

- Remember to mention your e-club in your e-mail signature file. This is an easy way to promote the list.

- If you are looking for a large distribution list, you might even register your mailing list with Topica (*http://www.topica.com/solutions/direct.html*) or other public mail lists.

## Your Communication with Your Mail List

To be successful with private mail list marketing, you have to have a great targeted list and you have to know how to communicate effectively with your subscribers. How often should they receive your messages? When do you start to become an irritant? What time and day are your recipients going to be most receptive? How should your communication be formatted? Should it be text or HTML? These all are important questions to be answered if you want to improve the response.

How often should you communicate? It depends on what you're sending and what they asked to receive. Newsletters should generally be sent out every couple of weeks or once a month. Special promotions, coupons, and e-specials generally will be sent out weekly or bi-weekly at a consistent time. What's new updates would generally be sent monthly unless you've got something "hot." Tips of the day should be sent . . . daily. Tips of the week should be sent . . . weekly. Last minute getaways from travel agencies are usually sent weekly.

The content should always be considered relevant, valuable, and useful to the recipient. You might consider sending different e-mail content to different target markets. You might also consider sharing the load—making this a joint project with other travel and tourism-related organizations or even other travel agents in your office. That way everyone will contribute a little. There are many sources for your e-mail content:

- Create it yourself

- Find syndicated content online

- Reprint articles with permission

- Ask your business partners to contribute an article

- Recap highlights of interesting articles

- Interview an expert.

There are many places that offer syndicated content online. A few suggestions on where to find free articles:

- iTravelSyndicate (*http://www.itravelsyndicate.com*)

- EzineArticles.com (*http://www.ezinearticles.com*)

- OSKAR Consulting (*http://www.oskar.com*)

There are also many places that offer subscriptions to travel and tourism articles:

- Amazines (*http://www.amazines.com*)

- Copyright Clearance Center (*http://www.copyright.com*)

- Scoop ReprintSource (*http://www.scoopreprintsource.com*)

When should your communication be delivered? There have been many studies on this topic, and consensus has it:

- Never send your message late in the day or first thing in the morning. If you do, your e-mail is included in that large group that is in the recipient's in-box first thing in the morning. You know what happens to all that e-mail because you do it yourself—the first thing you do is see how much you can delete—starting with anything that looks remotely like an ad or promotion.

- Not after 2 p.m. on Friday or at all in the afternoon on Friday in the summer months. Being buried in that huge pile awaiting a recipient on Monday morning is the kiss of death for your e-mail.

- Lunch hour is best. Generally, people clean out their e-mail first thing in the morning and again before they go to lunch. After their lunch break they are a little more relaxed and the first thing they do is check their e-mail. This is the best chance for your e-mail to get noticed.

When it comes to the formatting of your correspondence, if you communicate through a newsletter, coupons, e-specials, or similar type of marketing content, an HTML message has a better chance of grabbing the viewer's attention. If your message is meant to look like a personal one-on-one message, then text-based is better. Your communications should be personalized using the recipient's first name appropriately throughout the correspondence and in the subject field.

Your content should always be valuable, fresh, relevant, and succinct. One bad message could result in many "Unsubscribes."

Each paragraph should be written so it can be easily scanned, containing no more than six or seven lines. Include calls to action.

Always encourage viral marketing—"Send a copy to a friend"—and provide instructions for the friend to subscribe to be included on your list.

Use a personal name in the "From" field. You want to build a relationship!

Take time with your subject field:

- Avoid ad copy

- Avoid gimmicky slogans

- Build business credibility

- Use action words

- Be positive.

Personalize your message with the recipients' first name in the subject field as well as the salutation and throughout the e-mail. Good mail list software makes this easy to do. Be sure to check the preview screen. Most e-mail programs these days have a preview screen which allows users to get a glimpse of the message before they actually open in. You want the most important information of your e-mail to show up in the preview screen so be sure to keep it simple and to the point.

Close your e-mail with a P.S. and use the P.S. to restate your offer, give it a sense of urgency, and make it easy for readers to respond. Use phrases like "while supplies last," "in the next 24 hours," "call now," "reply to this e-mail." You should always place your P.S. above your signature, as most people do not read past the signature.

Provide rich content with links back to your Web site. The more time people spend on your site the more your brand is reinforced and the more people start to get to know you, trust you, and see you as an expert in the field. People do business with people they know and trust. Differentiate yourself. Become the recognized expert.

## Stay under the Spam Radar

These days anywhere between 5 and 20 percent of legitimate, permission-based e-mail is filtered out by the spam detectors and never reaches the intended recipients. Always run your marketing messages through a spam checker before sending out. The spam checker will give you a spam rating score and tell you how you received that score. Today, if your score is 5.0 or higher it will be deemed to be spam by most of the spam filters. If your message scores too high, you should edit your message to eliminate or change the items that gave you the score. Then you should run your new message through the spam checker to make sure you have an acceptable score before sending your message out.

Many ASP mail list software programs have an integrated spam checker, like Professional Cart Solutions (*http://www.profcs.com*) pictured in Figure 14.2.

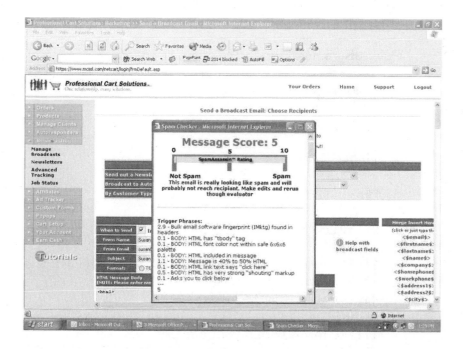

**Figure 14.2.** Professional Cart Solutions has a spam filter integrated into its software.

If yours does not, there are a number of free spam checkers online and others that charge a fee such as Site Build It! (*http://spamcheck.sitesell.com*) and ContentChecker (*http://www.lyris.com*).

Some of the e-mail elements that add points to your spam rating include:

- Using software and listservers that are commonly used by spammers. The header identifies the software that you are using.

- Spam words in the subject line. Things such as:

  - FREE in CAPS

  - GUARANTEED

  - Subject talks about saving

  - Starts with Hello

  - $

- Hyperlinks—Using links without the http:// prefix or using IP numbers instead of domain names.

- Color discrimination:

  - Color tags not formatted correctly

  - Using colors not in the 217 Web-safe colors

  - Hidden letters (same color as background)

- Background other than white

- HTML issues:

  - HTML message with more than 50 percent HTML tags

  - JavaScript within the message

  - HTML forms within your e-mail

  - HTML comments that obfuscate text

- Using excess capital letters

- Using large fonts and characters. Fonts larger than +2 or 3 can cause you to have points added to your score. Use H1, H2, H3 instead.

- Using spam words or phrases in the body of your message adds points to your score. There are way too many of these to list. Your spam checker lets you know what words are adding points. The following are the type of words and phrases that they are looking for:

    - Great offer

    - Risk free

    - You have been selected

    - Guarantee

    - Call now

    - Amazing

    - Act now

    - Millions

    - Order now

- Carefully word your Unsubscribe. Claims that a recipient can be removed, claims that you address removal requests, and list removal information, all add points to your score. Use text like "Use this link to unsubscribe."

- If your communication is a newsletter, say so. The spam rating also allows points to be deducted from your score for certain elements. When the subject contains a newsletter header, or contains a newsletter frequency, month name or date, you might be spared some unwanted points.

- Use a signature file. This is another element that can cause points to be deducted from your score. Spammers never include their signature file.

- Don't mention spam compliance—only spammers do this.

- Keep your message size over 20k. Spammers' messages are very small in file size because they often send millions in a mailing.

- Always make sure you update your list and do your housekeeping regularly. Remove any addresses that have bounced back to you as undeliverable if your software doesn't automatically do this for you. Remove any "spam flag" addresses in your database—those that begin with spam@, abuse@, postmaster@, or nospam@.

- Set up test accounts for yourself at the popular e-mail hosts to ensure that your mail is getting through. Set up test accounts at MSN, Hotmail, Yahoo, AOL, and some of the popular ISPs.

- Always monitor the ISP blacklists to make sure you are not included.

## Recent Legislation

It is essential to make sure you are in compliance with legislation regarding anti-spam (in the U.S.), privacy (in Canada), and other rules and regulations related to commercial e-mail throughout the world.

The U.S. legislation is called the Controlling the Assault of Non-Solicited Pornography and Marketing Act (CAN-SPAM). This legislation provides regulations for commercial e-mail. The full details can be found at *http://www.ftc.gov/bcp/conline/pubs/buspubs/canspam.shtm*.

These are the main rules for CAN-SPAM:

- You must provide accurate header information. The sender has to identify himself/herself/itself accurately.

- You must provide an accurate subject line for commercial e-mails.

- You must provide a functioning return e-mail address that is clearly and conspicuously displayed and permits a recipient to decline future commercial e-mails (opt-out) from that sender.

- Commercial e-mail must include the (snail mail) postal address of the sender.

- Commercial e-mail must include clear and concise identification that the content of the e-mail is an advertisement or solicitation.

- If a person opts out of your mailings you must remove that individual from your database within 10 days and you are not allowed to transfer, sell, or give that individual's contact information to anyone else after they have asked to be removed.

The Canadian legislation is the Personal Information Protection and Electronic Documents Act, commonly referred to as PIPEDA. The Canadian legislation establishes rules to govern the collection, use, and disclosure of personal information. It recognizes the "right of privacy" of individuals with respect to their personal information. Full details on the Canadian legislation can be found at *http://www.privcom.gc.ca/legislation/index_e.asp*.

The main rules for PIPEDA include:

- Accountability—An organization is responsible for personal information under its control and shall designate an individual or individuals who are accountable for the organization's compliance with the following principles.

- Identifying purposes—The purposes for which personal information is collected shall be identified by the organization at or before the time the information is collected.

- Consent—The knowledge and consent of the individual are required for the collection, use, or disclosure of personal information, except where inappropriate.

- Limiting collection—The collection of personal information shall be limited to that which is necessary for the purposes identified by the organization. Information shall be collected by fair and lawful means.

- Limiting use, disclosure, and retention—Personal information shall not be used or disclosed for purposes other than those for which it was collected, except with the consent of the individual or as required by law. Personal information shall be retained only as long as necessary for the fulfillment of those purposes.

- Accuracy—Personal information shall be as accurate, complete, and up-to-date as is necessary for the purpose for which it is used.

- Safeguards—Personal information shall be protected by security safeguards appropriate to the sensitivity of the information.

- Openness—An organization shall make readily available to individuals specific information about its policies and practices relating to the management of personal information.

- Individual access—Upon request, an individual shall be informed of the existence, use, and disclosure of his or her personal information, and shall be given access to that information. An individual shall be able to challenge the accuracy and completeness of the information and have it amended as appropriate.

- Challenging compliance—An individual shall be able to address a challenge concerning compliance with the above principles to the designated individual or individuals accountable for the organization's compliance.

## Measure, Measure, Measure

You want to improve your effectiveness as you learn from experience. This can happen only if you keep track of past performance. You want to track such things as delivery rate, number of undeliverables, number of unsubscribes, click-through rates, gross response, and net response. You want to compare response rates within different timings, different types of creativity, different formats, different segments of your list, and different target markets. Once you analyze what is working and what is not, you'll be in a better position to improve your conversion ratios.

## Why E-mail is Not Dead

There has been a bit of a debate lately that with the up-rise of RSS and everyone jumping on the RSS bandwagon, that e-mail is, well, dead. While the current situation is showing us that open rates are declining, spam filters are blocking good e-mails, click-through rates are low, people are experiencing list fatigue, legislation is putting stricter rules and regulations in place concerning sending e-mail, and that RSS is an alternative (see Chapter 22 for the pros and cons of RSS), e-mail is still the killer App and will not be replaced by RSS. There are a few very important pros to e-mail that RSS just does not deliver:

- E-mail is trackable (open rates, CTRs, etc.) down to the individual level.

- ROI is easily understood and measurable.

- It is a mature channel with industry standard metrics.

- E-mail can be personalized. You can include such elements as the recipient's name, company, and city, in the Subject field, the To field and in the content of the message.

- E-mail can be segmented.

- E-mail can be highly targeted, designed and branded with rich content.

- E-mail can and should incorporate viral marketing.

With a private mailing list you can plan how you will measure and quantify success before you start. RSS does not allow you to test different elements of your campaign to see which yield the highest conversions. Private mail list marketing does allow for such testing of things like:

- Timing—day of the week, time of the day, etc.

- A/B creative

- Format—HTML versus text, long paragraphs versus bullet points

- Segment

- Response rates

- From line—company name, person's name, destination

- Subject line

- Top offer

- Featured offer

- Bottom offer

- Ad copy effectiveness

- Headlines

Your private mailing list gets you in front of your target customer on a regular basis and it helps build repeat traffic to your site. With private mailing lists you are able to promote your destination, attractions, or operation which helps bring visitors to your Web site. Private mail list marketing helps reinforce branding and conserves your contact base.

## E-mail as the Killer App—The Latest

E-mail has been around for many years. Just like other Internet marketing techniques, the way in which we go about using it has evolved dramatically since its introduction. When using e-mail today it is important to have a plan and quantify success, provide consistently valuable content, and build a profile of everyone in your database.

With today's sophisticated mail list programs you are able to build a profile of everyone in your mail list database. You can do this in one of three ways:

- Track the click

- Ask the question

- Track the behavior.

By building a profile you are able to distinguish which of your customers are interested in golf packages, which are interested in family vacations, spa retreats, or any combination of packages. Once you have these profiles in place you will be able to send out messages that employ dynamic personalization. With dynamic personalization you can use each customer's profile to send them targeted e-mails based on their individual preferences.

Dynamic personalization is being used by many tourism operations to track users' clicks in order to determine which packages they prefer—golf packages, family vacations, and/or spa retreats. Using this information you are able to send customized e-mails based on the customer's individual preferences. If someone in their database has shown interest in the golf packages and nothing else, then this person would receive customized e-mails about the golf packages and nothing else. If, however, someone in their database has shown interest in both their golf and spa packages, then this person would receive customized e-mails that listed both golf and spa packages. These dynamically personalized e-mails are customized and personalized to also include the individual's name and other information based on their priorities—all of this information is provided in their profile.

Another great application of direct mail list marketing is the ability to perform behavioral targeting. While dynamic personalization focuses on the individuals' preferences and priorities, behavioral targeting focuses on the actual behavior. Behavioral marketers target consumers by serving ads to predefined categories. Let's say a user visits several Web pages related to travel and golf. On the next page the user goes to, they will be presented with a golf getaway package ad. The key for this ad is not the actual profile, but the user's behavior. Had the user visited several pages related to amusement parks, there may have been an ad for Six Flags Amusement Parks. Amazon.com, for example, uses a type of behavioral targeting. On Amazon.com when you search for, or purchase, a book you are presented with "people who bought this item also bought..." and a list follows.

With the introduction of spam, spam filters, new legislation and ISP blacklists, there are things that you can do to help you get your e-mail message through to the intended recipient. As mentioned earlier, always, always, run your message through a spam checker before sending.

## The Good News—RSS and E-mail are Not Mutually Exclusive

A better alternative to choosing one over the other is to incorporate both e-mail and RSS as part of your marketing mix. It is not a bad idea to make your content available through both means or offer some of your content through e-mail and other content through RSS.

## Internet Resources for Chapter 14

I have developed a great library of online resources for you to check out regarding private mail list marketing. This library is available on my Tourism Internet Marketing University Web site *http://www.TourismInternetMarketingU.com/ max* in the Resources section where you can find additional tips, tools, techniques, and resources.

I have also developed courses on many of the topics covered in this book. These courses are also available on my Tourism Internet Marketing University Web site *http://www.TourismInternetMarketingU.com/max*. These courses are delivered immediately over the Internet or can be ordered as a CD.

# 15

## Effective Promotion Through Direct Mail Lists

Direct marketing has been around for years. It involves sending promotional messages directly to consumers. There are many reputable companies that specialize in direct marketing and there are many marketers who rent mailing lists from these companies. These traditional direct marketing companies take their customers' marketing materials and manage the process of printing labels, affixing the labels, postage, and sending the materials out. This same type of service is now available online but instead of being sent by snail mail, the marketing message is sent by e-mail. In this chapter, we cover:

- How direct mail list companies work

- How to select a company to work with

- How you work with a direct mail list company

- Costs related to direct mail list marketing

- Tips on how to make the most of your direct mail list marketing.

## How Direct Mail List Companies Work

Both online direct mail list companies and offline direct mail list companies work based on the same foundation. They provide a service to travel and tourism businesses and organizations that want to market directly to a particular demographic and/or geographic segment of the population. In order for these direct mail list companies to do this effectively, they develop large permission based databases containing information on individuals who fit certain criteria.

As with many business practices, how they generate these databases is what differentiates the good companies from the bad. Some direct mail list companies use software programs designed to "grab" e-mail addresses from newsgroups, public mail lists, and a number of other places on the Internet. They have not been given permission to send anything to the people who own these e-mail addresses. The more reputable companies, on the other hand, use a number of strategic ways to build their lists of people interested in receiving information on specific topics. For example, some companies partner with sites that have significant targeted traffic. They then offer the site's visitors relevant and interesting information and the opportunity to "opt in" to receive updates or information on a specified topic.

When a Web site visitor requests information on a specified topic, the visitor has to ask to be put on the list or opt-in; they then provide their e-mail address, and often they are asked to provide their first name. It is important to the list company that the visitor provides his or her first name so that future correspondence with them can be personalized.

Some of the more reputable companies use a "double opt-in" method of collecting names to help increase the value and validity of the names on their list. As with a single opt-in, the site visitor asks to be put on the list to receive updates or information on a particular topic. However, with a double opt-in, when the mail list company receives the request to be added to the list, it follows up with an e-mail to the individual notifying them that the request has been received and asks the individual to confirm the request by replying to the e-mail.

These direct mail list companies organize their databases by area of interest and are continually trying to improve their lists and add to the profile of everyone in their database. They use different methods to try and improve their lists, such as data mining with their correspondence. Sometimes they use tracking techniques to hone in on specific areas of interest, sometimes they ask a question or two to access more demographic or psychographic information about the individuals on the list, and sometimes they send a detailed survey-type questionnaire asking for feedback so they can better tailor the information being sent to the individual.

## How to Select a Direct Mail Company

When selecting a direct mail list company to work with, there are a number of factors that need to be considered. First and foremost, the company must be reputable. Second, the mail list company you choose to work with should have a topic list that fits with your specified target market.

Once you have narrowed down the reputable companies that have topic lists that fit with your target market, you should look at the company's costs, tracking capability, policies on content, and opt-in policies. It is important to work with a company that allows correspondence with the individuals on the list to be personalized, since you get a much higher response rate from personalized e-mail than generic e-mail. It is also important to work with a company that does not place any restrictions on hypertext links, as you want to be able to encourage recipients to visit your Web site. You also want to be able to find out how many people read the message you sent, and how many people merely "clicked through" to your Web site rather than taking the action you wanted them to, which is why you should look for a company that provides tracking statistics.

## How to Work with a Direct Mail List Company

Once you have selected the direct mail list company or companies you want to work with, you should:

- Fine-tune the specific list to receive your message

- Provide the message content to the direct mail list company

- Approve the sample message

Then, the mail list company will:

- Compile the specific list

- Develop or format the message you provided

- Send you a sample for final approval

- Merge the list with your message so that each person on the list receives a personalized message

- Send out the message to the list

- Track specific actions taken by recipients once they have received the message.

You will work directly with the direct mail list company to develop a list that meets your objectives and fits your budget. You might want your message to go out to people interested in golf or white water rafting or RVing or travel to Mexico—whatever relates to your business. The lists are usually rented on a per name basis—the more names and e-mails, the more you pay. If the list you are requesting provides more names than your budget can afford, the list might be able to be segmented further to include only white water rafting enthusiasts (or whatever your target market is) in specific income brackets.

## Costs Related to Direct Mail List Marketing

Often there is a sliding scale based on volume, but most mail list companies charge on a per-name basis. Generally, all the services you need from the direct mail list company, including segmenting the list, merge and personalization, and delivery of the message are all included in the cost per-name. Of course different companies charge different amounts per name so you should find a reputable company that fits within your budget.

Postmaster Network (*http://www.postmasternetwork.net*) is one of the oldest and most reputable direct mail list companies around (see Figure 15.1). It has more than 400 topic lists, with more than 20 million double opt-in e-mail addresses. It has the largest database of business-to-business double-opt-in e-mail addresses, and partners with sites like CNET, MSNBC, OSTG, Webshots, Experience.com, and many more. Fees range between $100 per thousand for consumer lists to $250 per thousand for B2B lists with a minimum order of 5,000 names. When doing your research you will notice that there are a number of direct mail list companies to consider. I have provided a link to many of them in the free Internet Resources section of my Web site (*http:// www.TourismInternetMarketingU.com*). Although the pricing information and numbers of topic lists or categories were correct at the time of printing this

**Figure 15.1.**   Postmaster Network is one of the oldest and most reputable direct mail list companies around.

book, check the direct mail list company sites for updates before making any decisions.

## Make the Most of Your Direct Mail List Marketing

Direct mail list marketing is a great way to get your message to a significant number of people in your target market in a short period of time. Ideally, you would like to have each of these names on your private mail list. If you're smart about the content of the message you have the direct mail list company send out, you can go a long way toward converting the direct mail list recipients to your own private mail list subscribers.

Be sure to give the recipients of your mail list message a compelling reason to visit your Web site. The hypertext link in your direct mail message should take them to a page of your Web site that not only gives them the content they are expecting, but also gives them a compelling reason to join your private mail list and an opportunity to easily sign up.

The key to getting your message opened and read is a dynamite subject line. You should consider personalizing the subject line with the recipient's name and make sure the subject line copy does not read like an ad. Ads and junk mail are the first to be deleted.

Busy people do not read their e-mail, they scan it. So it is important that your message follow suit and is written so it can be easily scanned. Be sure to grab the reader's attention in the first sentence. If you don't, he or she won't read any further.

Your e-mail is a reflection of the attention to detail you give everything in your business. So be sure your message is grammatically correct, that you use the proper upper and lowercase letters and correct spelling.

Make sure you access and analyze any tracking information available from the direct mail list company. Notice what copy works best. Notice what subject lines give a better response rate. Notice the different responses from different direct mail list companies.

## Internet Resources for Chapter 15

I have developed a great library of online resources for you to check out regarding direct mail list marketing. This library is available on my Tourism Internet Marketing University Web site *http://www.TourismInternetMarketingU.com/max* in the Resources section where you can find additional tips, tools, techniques, and resources.

I have also developed courses on many of the topics covered in this book. These courses are also available on my Tourism Internet Marketing University Web site *http://www.TourismInternetMarketingU.com/max*. These courses are delivered immediately over the Internet or can be ordered as a CD.

# 16

## Developing a Dynamite Link Strategy

The more strategically chosen **links** you have to your site, the better. Increase your traffic and improve your search engine ranking by orchestrating links from related travel and tourism Web pages. In this chapter, we cover:

- Developing a link strategy

- How to arrange links

- Getting noticed—providing an icon and tag line hypertext for links to your site

- Link positioning

- Tools to check your competitors' links

- Using links to enhance your image

- Web rings and meta-indexes

- Getting links to your site

- Reciprocal link pages

- Associate programs

- How links can enhance your search engine placements.

## Links Have an Impact

Developing your link strategy is one of the most crucial elements of Internet marketing. It is a time-consuming task, but it is time well spent. Links are important for several reasons.

1. Strategically placed, they can be a real traffic builder.

2. The most popular search engines use link popularity and link relevancy as part of their ranking criteria. The more links to your site, the more popular it is, so the number of links you have to your site can significantly impact your placement with those search engines.

3. The more links you have to your site, the more opportunities search engine spiders have to find you.

## Links Have Staying Power

When you post a message to a newsgroup where you promote your tourism Web site through your brilliant contributions and your signature file, you receive increased traffic while the message is current and is being read by participants in the newsgroup. As time passes, your message appears farther and farther down the list until it disappears, and then your traffic level returns to normal. The same goes for a promotional effort in a mail list. You can expect increased traffic for a short while after your mail list posting, but as soon as everyone has read your posting and visited your site, traffic levels return to normal.

This is not the same for links. Traffic from links does not go away as easily as other forms of Internet marketing. Links generally stay active for a long time. When a link to your site is placed on another Web site, you hope people see it and are enticed to click through to visit your site. As long as the site that hosts your link has new traffic, you continue to receive traffic through it. The beauty of links is that in three months, that link will still be there and people will still be clicking through!

**Links**
Selectable connections from one word, picture, or information object to another.

Links are very important because if you have links placed on a high-traffic Web site, they can turn into traffic builders for your own site. They also are important because they can have a major impact on your ranking in search engines, because some of the busiest ones use link popularity in their ranking criteria. Some of these search engines include:

- Google (*www.google.com*)

- Yahoo! Search (*www.search.yahoo.com*)

- AltaVista (*www.altavista.com*)

- HotBot (*www.hotbot.com*)

- MSN (*www.msn.com*).

Once your link strategy is implemented and you begin to see an increase in the number of sites linking to your Web site, you will see your ranking in the previously mentioned search engines improve. For more information on search engines and their ranking criteria, see Chapter 2.

## A Quick Talk about Outbound Links

The more links to your site, the better chance that someone will be enticed to visit. However, a quid quo pro usually applies, and this means providing reciprocal links, giving people the opportunity to leave your site with the click of a button. To minimize this "flight effect," make sure you place outbound links two or three layers down in your site. Never place outbound links on your home page. You want your visitors to come into your site and see and do everything you want them to before they have the opportunity to go elsewhere.

There are two ways you can provide outbound links. The first is by providing a hypertext link, which transports the visitor from your site to someone else's with a single click. The second and preferred method is to have each outbound link open a new browser window when clicked. This way your visitors get to see the referred Web site, but when they are finished and close that window, the original browser window with your Web site is still active. The browser window with your site should still be visible on the task bar during their visit to the referred site.

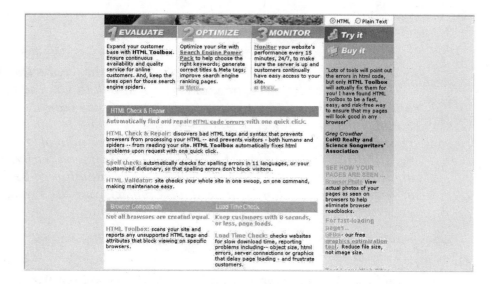

**Figure 16.1.** The NetMechanic site provides many valuable tools. Its HTML Toolbox can be used to find out if you have dead links on your site or if you have any HTML errors that need correcting.

Regularly test all of the links from your site to ensure that they are "live" and are going to the intended locations. Dead links reflect poorly on your site even if they are out of your control. There are tools available online to help you determine whether you have dead links. These tools include NetMechanic at *http://www.netmechanic.com* (see Figure 16.1). NetMechanic is discussed in more depth in the Internet Resources section of my Web site, referenced at the end of this chapter.

## Google Webmaster Guidelines on Link Schemes

All things in moderation—including links. We know that link popularity and link relevance are very important in the search engine ranking algorithms. We also know that the major search engines hate anything that smells of manipulation. You need to walk a fine line with your link strategy. I provide you with several link strategies in this chapter but it is important that you know what Google has to say about link schemes before you decide how you will proceed with your link strategy. The following was taken verbatim from Google webmaster guidelines.

*"Your site's ranking in Google search results is partly based on analysis of those sites that link to you. The quantity, quality, and relevance of links count towards your rating. The sites that link to you can provide context about the subject matter of your site, and can indicate its quality and popularity. However, some webmasters engage in link exchange schemes and build partner pages exclusively for the sake of cross-linking, disregarding the quality of the links, the sources, and the long-term impact it will have on their sites. This is in violation of Google's webmaster guidelines and can negatively impact your site's ranking in search results. Examples of link schemes can include:*

- *Links intended to manipulate PageRank*

- *Links to Web spammers or bad neighborhoods on the Web*

- *Excessive reciprocal links or excessive link exchanging ("Link to me and I'll link to you")*

- *Buying or selling links*

*The best way to get other sites to create relevant links to yours is to create unique, relevant content that can quickly gain popularity in the Internet community. The more useful content you have, the greater the chances someone else will find that content valuable to their readers and link to it. Before making any single decision, you should ask yourself the question: Is this going to be beneficial for my page's visitors?*

*It is not only the number of links you have pointing to your site that matters, but also the quality and relevance of those links. Creating good content pays off: Links are usually editorial votes given by choice, and the buzzing blogger community can be an excellent place to generate interest. In addition, submit your site to relevant directories such as the Open Directory Project and Yahoo!, as well as to other industry-specific expert sites."*

## Strategies for Finding Appropriate Link Sites

Ideally, you should be linked from every high-traffic site that is of interest to your target market. Develop a strategy to find all of these sites and arrange links.

Start with the popular search engines. Most people use search engines and directories to find subjects of interest on the Internet. Most of the people searching never go beyond the first 10 to 20 results that the search engine returns. Thus, these top 10 to 20 sites get a lot of traffic. Search your most relevant keywords in all the popular search engines and directories, and investigate these top sites for link possibilities. Some of these sites will be competitors and might not want to reciprocate links. The best opportunity for links is with non-competing sites that have the same target market. I suggest you take your most important keywords, do a keyword search in the 20 most popular search engines and directories, and review the top 30 sites in each for potential link sites.

Another strategy to find useful link sites is to see where the leaders in your industry and your competitors are linked. I use the term *competitors* very loosely. It would include your direct competitors, your industry leaders, companies selling non-competing products to your target market, companies selling similar types of products or services to your target market, and companies that compete with you for search engine ranking. See what your competition is doing. Determine where they are linked from, and decide whether these are sites that you should also be linked from. Learn what they are doing well, and also learn from their mistakes. You should be linked everywhere your competition is appropriately linked, and then some.

## Explore These URLs

There are many tools on the Internet to help you identify a Web site's links. These tools can be used to see which sites are linking to your Web site. But they can also be used to see what sites are linking to your competition. This is a great way to research where your site could be linked from but isn't—yet! Let me walk you through a step-by-step process to increase the number of links to your Web site.

When determining which sites you should be linked from, you first have to develop a lengthy list of competitors. A competitor can be any business or site that offers the same travel-related products or services as you do or anyone targeting the same demographic group or any tourism operator in your geographic area. Because the Internet creates a level playing field for all businesses, you are competing against large and small companies from around the globe. Someone using a search engine to find information on services that your company can provide might see results from companies from all across the world in the top ten results.

Once you have developed your extensive list of competitors and have gathered their URLs, you must then find out what sites they are linked from. Tools have been developed to assist you in finding who is linking to your site. I have provided a list of some of these tools in the next section. For more resources visit the Resources section of my Web site at *http://www.TourismInternetMarketingU.com/max*. In most cases, you enter your URL, and then these tools provide a list of sites linking to it. However, by entering the URL for a competitor's site you can just as easily determine which sites are linking to your competition and industry leaders.

The more organized you are for this exercise, the better. I suggest that you:

1. Gather an extensive list of competitors and their URLs.

2. Choose the tool(s) from the next section that you are going to use for this exercise.

3. Enter the first competitor URL to find the sites linking to it.

4. Copy and paste the results into a Word, Notepad, or other file that you can access later.

5. Enter the next competitor URL to find the sites linking to it.

6. Copy and paste the results into the same Word, Notepad, or other file, adding to your list of potential link sites.

7. Repeat steps 5 and 6 until you have found all the sites linking to your competition. When this is done, you have your potential link sites list.

8. Now develop a link request (see below for details) and keep it open on your desktop so that you can copy and paste it into an e-mail when you find a site you'd like to have a link from.

9. Next, visit every one of the potential link sites to determine whether the site is appropriate for you to be linked from. If so, send your link request. If the site is not appropriate for whatever reason, delete it from your list. Also delete duplicates. When you get to the bottom of your list, it has changed from a potential links list to a request links list.

10. Follow through and follow up. Follow through and provide an appropriate link to those who agree to a reciprocal link. Follow up to make sure that they provide the link to your site as promised, that the link works, and that it is pointing to the correct page on your site.

11. Submit the Internet address of the page that has provided the link to the popular search engines so that they know it's there. This will help boost your link popularity scores.

## Tools to Identify Your Competitors' Links

The following tools can be used to obtain a list of locations on the Internet that are linked to your competitors' Web sites:

### AltaVista
*http://www.altavista.com*
To find out where your competitors are linked using AltaVista, simply enter the competitor's URL in the search area like this: *link: yourcompetitorsdomain.com.* This returns all pages in AltaVista with a link to your competitor's Web site.

### Excite and Other Search Engines
*http://www.excite.com*
Just enter your competitors' URLs and see what comes up. (Be sure to include *http://*.) If anything, the search query will include all indexed Web sites that contain the URL searched.

### Google
*http://www.google.com*
Enter your competitor's URL in the search box like this: *link: yourcompetitorsURL.com.* The results will contain all Web sites linking to your competitor's Web site.

### HotBot
*http://www.hotbot.com*
Enter your competitor's URL in the search box and change the default from "all the words" to "links to this URL." When you type in the URL, remember to include *http://*. The results will contain all Web sites linking to your competitor's Web site.

### Link Popularity
*http://www.linkpopularity.com*
Simply type in your competitor's URL and it will give you a list of all the sites linking to that particular site (see Figure 16.2).

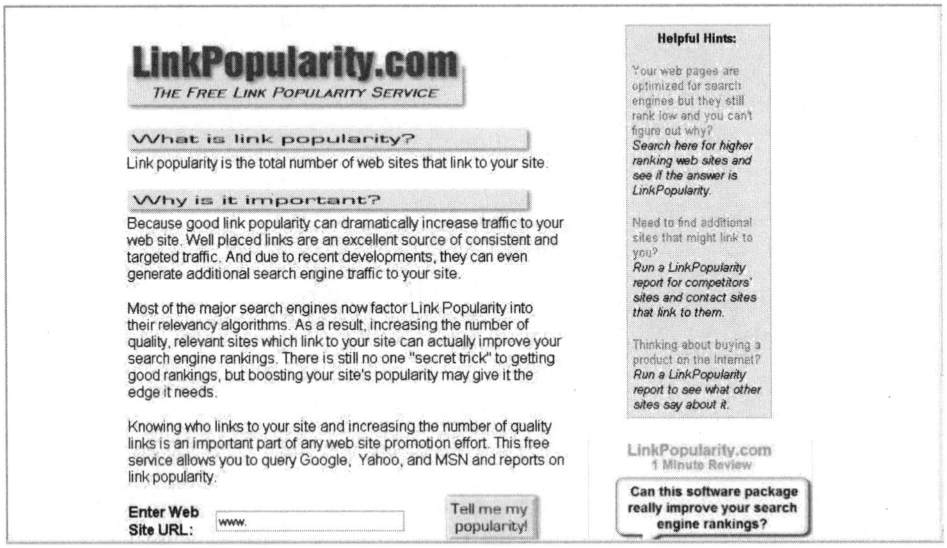

**Figure 16.2.**   LinkPopularity.com offers a free link popularity check service.

## Other Potential Link Strategies

Another strategy for finding potential link sites is to visit the many different search engines and do a search on keywords you feel people would search on if they were looking for your site. The top results get a lot of visits from your target market, so they are always good potential link sites.

The following is a step-by-step strategy to get linked from these sites.

1. Make a list of your most important keywords for your Web site using your master keyword list and meta-tags (see Chapter 2).

2. Develop a list of the top five search engines (check SearchEngineWatch.com).

3. Go to each of the five search engines and input your most important keywords as identified in step 1.

4. Copy and paste the top 30 results into a Word, Notepad, or other file that you can access later.

5. Enter the next keyword and copy and paste the results into the same Word, Notepad, or other file, adding to your list of potential link sites.

6. Repeat step 5 until you have used all the keywords in your list. When this is done, you will have 150 potential sites for each keyword. You now have your potential link sites list.

7. Now develop a link request (see the next section for details) and keep it open on your desktop so that you can copy and paste it into an e-mail when you find a site you'd like to have a link from.

8. As stated above, visit every one of the potential link sites to determine whether the site is appropriate for you to be linked from. If so, send your link request. If the site is not appropriate for whatever reason, delete it from your list. Also delete duplicates. When you get to the bottom of your list, it has changed from a potential links list to a request links list.

9. Again, as already stated, follow through and follow up. Follow through and provide an appropriate link to those who agree to a reciprocal link. Follow up to make sure that they provide the link to your site as promised, that the link works, and that it is pointing to the correct page on your site.

10. Submit the Internet address of the page that has provided the link to the popular search engines so that they know it's there. This will help boost your link popularity scores.

## Winning Approval for Potential Links

Now that you have a list of Web sites you would like to be linked from, the next step is to determine from whom to request the link. Usually this can be found on the site. Titles such as Webmaster@ or any variation on that theme are usually a safe bet. If the site does not have an obvious contact, try feedback@. You can either send the request there or ask for the e-mail address of the right person.

If you cannot find an e-mail address on a Web site, you can visit a domain registration service such as Network Solutions (*www.networksolutions.com*) to find out contact information for that domain name. Click on the "WHOIS Lookup" link and submit the URL to do a search. The results will include the contacts, both technical and administrative, for that Web site. The technical contact most likely is the person you are looking for, because that is who most likely looks after the Web site. The administrative contact is usually responsible for the renewal of the domain name, and the billing contact is usually the bill payer for the domain name.

Generally, a short note with the appropriate information in the subject line is most suitable. Your note should be courteous; briefly describe your site's content, and provide the rationale for why you think reciprocating links would result in a win-win situation. It doesn't hurt to compliment some aspect of the site that you think is particularly engaging.

It is a good idea to develop a generic "link request" letter that you can have on hand when you are surfing. You should always keep this letter open on your desktop when surfing the Internet so that you can easily copy and paste the letter into an e-mail.

Here is an example of a link request e-mail:

*Dear Web Site Owner,*

*I have just finished viewing your site and found it quite enjoyable. I found the content to be very valuable, particularly (customize here). My site visitors would appreciate your content as I think we appeal to the same demographic group. My site, http://ww.mysitename.com, focuses on (my site content) and would likely be of value to your visitors. I'd like to suggest we trade links.*

*Sincerely,*

*John*

A typical response might say that they would appreciate the link to their site, and offer to provide a reciprocal link. To facilitate this, you should either have the HTML for the link ready to send or have it available on your site, or both. Make sure you have your most important keyword in the text around the link to your site to ensure that you score as high as possible in the link relevancy category.

Make sure to follow through and follow up. If you said that you would provide a reciprocal link, do so within 24 hours. Follow up to make sure that your site has been linked from theirs, the link works properly, and it is linked to the right page on your site.

Then remember to send a thank you. Because they are doing you a favor by adding your site to their Web site, you should strive to develop a good relationship with them. This way they might be more generous with the link they give you. They might place it higher on the page, or even offer you the opportunity of having a small graphic link on their page, which would be dynamite for increasing traffic to your site. These graphic links are explained in more detail later in the chapter.

Another way to get links is to ask for them on your site. In a prominent location on your site, place a link that says something like, "Would you like to provide a link to this site? Click here." Link this message to a separate page that holds several options for links. You can provide viewers with several different sizes of banner ads they could place on their Web site. You can also provide them with a thumbnail icon, the HTML, and your tag line, which they could simply copy and paste into the HTML code on their Web site. Again, remember to select appropriate keywords to include in the text around the link to increase your link relevancy score with the popular search engines.

Quite often, if you offer viewers these opportunities for links, you have a better chance of receiving these enhanced link features. If you make it easier for them to add the link, they will be more willing to provide it. Figure 16.3 shows an example of a site that provides the relevant coding and images for people who want to provide a link.

You might want to offer an incentive to people who provide you with a link. Include viewers who provide a link to your site in a drawing for a prize. You might run a contest such as "Provide a link to us and win," where you include all those sites linking to you in a drawing once a week or once a month, depending on the size of the prize.

**Figure 16.3.** By providing the HTML text and icons on your site, you can make it very easy for visitors to add your link to their sites.

Meta-indexes are another source for links. For a complete discussion of meta-indexes, see Chapter 17.

You might need to prompt sites to provide promised links. If you have made an arrangement for a link and find that the link is not there, it is appropriate to send an e-mail reminder. When sending the follow-up e-mail, include your icon, HTML, URL, and any other helpful information.

## Making Your Link the Place to Click

There are links and then there are links. Usually links are your company name hyperlinked to your home page, and your company's site link is listed with a number of other companies' links. Sometimes, if you are lucky, there is a brief description attached to the link.

You should take a proactive approach with linking arrangements. Explore every opportunity to have your link placed prominently and, if possible, to have it differentiated from the other links on the page.

Once you have an agreement with a site willing to provide a link, you

---

**Icon**

An image that represents an application, a capability, or some other concept.

---

should ask if you could send them an **icon** and the HTML for the link. The icon (GIF or JPG format) should be visually pleasing and representative of your business. Within the HTML, include a tag line or call to action that entices people to click on the link. With the icon or logo, the tag line, and your company's name, your link will stand out. Again, remember to include appropriate keywords in the text around the link to add to your link relevancy score to improve your search engine ranking.

If another Web site is generous enough to provide a link to your site, your image should be only a thumbnail, for you don't want to take up too much space. This image could be your corporate logo or a graphic from a current promotion for one of your products or services. By having this image and tag line strategically placed on a Web site, the chances that a viewer will click through to visit your Web site are much higher.

## To Add or Not to Add with Free-for-All Links

There are thousands of free-for-all links sites on the Net. These sites allow you to add your URL to a long list of links, but they provide little traffic and the search engines don't like sites that try to manipulate the search placement. I'd suggest you stay away from these types of link sites.

## Add Value with Affiliate Programs

Another way of benefiting from links to your Web site is by developing an affiliate program. Affiliate programs (also called reseller, partnership, or associate programs) are revenue-sharing arrangements set up by companies selling products and services. When another site agrees to participate in your affiliate program, it is rewarded for sending customers to your business. These customers are sent to your site through links on your associates' or affiliates' Web sites. By developing and offering this type of program, you generate increased business and increased links to your site and increased link popularity for search engines.

## Maintaining a Marketing Log

Record all new links to your site in your Internet marketing log. It is important to maintain this log and review it regularly. You must periodically check to make certain that links to your site are operational and are going to the appropriate location. Along with the URL where your site is linked from, you should also keep track of all contact information gathered when communicating with the Webmaster.

## A Word of Caution with Link Trading

You must be aware when trading links that all links are not created equal.

- If you provide a prominent link to another site, make sure you receive a link of equal or greater prominence.

- Be aware when trading your links with sites that receive substantially less traffic than you do that you will probably have more people "link out" than "link in" from this trade. Consider trading a banner ad and a link from their site for a link from your site, thus making it more of an equal trade. If their site has more traffic than yours, don't mention it unless they do.

- Never put your outbound links directly on your home page. Have your outbound links located several levels down so that visitors to your site will likely have visited all the pages you want them to visit before they link out.

- When incorporating outbound links, make sure that when the link is clicked, the Web page is opened in a new browser window so that the visitor can easily return to your Web page.

- Sometimes when people update their site, they change the Internet address or delete a page altogether. If you have placed a link on your page to that page, and one of your viewers tries to link out to that page and receives an HTTP 404 error, this reflects badly on your site. You should frequently check your Web site for dead links.

- When you change content on a page within your site, don't create totally new pages; just update the content on your current pages and keep the same file names. There might be links to your pages and if you delete them, anyone trying to click on a link to your site from another site will get an HTTP 404 error. This results in a dead link on the referring page as well as in any search engine listings you might have.

## Internet Resources for Chapter 16

I have developed a great library of online resources for you to check out regarding link strategies. This library is available on my Tourism Internet Marketing University Web site *http://www.TourismInternetMarketingU.com/max* in the Resources section where you can find additional tips, tools, techniques, and resources.

I have also developed courses on many of the topics covered in this book. These courses are also available on my Tourism Internet Marketing University Web site *http://www.TourismInternetMarketingU.com/max*. These courses are delivered immediately over the Internet or can be ordered as a CD.

# 17

# Maximizing Promotion with Meta-Indexes

Meta-indexes and directories are designed to be useful resources for people who have an interest in a particular topic. Meta-indexes provide Internet marketing opportunities for the travel and tourism industry to reach your target audiences and they should be utilized to their full potential. In this chapter, we cover:

- What meta-indexes are

- Why meta-indexes are useful for travel and tourism businesses

- How to make the links to your site stand out

- Creating your own meta-index.

## What Are Meta-Indexes?

Meta-indexes are lists of Internet resources pertaining to a specific subject category and are intended as a resource for people who have a specific interest in that topic. These lists, such as the one for golf courses in North Carolina shown in Figure 17.1, consist of a collection of URLs of related Internet resources that

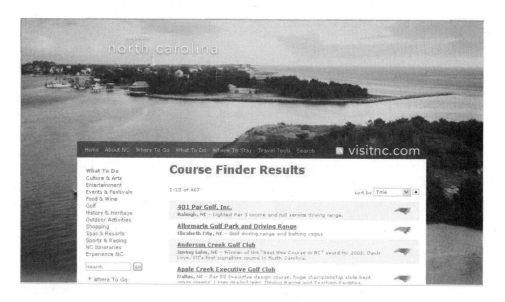

**Figure 17.1.**   VisitNC.com provides a meta-index with links to Web sites of golf courses in North Carolina.

are arranged on a Web page by their titles. The owners or creators of meta-indexes put a lot of effort into compiling these lists and are eager to find new sites to add to them. It used to be that the owners of these sites would list your site for free because they desired to have the most meta of the meta-indexes—they strived to have the largest of the large indexes, and more sites mean a larger index. Today, many of these meta-indexes are commercial and charge a fee for the link to your site.

Some of these meta-indexes have a "Submit" or "Add Your Site" area; otherwise you have to develop a request for inclusion e-mail and send it to the owner of the site. In your inclusion request e-mail, let the owner know that you visited the site and feel that your site would be appropriate to be included. Give the reasons you think your site is appropriate and request the link. You should provide the HTML for the link as well. Review the techniques discussed in Chapter 16 to have your link stand out with a graphical icon, hypertext link, and tag line, as well as including targeted keywords to enhance your link relevancy scores for enhanced search engine placement.

Meta-indexes are directed at a specific topic, such as "Connecticut country inns" or "Tucson golf courses." Meta-indexes provide easy access to a number of sites on a specific topic, and they are a great way to draw targeted, interested people to your Web site. In addition, some users might rely on meta-indexes as their only search effort. They might not use a search engine to perform a query on Mexican resorts, for example, if they know a certain meta-index contains 200 sites on Mexican resorts. Where search engine results will show links to actual Mexican resorts, they might also show books on Mexican resorts, or personal Web pages relating to family vacations at Mexican resorts. Experienced Web users know that meta-indexes provide only links to the actual Web sites of Mexican resorts. Meta-indexes can increase your chances of being found by people who are interested in your destination or travel packages.

You might want to consider placing a banner ad on one or more of the meta-indexes you find, given that the target audience you want to reach will be the people using these indexes. Choose carefully, though; you don't want to buy a banner ad on a meta-index that is not up to par and doesn't provide the traffic you are looking for. Take your time and investigate the meta-index before advertising on it. Does it appeal to the eye? Is it of good quality? Are there many dead links? Is it updated frequently? Does it have sufficient traffic?

Meta-indexes can be an effective way to increase traffic to your Web site. Word spreads quickly about the best meta-indexes because they are a great resource. Your target market will tell two friends and they will tell two friends, thus increasing traffic. In addition, more people may add links to your meta-index, and the more links you have to your Web site, the more traffic your site gets.

## How to Find Appropriate Meta-Indexes

Now that you know what a meta-index is, how do you find one? One way would be to simply browse the Web and just happen to come across one. A better way to find meta-indexes is through the search engines and directories.

To perform a search for meta-indexes you need to know how your particular search engine of choice works. Most search engines have advanced search capabilities, so be sure to explore them. When you're looking for meta-indexes, we recommend that you create a more focused search by adding an extra word to your search term(s) such as *directory, list, index, table, resource, reference,* or *guide.* By adding one of these words in conjunction with another word—for example, *travel*—you're increasing your chances of finding appropriate meta-indexes. Performing a search on *travel* alone will return far less-targeted results.

Alternatively, looking for a travel directory alone might not work for you either. Why not? A search for a travel directory on the search engines often means looking for all sites that contain the word *travel* and all sites that contain *directory.* You should refine your searches to achieve more accurate results. Some general techniques that use the words *travel* and *directory* as examples that you can apply in your search for meta-indexes are:

- Entering *travel directory* generally means: Look for all sites containing the word *travel* or *directory,* but try to gather those sites with *travel* and *directory* together.

- Entering *"travel directory"* (with quotation marks) often means: Look for all sites containing the words *travel* and *directory* next to each other.

- Entering *+travel directory* generally means: Find all sites with the word *travel* and preferably the word *directory* as well.

- Entering *+travel+directory* generally means: Find all sites with both words.

Most search engines look for information in different ways and allow different techniques to be applied in order to narrow or broaden the search criteria. This information can be obtained by looking at the respective search engines' Help pages (Figure 17.2).

Ideally, when searching for appropriate meta-indexes, you will be very niche targeted. You will be looking for your most important keyword phrases in conjunction with the word meta-index or directory or directories. For example, if you are a golf course in North Carolina, your search will be for "North Carolina Golf Course Directory."

Many search engines and directories offer an Advanced Search or Search Options page that lets you perform more detailed searches without using the

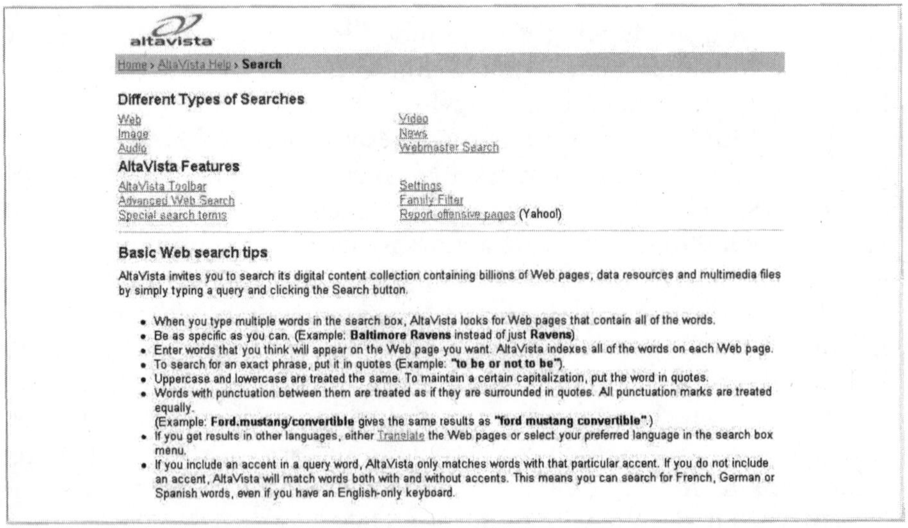

**Figure 17.2.**  AltaVista's Help page and quick-search guide.

parameters outlined above. Yahoo! (Figure 17.3) and Google (Figure 17.4) are two such sites.

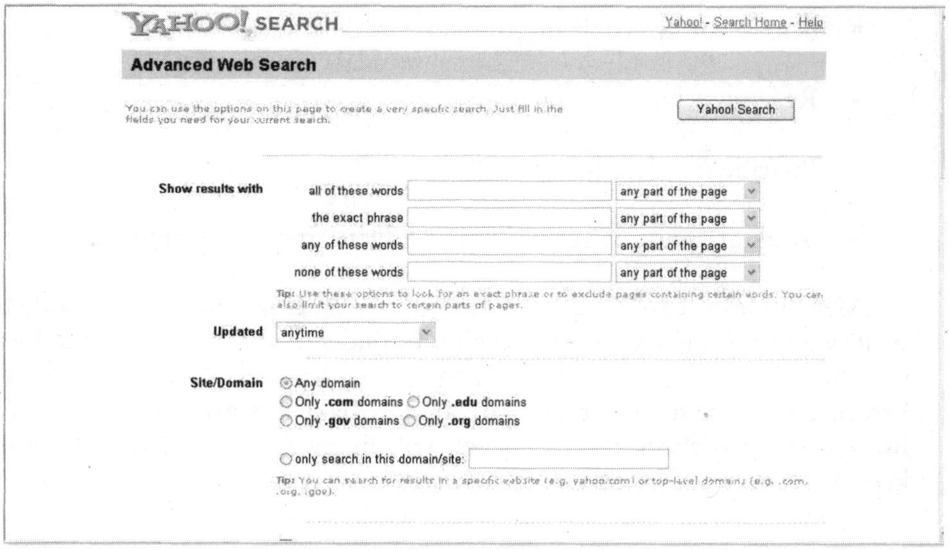

**Figure 17.3.** Yahoo!'s advanced search options.

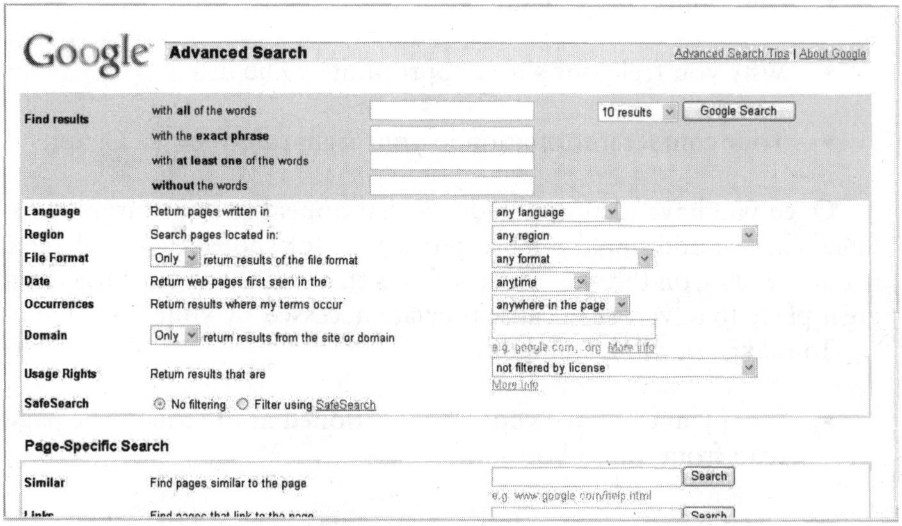

**Figure 17.4.** Google's advanced search options.

## Enlisting Meta-Indexes for Optimal Exposure

To ensure that you are taking full advantage of meta-indexes:

- Search for appropriate tourism and destination meta-indexes.

- Request a link.

- Provide the details necessary.

- Look at sponsorship or banner advertising opportunities.

Meta-indexes can be arranged by subject (such as sites that provide links to white water rafting operations, ski hills, or dude ranches) or by geography (North Carolina golf courses, Costa Rica eco-tour or Las Vegas shows). As mentioned before, the major search engines are a good place to start. Once you find a good list and start to check the links, you will likely find other lists. Bookmark or keep a record of the meta-indexes you like for future reference.

When requesting a link to your site, send an e-mail with "Site addition request" in the subject area of your message. Include the following in the body of the message:

- URL

- Description of your site

- Why you feel your site is appropriate to be listed

- Your contact information in your signature file (see Chapter 11).

Once you have identified indexes that appeal to your target market, determine whether additional opportunities exist for sponsoring or purchasing banner advertising on the site. Meta-indexes that relate to your target market are a great place to advertise because they are accessed by your potential customers.

To make your link stand out:

- See if you can have your link positioned at the top of the page—people read from top to bottom.

- See if you can add a graphic—people's eyes are drawn to graphics.

- Provide a call to action to get people to visit your site.

- Grab the visitor's attention with the text or description you use.

- Consider buying the banner ad space at the top of the page—get whatever attention you can, as the visitors to this page are your potential customers looking for what you have.

Try as well to get your most important keywords in the text around the link to your site as this will help with your search engine relevancy score and your search engine positioning.

Keep in mind that the compilers of the free meta-indexes are motivated by noncommercial reasons and are under no obligation to add your site to their list or process your request quickly.

More and more meta-index sites are moving to a more commercial focus. A simple text listing on a meta-index might be free, but there could be a fee charged for placing a hypertext link within the listing. If you are considering paying a fee to be included in a meta-index, consider the volume of traffic the meta-index receives, whether the traffic is targeted, and the cost involved in relation to the return on investment. It might be wise to contact those already listed in the meta-index to see if the listing has been a good investment for them.

## Internet Resources for Chapter 17

I have developed a great library of online resources for you to check out regarding meta-index marketing. This library is available on my Tourism Internet Marketing University Web site *http://www.TourismInternetMarketingU.com/ max* in the Resources section where you can find additional tips, tools, techniques, and resources.

I have also developed courses on many of the topics covered in this book. These courses are also available on my Tourism Internet Marketing University Web site *http://www.TourismInternetMarketingU.com/max*. These courses are delivered immediately over the Internet or can be ordered as a CD.

# 18

# Winning Awards, Cool Sites, and More

There are literally hundreds of awards and listings for Cool Sites, Sites of the Day, Hot Sites, and Pick-of-the-Week Sites. Sometimes you are required to submit your site for consideration; many times these sites are selected based on such things as:

- Awesome graphics

- Dynamite content that is useful and interesting

- Uniqueness

- Fun features.

If you are selected for one of these sites, it can mean a huge increase in the number of visitors to your site. You must be prepared for the increased traffic flow as well as the increased demand for online offerings. In this chapter, we cover:

- Where to submit your travel and tourism site for award consideration

- How to win Site of the Day—tips, tools, and techniques

- Getting listed in What's New

- Posting your awards on your site

- Hosting your own Site of the Day.

## It's an Honor Just to Be Nominated

There are sites that actively find and evaluate other sites on the Internet and recognize those that are outstanding by giving them an award. The award sites are generally quite discriminating in terms of selecting which sites are the recipients of their award. They have established criteria defining what they consider "hot" or "cool" and base their award selection on those criteria. Figure 18.1 shows a variety of awards.

What's New Web sites are designed to inform Internet users of new sites and updates to existing sites, and are often selective in terms of which new sites they promote. The owner of each site also chooses awards for Site of the Day, Week, Month, and Year. As mentioned earlier, some of these sites require you to submit an announcement or site description, and the awards are granted based on criteria such as graphics, dynamic content, uniqueness, and the "fun" quality of your site. Other sites grant their awards based solely on the personal likes and dislikes of the owner of the site and do not adhere to any criteria at all.

Some Web site awards are taken just as seriously as the Academy Awards. The Webby Awards have a very comprehensive nomination procedure. Information regarding the Webby is available on their Web site at *http:// www.webbyawards.com.*

**Figure 18.1.**   A collage of some of the more popular award sites.

When you win an award, you will be presented with an award icon to post on your site for all to see. The award icon is usually a link back to the site that bestowed the honor on you.

## Choosing Your Awards and Submitting to Win

There are different levels of prestige associated with different award sites. Some are an honor to receive and some are highly competitive because of the number of submissions they receive. To find these award sites you can do a Google or Yahoo! Search on "travel awards" or "tourism awards." Another option is to visit the awards page on sites like Travelocity (*http://www.travelocity.com*) and follow the links to awards they have won.

Some awards are easier to receive than others, such as those from commercial sites that give out awards in an attempt to increase the traffic to their own site. They can increase their traffic because the awards they give are graphic links displayed on the winner's site and visitors who visit the award-winning site can follow the link back to the award giver's site. On the other hand, there are Webmasters who give out awards to anybody and everybody who makes a submission. The award is granted with the sole purpose of building traffic.

The bottom line is that awards can be valuable assets. The average Web user cannot tell which awards are the prestigious ones and which are given to anyone who submits. So, submit for any awards that you choose to, as long as your site is ready.

Where you place these awards is important. If you win many awards, consider developing an Awards page to house them with a link from your navigation bar.

Always determine if the marketing tools and techniques will increase visitors from your target market before deciding to include them in your online marketing strategy.

Getting mentioned on one of the popular Cool Sites lists is probably the single biggest way to draw a tremendous amount of traffic to your site. However, that traffic is like a flash flood—fast and furious. Be careful what you wish for—you just might get it! Be prepared! Have a plan that you can implement on a moment's notice. If you offer something free from your site, be sure that you can access a huge volume of whatever it is and that you have a plan to distribute quickly. If you offer a free download from your site, plan to have a number of alternative **FTP** sites available to your visitors. If you have a call-in offer, make sure you have a telephone response

**FTP (File Transfer Protocol)**
The simplest way to transfer files between computers on the Internet.

system in place and staff to handle the huge volume of calls you might get. You need a plan to handle a huge volume of e-mails as well.

Once you have decided that the type of traffic that comes along with winning awards fits with your marketing strategy, make sure your site has the makings of a winner and then submit to as many award sites as you can.

- First, make a list of the URLs of the award sites you are interested in.

- Understand the submission form and guidelines. Review a number of forms to determine the information commonly requested.

- To save time, develop a document with the answers to the various questions from which you can copy and paste into the different submission forms.

- Submission forms capture the following types of information:

  - URL

  - Title of your site

  - Contact person (name, e-mail, phone, address)

  - Owner of the site.

- Submission guidelines tell you what types of sites can be submitted. (Some awards do not accept personal pages; others do not include commercial sites.) The submission guidelines also tell you what meets the definition of "cool" or "new" and what doesn't.

- Some award sites require that you display their award icon on your site. Posting an award on your site can provide a number of positive results—including enhanced credibility.

## What's Hot and What's Not in the Name of Cool

Most of the award sites provide their selection criteria. Some base their selection on valuable content; others look for innovative and unique capabilities. Sites vary on what they consider "hot" or "cool," but they are fairly consistent on what doesn't make the grade, as summarized next.

| What's Hot | What's Not |
| --- | --- |
| Awesome graphics, animation, audio, video | Single-page sites |
| Great, original content | Single-product promotion |
| Broad appeal | Offensive language or graphics |
| Fun features | Lengthy download time |

## Posting Your Awards on Your Site

If you have managed to collect a few awards for your travel and tourism Web site, you want to display them. After all, any award is a good award, and the site that granted you one expects you to display it in return for the recognition. Posting the awards on your home page might not be the best idea, though. For one thing, the additional graphics that will have to be downloaded will slow the load time for your home page. Second, by posting the awards on your home page, you are placing links leading out of your site on the very first page people land on. Thus, you are giving people the opportunity to leave your site before they have even had a chance to explore it. Where should you post your well-deserved awards, then? The simplest way is to create an awards section on your Web site. Here, you can list all of your awards without adversely affecting the load time of your home page or losing traffic.

## Becoming the Host of Your Own Awards Gala

You can also create your own awards program to draw traffic to your site; however, this requires a considerable amount of work to maintain. Hosting awards may be a very appropriate strategy for a destination marketing organization or industry association.

The benefits of having your own awards program include having links back to your site from the awards placed on winners' sites. Having links back to your site is important for search engine placement because of link popularity. If you are the host of the awards program you control the text around the link that takes people back to your site, so make sure you include your most important keywords to enhance your link relevancy score to further improve your search engine ranking.

There are also great opportunities for permission ("Click here to be notified via e-mail when we have a new award winner") and viral marketing ("Tell a friend about this award—click here").

In addition, having your own awards program provides you with "bragging rights" and the opportunity for press releases to announce your awards, which gain exposure for your Web site and increase traffic. You need to work at it daily or weekly, so you must be committed to it.

Be sure there is a benefit from a marketing perspective before you design and develop your own awards program. You must also be prepared to conduct your own searches to find sites worthy of your award if the quality of sites being submitted to you is not up to your standard.

There are a number of steps involved in getting your awards program up and running:

- Develop the criteria to use in your site selection.

- Develop several Web pages related to the award including information on selection criteria, submission forms, today's or this week's award winner and past award recipients' page, in order to promote the award. (Be sure that you stipulate whether you are looking for submissions from commercial sites or personal pages and what criteria will be used in judging submissions.)

- Develop your award icon. Have this icon link back to your site. The award distinguishes the winners; thus, the link might be displayed prominently on their sites. This is a great traffic builder.

- Finally, announce the award and market, market, market.

## Internet Resources for Chapter 18

I have developed a great library of online resources for you to check out regarding awards. This library is available on my Tourism Internet Marketing University Web site *http://www.TourismInternetMarketingU.com/max* in the Resources section where you can find additional tips, tools, techniques, and resources.

I have also developed courses on many of the topics covered in this book. These courses are also available on my Tourism Internet Marketing University Web site *http://www.TourismInternetMarketingU.com/max*. These courses are delivered immediately over the Internet or can be ordered as a CD.

# 19

# Online Advertising

The world of banner advertising is changing rapidly. In the early days when banner advertising was in vogue, visitors were clicking through, good banner space was hard to find, and prices were rising. Then we saw the big decline. Click-through rates were poor and, as a result, advertisers were looking at alternative online advertising mediums. We saw banner advertising prices decline significantly. Quality space was not difficult to obtain and banner advertising was being used primarily to meet branding objectives. Over the last few years we have seen more and more pay-per-click targeted advertising opportunities, and this type of advertising is now on the rise. I have chosen to discuss the two types separately. I deal with pay-per-click or pay-to-play search engine advertising in Chapter 9, and deal with other forms of online advertising, including traditional banner advertising, in this chapter.

Despite all the doom and gloom and bad press, traditional banner ads can still be an effective advertising medium for travel and tourism organizations if the banner ad is properly developed and is placed on a well-chosen site.

We are starting to see a shift toward ads using rich media. Advertising online provides visibility—just as offline advertising does. You must develop an online advertising strategy that works with your packages, vacation specials, your destination, your marketing objectives, and your budget.

In this chapter, we cover:

- Your online advertising strategy

- Advertising opportunities on the Web for travel and tourism organizations

- Banner ad design and impact on click-throughs

- Banner ad sizes and locations

- Placing classifieds

- Tips to creating dynamite banner ads that work

- The cost of advertising online

- Measuring ad effectiveness

- Banner ad exchange networks

- Using an online advertising agency

- Sources of Internet advertising information

- Behavioral advertising

- Retargeting

- Content integration.

## Expanding Your Exposure through Internet Advertising

Today, Internet advertising is being recognized in the advertising budgets of travel, tourism, and destination businesses around the globe. Banner ads are a way to create awareness of your Web site and increase the traffic to it. Banners are placed on the sites that your target market is likely to frequent, thus encouraging this market to click-through and visit you.

The Internet offers many different advertising spaces. Banner ads can be placed on search engines, content sites, advertising sites, portals, and online magazines. The choice of where your ad is displayed is based on the objectives you wish to achieve with your online advertising strategy.

There are a number of advantages to online advertising:

- The response from these ads can easily be measured within one day through Web traffic analysis.

- The amount of information that can be delivered, if your Web site is visited, far surpasses that of a traditional advertising campaign.

- The cost of developing and running an online advertising campaign is much less than using traditional media.

Let's compare online advertising to traditional advertising. In traditional offline advertising, you generally work with a public relations (PR) firm or advertising company to come up with your marketing concept. As a client, you would review and approve the concepts (usually after several attempts) before they are ever released to the public. The PR or advertising firms are responsible for developing TV, radio, and print ads for your travel business. They come up with the media-buy strategy after reviewing appropriate publications, editorial calendars, pricing, and the discounts that they receive for multiple placements. The ads are then gradually released over the period of the campaign and finally are viewed by the public. At the end of the campaign, the PR or advertising company evaluates the success of the marketing campaign. This is very easy if the objective of the campaign is to achieve X number of sales, but it is much more difficult if the goal of your campaign is to generate company awareness.

Today, online banner ads are developed in much less time and are placed on Web sites quickly. Web traffic analysis software can tell you the next day if the banner ad is working or not by tracking the number of visitors who clicked through and visited your site through the ad. This provides you with the opportunity to change the site on which you are advertising or to change the banner ad to see if it attracts a greater audience.

## Maximize Advertising with Your Objectives in Mind

When developing your online advertising strategy, start with the objectives of your overall advertising campaign. The most common objectives for an online advertising campaign for a travel and tourism operation include:

- Building destination awareness

- Increasing Web site traffic

- Generating leads, bookings, and sales.

You have a number of choices to make, such as what type of advertising to use and where to advertise. These decisions should be based on your objectives. If your objective is to increase overall destination recognition, a nicely designed banner ad on several of the high-traffic search engines would be effective. If you would like to develop leads and find new customers, then a more targeted approach should be taken, such as placing a banner ad on a high-traffic Web site that is frequented by your target market.

When deciding how to proceed with your online advertising strategy, consider how many people you want to reach. Do you want a high-quality response from a small number of much targeted people, or do you want to reach a mass audience of grand proportions?

Always keep your budget in mind when you are devising your online advertising strategy. If you have a reasonable budget, you may want to work with several online advertising agencies. If your budget is small or nonexistent, there are many ways to stretch your advertising dollar. If you have the time, you can find promising sites to trade banners with.

## Online Advertising Terminology

### Banner Ads

Banner ads are small advertisements that are placed on a Web site. Travel and tourism companies usually develop their banner ads, find sites for placement, and then either purchase or trade banner space.

### Click-Throughs

When a viewer clicks on a banner ad with their mouse and goes to the site advertised, it is called a "click-through." Sometimes banner advertising prices are determined by the number of click-throughs. You don't pay every time your ad is displayed. You pay only when someone actually clicks on your ad and is delivered to the appropriate page on your Web site.

### Hits

Hits to your site are the number of times that another computer has accessed your site (or a file on a site). This does not mean that if a page on your site has 1,000 hits, 1,000 people have visited it. If your home page has a number of graphic files on it, this number could be misleading. A hit is counted when the home page main file is accessed, but a hit is also counted for every other file that loads along with the home page. Each one of your pages will have a number of files on it—you have a file for each graphic, a file for each banner you display and often a different file for each navigation button on the page. So if a person visits 10 pages on a site and each page has 15 files included on it, then at least 150 hits would be generated.

### Impressions or Page Views

When a banner ad is viewed, it is called an impression. Banner advertising prices are often calculated by impressions. If a person visits a page where your ad is displayed six times, this generates six impressions.

### CPM

Cost per thousand, or CPM, is a standard advertising term. CPM is often used to calculate the cost of banner advertising if a site sells advertising based on impressions. If the CPM of advertising your ski package banner ad on another site is US$40 (that is $40 per thousand impressions) and the number of impressions your ad generated was 2,000, then you, the advertiser, would have to pay US$80 for displaying the ad.

### CPA

Cost per action, or cost per acquisition, is an ad payment model in which advertisers only pay when their ad leads to a complete conversion—sale, registration, download, or booking. Almost all affiliate advertising is based on the CPA model. This type of advertising model is best suited to high-volume sites as it needs a large number of banner displays to generate actual sales.

### Keywords

You can purchase keyword advertising on search engine (see Chapter 9) sites that have sophisticated advertising programs, or sites whose advertising real estate is maintained by online advertising agencies that have sophisticated advertising programs. Your ad appears when someone does a search on the keyword that you purchased. This is good for zooming in on your target market.

## Geo-targeting

Purchasing geographically targeted banner advertising is one of the latest trends in Internet marketing. This is done by purchasing banner advertising for a range of IP addresses. Every device that connects to the Internet has its own unique IP address. These are assigned centrally by a designated authority for each country. We are now seeing search engines sell advertising by IP addresses to help businesses pinpoint their target geographic group. For example, John Doe is planning a family vacation in Florida and is searching for a campground in that area. Toby's RV Resort, a camp ground in Arcadia, happens to be marketing over the Internet, and as part of Toby's RV Resort's advertising campaign they have purchased ads by keyword and by IP address. Simply stated, they have said that they want their ad to appear only when the keyword *camping* is searched on by individuals whose IP address is within a certain range (the range being those existing in Florida). When John Doe does his search on the word *camping,* the Toby's RV Resort ad is displayed at the top of the page holding the search results. Someone in Michigan searching for camping would see a different ad.

## Jump on the Banner Wagon

Banner advertising is the most common and most recognized form of online advertising. Banner ads are available in various sizes. (See Figure 19.1 for some of the more popular banner ad sizes.)

Banners usually have an enticing message or call to action that coaxes the viewer to click on it. "What is on the other side?" you ask. The advertiser's Web site, of course. Banner ads can also be static, just displaying the advertiser's logo and slogan, or can be animated with graphics and movement.

If you use an advertising or PR company to develop your offline ads, quite often they can provide you with a library of banner ads that you can use for your online advertising campaign. If you choose not to use an advertising or PR company, you can outsource the creation of a banner ad to another company or create your own.

The banner ad should be designed to have a direct impact on the number of click-throughs it achieves. There are a number of resources on-line to assist you in developing dynamic banner ads. Animation Online at *http:// www.animationonline.com* allows you to create banners on-line at no charge. Other resources to assist you in designing and building banner ads are identified in the Internet Resources section of my Web site, referenced at the end of this chapter.

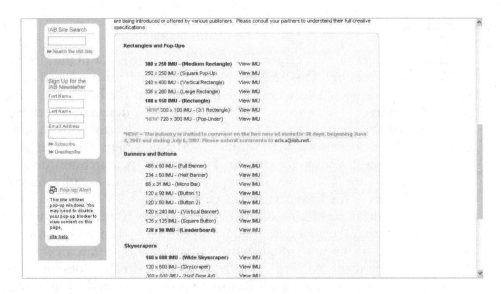

**Figure 19.1.**   The Interactive Advertising Bureau (*http://www.iab.net*) is a great online resource that reviews the popularity of different sizes and types of banner ads.

As noted previously, there are a wide variety of banner ad sizes available. You should consult with the owners of the Web sites on which you want to advertise before you create your banner ad or have one created professionally for you.

The objective of your banner ad is to have someone click on it. Do not try to include all of your information in your ad. A banner that is too small and cluttered is difficult to read and is not visually appealing. Many banners simply include a logo and a tag line enticing the user to click on it. Free offers or contest giveaways are also quite effective for click-throughs because they tend to appeal to the user's curiosity.

## Exploring Your Banner Ad Options

Static banners are what the name suggests. They remain static on the same Web page until they are removed. Your banner ad will be visible on that particular page until your reader moves to another page.

Animated banners are banners that move on a Web site. Animated banners are usually in **GIF** format and contain a group of images in one file that are presented in a specific order (see Figures 19.2a through 19.2c). When using animated banner ads, you can choose to loop the file so that the banner continues to move between the images in the files, or you have the option to make it stop after a complete cycle.

Rotating banners are banner ads that rotate among different Web pages on the same site. Some rotating banners rotate every 15 or 30 seconds, so a visitor might see several ads while remaining on the same page. Other rotating banner ads rotate every time there is a new visitor to the page. Rotating banners are commonly used in high-traffic Web sites.

**GIF**
Graphics Interchange Format.

Scrolling banners are similar to modern billboards. Here the visitor sees a number of billboard ads, scrolled to show a different advertisement every 10 to 30 seconds.

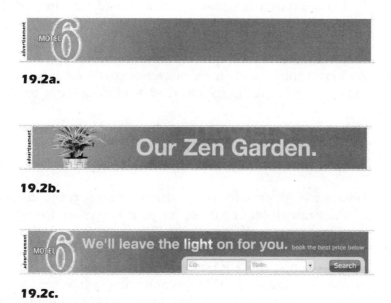

**19.2a.**

**19.2b.**

**19.2c.**

**Figure 19.2.**    a) This is the first stage in an animated banner ad for Motel 6. It captures the readers' attention because it is so simple. b) This is the second stage in the animated banner ad. c) This is the final stage in the animated banner ad series. It captures the readers' full attention and offers the chance for the reader to do a search.

## Banner Ad Tips

Follow these tips to ensure that your banner ad achieves your marketing objectives:

- Make sure that your banner ad is quick to load. If the Web page loads in its entirety before the banner, then the viewer might click away before ever seeing it. Ideally, you should have a very fast banner ad on a relatively slow-loading site. This way, your viewers have nothing to do but read your banner ad while they are waiting for the site to load. You should always try to keep your banner ad size under 5K.

- To see how big files are when using any version of Internet Explorer, you can follow these steps:

  - Right-click on the banner ad.

  - Select Properties.

  - In the Properties window you will see a Size line which will tell you the banner size.

- Keep it simple! If your banner contains too much text or animation, or too many colors and fonts, viewers experience information overload and will not be encouraged to read or click on your banner.

- Make sure your banner ad is easily viewed. Many banners on the Internet are nicely designed but difficult to read. Use an easy-to-read font with the right size type. Be careful in your choice of color.

- Always use Alt tags for those visitors who surf the Internet with their graphics turned off or cannot see your banner ad for whatever reason.

- Make sure your banner ad links to the optimum page on your site. It is not uncommon to click on an interesting banner only to find an error message waiting for you. This is annoying to Internet users and counterproductive for your marketing effort. Check your banner ads on a regular basis to verify that the link remains active and is pointing to the right page on your Web site.

- If you are using animated banner ads, limit your ads to two to four frames.

- You should always include a call to action such as "Click here." It is amazing how many people do what they are told. However, you still have to make your ad interesting and one that grabs their attention. Don't simply say "Click here"—give your audience a compelling reason to do so.

- Test your banner ads with the different browsers, the different versions of these browsers, and at different screen resolutions to make sure that they look the way you want them to.

- If you know absolutely nothing about advertising and graphic design, do not try to create a banner on your own. Go to a professional. If you do design your own banner, get a second opinion and maybe a third.

- Have your link send your target customer to an appropriate landing page rather than your home page. (See Chapter 7 for tips on landing pages.)

## Interesting Banner Ads

The following are more technologically advanced forms of banner advertising. They are interesting to viewers because they have attributes that are unique or unusual in some way. These attributes might be more apt to grab viewers' attention and entice them to click on the banner ad.

- Expanding banner ads. An expanding banner ad (see Figures 19.3a and 19.3b) is one that looks like a normal banner ad but expands when you click on it, keeping you on the same site rather than transporting you to another site on the Internet. Usually these say "Click to Expand," and the viewer then can learn more about what the banner is promoting.

- Animated banner ads. Animated banner ads contain a group of images in one file that rotate in a specific order. These banner ads are more likely to receive a higher click-through than a normal banner ad because moving images increase chances of viewers reading the banner. These banners also allow you to deliver more information than in a normal banner ad because you can show different files, which contain different data. Limit your banner ads to two to four frames to keep your load time fast and to make sure your viewers read your information before they continue to surf the Internet.

**Figure 19.3.**   a) This is an example of an expanding advertisement with video. It displays the ad and then prompts the viewer to roll over to see the videos. b) When the banner expands, you have a choice of videos to watch.

- Drop-down menu banner ads containing embedded HTML. Lately we are seeing an increase in banner ads containing embedded HTML (see Figure 19.4). This allows viewers to select from a drop-down menu which site they want to visit. These banners are great because instead of making viewers click through and then navigate through your site, as with a

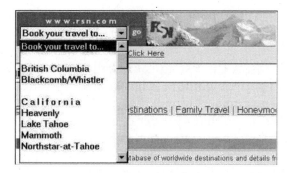

**Figure 19.4.** An embedded HTML banner ad with selection capability.

conventional banner, these direct your viewers to the page of interest on your site. This type of banner ad also is great for co-op advertising programs. Several travel and tourism companies targeting the same target market, in a non-competing way, can use this type of banner advertising to get more exposure for their dollar.

- Interstitial ads. These are advertisements that appear in a separate browser window while your visitors wait for a Web page to load. Interstitial ads are more likely to contain large graphics, streaming presentations, and more applets than a conventional banner ad. However, some users have complained that interstitial ads slow access to destination pages.

- Java, Flash, and Shockwave ads. These banner ads allow you to use rich media in your advertisements. By using these technologies, you can incorporate animation and sound into your banner advertisement. Although Java banners are more technologically advanced and offer more features, they also take longer to download and risk not being viewed. Flash was designed to generate faster-loading Web sites, online animation, and advertising. If you want to incorporate rich media into your banners, you may want to go with Flash or Shockwave because you want your visitors to see your banner ads as quickly as possible.

- Floating ads and DHTML. These ads appear when you first view a Web page, and they appear to "fly" or "float" over the page for anywhere from 5 to 30 seconds. They tend to obscure your view of the page, and they often disable mouse input until the ad is finished loading so that you must watch it before being able to access the page content. They have a high click-through rate and are great for branding, although their intrusiveness has been questioned.

- Unicast ads. A Unicast ad is basically like a television commercial that runs in a pop-up window. It has animation and sound and can last from 10 to 30 seconds. Although they are like television commercials, they go a step further in that a viewer can then click on the ad to obtain further information. They have a higher-than-average click-through rate.

- Rich Media ads. These advertisements are banner ads that use dynamic tools such as Flash, HTML forms, Java, ASP, Shockwave, Javascript or other programming languages or applications that increase the appearance and/or the functionality of the ad. A rich media ad may include sound or a registration form and usually commands higher CPM levels than other banner ads.

## Location, Location, Location

As with all types of advertising, the location of the ad is extremely important. There are any number of targeted travel and tourism-related sites where you can place your banner ads. Always make sure that your banner advertising location is consistent with your objectives and always make sure your banner ads appear above the fold or above the scroll. That is, be sure your ad is positioned on a Web page so that it can be viewed without having to scroll.

### Search Engines

Advertising with search engines is covered in Chapter 9.

### Content Sites

If your objectives include bringing interested people from your target market to your site, then advertising on strategically chosen content sites would be extremely effective. These are sites that concentrate on a specific topic. The CPM of advertising on content sites ranges drastically depending on the traffic volume they see and the focus of their visitors.

## Banner Ad Price Factors

The price of banner ad space varies from site to site. Banner ads are most often sold based on the number of impressions or number of click-throughs. However, there is also the option of them being sold on the cost per acquisition. As stated earlier, an impression is an ad view, and click-throughs are the actual clicking on the banner ad and being sent to the advertiser's Web site. The price per impression should be less than the price per click-through, whereas the price per acquisition should be much greater than either to make it worth the while for the Web publisher.

When site owners charge per impression, there is usually a guarantee that your ad will be seen by a certain number of people. The burden is on the seller to generate traffic to its site. When the charges are per click-through or per acquisition, the responsibility is on you, the advertiser, to design an ad that encourages visitors to click on it and then follow through with the desired conversion. Sites that charge per impression are more common than those that charge per click-through or per acquisition.

There are obvious advantages to you, the advertiser, when paying per click-through. You do not have to pay a cent for the 10,000 people who saw the banner but did not pursue the link. Sites that do not have a large volume of traffic often charge a flat rate for a specified period of time.

## Considerations When Purchasing Your Banner Ad

Before you sign on the dotted line to purchase banner advertising, there are a few things you should consider:

- How closely aligned to your target market is the target market of the site you want to advertise on?

- How many sites are there like the one you are considering advertising on? Are there other sites you could use to reach the same audience?

- What banner sizes are allowed? Generally, the larger the banner, the more it costs.

- How many ads are on each page? The more ads on a page, the lower the click-through rate for any particular ad on that page. Generally, the more ads on a page, the lower the price per ad.

- Where on the page will your ad appear? Top? Bottom? Side? Above the fold or below?

- What banner rotation system is being used? Is there a comprehensive program that automatically profiles the visitors and provides the best banner? The more targeted the audience, the more expensive the ad; these profiling systems can provide ads to a very targeted audience.

- What are the site's competitors charging?

- Does the site have a sliding-scale ad rate?

## Make Sure Visitors Can See Your Banner

A major fact that is often overlooked is that some people still surf the Internet with their graphics turned off. Not a big deal, right? What if you purchased a banner ad and you're paying based on impressions? They are not going to see it, so how could they click through? An easy way to make sure that the viewer still knows that your banner is there is to attach an Alt tag to your banner. An Alt tag is a small piece of HTML code that is added to a Web site. It tells the browser what is supposed to be displayed if the graphic cannot be viewed. It is here that you should develop a clever tag line that still entices the viewer to click through to your Web site. Remember that it is important to include an Alt tag on all of the graphics on your Web site.

## Making It Easy with Online Advertising Networks

If your objective is to reach a large number of users through a wide variety of sites, Internet ad networks could be right for you. Ad networks manage the banner advertising real estate on a wide range of different Web sites that people look at every day. If you are going to join an ad network, you are known as an advertiser. You supply your banners to the ad network and determine how you want it to promote you.

ValueClick (*http://www.valueclick.com*) is an example of a popular ad network (see Figure 19.5). ValueClick has 21 channels in its network and is emerging as an ad network leader. It can target the travel industry or any other specific industry of your choice, or advertise your banner to a mass audience. For a

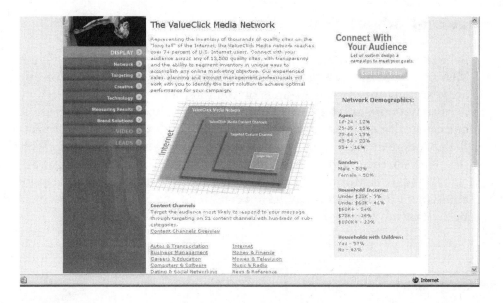

**Figure 19.5.** ValueClick is a large ad network offering advertisers the opportunity to target their audience using ValueClick's network.

more targeted audience, your CPM would be higher. Even though you have to pay a little more initially, it saves you in the long run. Run of network (RON) or run of network buy, means that you, as the advertiser, purchase banner inventory across an ad network's entire range of sites or a cluster of specified sites in the network designed to reach a specific audience.

The benefit of joining an ad network is that the network not only targets your audience, it also provides you with real-time reports that indicate the success of your banner ads. This allows you to evaluate the success of your current banner ad campaign and offers you the chance to change your marketing strategy if you are not happy with your results. Maybe you want to take a different approach, or maybe a different banner design might work better for you. Whatever it might be, the data that the ad network can provide you with is beneficial to determining the strength of your banner ad campaign.

You can also join an ad network as a publisher. Publishers are the Web sites that banners are placed on. If you would like to make some additional online revenue from your site without the administrative and technical headaches, you can join an ad network which will place banner ads on your site and pay you for the usage of this space. Very similar to an affiliate program or banner exchange, when you join an ad network you can dramatically increase your online revenue.

## Behavioral Advertising

Behavioral advertising, also known as behavioral targeting, is advertising to Web site visitors based on their own behavior and the behavior of others that are searching for the same things on the Internet.

Behavioral marketers target consumers by following Web site users around and categorizing them based on their searches. For example, if a user visits several Web pages related to travel and golf and then visits a car dealership Web site, on that Web site there will be an ad for a golf getaway. The key for this ad is not the actual profile, but the user's behavior. Had the user visited several pages related to amusement parks, there may have been an ad for Six Flags Amusement Parks. Behavioral advertising is covered in more detail in Chapter 14.

## Re-targeting

Targeting, in terms of advertising, refers to an advertiser's attempt to reach a desired audience. Re-targeting, also called re-marketing, is the process of targeting those visitors who have been to your site but left without completing the desired conversion.

Re-targeting works by observing your Web visitors' behavior while they are on your site. If the Web site visitor leaves your site without completing the desired conversion, purchasing one of your packages, booking a hotel room, or signing up for your newsletter, then targeted messages are delivered to these visitors when they visit other areas of your site or when they visit any other site in the advertising network.

The possibilities of re-targeting can be enormous. Re-targeting can also be done with Web site visitors who have been to your site and completed the desired conversion. These customers can be re-targeted with ads for travel-related products that complement their previous purchase or they can be re-targeted with new vacation packages and destinations.

## Bartering for Mutual Benefits with Banner Trading

When you use this technique, you barter with other travel and tourism related Web sites to trade banners with their sites. If you are browsing the Internet and find a site that you think appeals to your target market, but is not a direct competitor, then ask for a trade. Send the Webmaster an e-mail outlining your proposition. Include the reason you think it would be mutually beneficial, a description of your site, where you would place that site's banner on your site, and where you think your banner might go best on its site.

When you make arrangements like this, be sure to monitor the results. If the other site has low traffic, then more visitors could be leaving your site through its banner than are being attracted. Also, check the other site regularly to make sure that your banners are still being displayed for the duration agreed upon.

## Form Lasting Relationships with Sponsorships

Sponsorships are another form of advertising that usually involve strong, long-lasting relationships between the sponsors and the owners of the sites. Sponsors might donate money, Web development, Web hosting, Web site maintenance, or other products and services to Web site owners in exchange for advertising on their site—this creates a mutually beneficial relationship. By sponsoring other travel, tourism, and destination-related Web sites on the Internet, you can achieve great exposure for your own travel site. The benefits of sponsorships on the Internet are that you can target a specific audience, you usually get first call on banner ad placement, and you show your target market that you care about their interests. Overall, by sponsoring other travel, tourism, and destination-related sites on the Internet, you have the opportunity to get directly in the face of your target market.

There are a number of ways in which you can advertise online through sponsorships. The following is a list of the more common forms of online sponsorship:

- E-zines and newsletters. An example would be Kiawah Island Golf Resort sponsoring a Golf Digest e-zine.

- Content sites. An example would be Best Western sponsoring a NASCAR racing Web site.

- Online chat sessions. An example would be Sandals sponsoring a chat on the WeddingChannel.com.

- Events. An example would be an airline such as Continental Airlines sponsoring a seminar on vacation planning and booking.

## Commercial Links

Another form of online advertising is commercial links. A number of targeted sites provide lengthy lists of URLs related to a specific topic. See Chapter 17 on meta-indexes. These sites sometimes provide your listing for free but charge a fee to have a hypertext link activated from their site to yours. These are great sites, especially because they are targeted toward your demographic group.

## Sponsoring a Mailing List

Another online advertising opportunity is presented by mailing lists. Mailing lists provide a much-targeted advertising vehicle. Mailing list subscribers are all interested in the list topic and are therefore potential clients, if you select the mailing list carefully. The rates for sponsoring lists can be quite low. The cost would be determined on a price-per-reader basis and is usually between one and 10 cents per reader. Subscribe to the lists that appeal to your target market and read the FAQ files to determine whether advertising or sponsorship opportunities exist for each mailing list. If the mailing list allows sponsorship, contact the mailing list administrator to inquire about the cost of sponsoring and, if the cost is reasonable, check availability and sponsors. All of the members of the mailing list have subscribed and want to be on the list; therefore, they are likely to read your e-mail. This is an excellent opportunity for you to expose your travel specials, packages, or destination to these potential consumers. A good example would be Trip.com sponsoring a mailing list about vacation destinations around the world. Readers are interested in the topic, so they might be encouraged to click through and book a trip.

## Online and Offline Promotion

Your advertising strategy shouldn't be limited to online activities. It is important to integrate your offline advertising strategy with your online advertising strategy. When you run an online campaign, you will want to consider running a consistent campaign offline.

## Advertising Through Content Integration

Web surfers have been inundated with so many banner advertisements that they are becoming oblivious to them. Web surfers no longer want to be advertised to. A new trend for advertisers now is content integration. Content integration takes product placement one step further than ever before.

With content integration your destination, travel agency, getaway packages, or travel products become part of an article or part of the topic of discussion in an e-magazine, e-zine, newsletter or other online publication. For example, if *Southern Living*'s online magazine was running an article on best golf practices, the article would incorporate links out to various Web sites such as Pebble Beach Golf Resort (*http://www.pebblebeach.com*). The article would either recommend or simply inform the reader of Pebble Beach and the link out would allow the visitor to link over to their Web site for more information.

## Video Advertising

Another great new online advertising vehicle is video. Online video advertising is still relatively new and it is generating quite a bit of excitement in the travel and tourism industry as more and more operations are recognizing the combined branding and direct response value. In fact, according to eMarketer, spending for online video advertising in the U.S. will come in at around $640 million this year as opposed to $225 million last year (see Figure 19.6).

With video advertising you can transition your television, or other offline advertising, to online. Make your video ad easy to download, redistribute, and even allow other travel and tourism related Web sites to publish it on their own site. Video advertising can open up a huge number of online distribution channels. There are literally thousands of travel and tourism Web sites looking for content, blogs, search engines, directories, and content distribution services that are available. To maximize your online video campaign, incorporate such viral marketing techniques as forward to a friend and allow users to turn the volume down or mute the video sound.

Video advertising is fast becoming a key component of any new cutting-edge and effective communication campaign.

## Social Network Advertising

It has been estimated that about two-thirds of the U.S. population is using some sort of online social network. With new social networking sites emerging all the

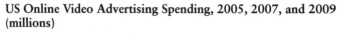

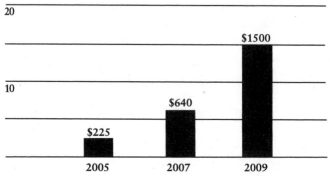

**Figure 19.6.** eMarketer's U.S. online video advertising spending projections for 2009.

time, like Classmates.com, MySpace.com, and Facebook, and with their seemingly overnight success, it's hard to dispute the notion that people want to be socially connected online.

More and more companies are holding on to that notion. eMarketer estimates that in 2007 companies will have spent $900 million in the U.S. and $330 million outside the U.S. on social network advertising. They estimate that social network ad spending will account for 6.3 percent of all of the money spent on U.S. online advertising and that it will be a $2.5 billion business by 2010 (see Figure 19.7).

As with any online marketing, if you are considering advertising on social networks, you want to target your audience, track your investment, and measure your return on investment. Research the social network sites' traffic, their members, and their niche. Go after the ones that have the type of audience you are targeting. Some social network sites allow you to specify who to serve your ads to based on the configuration of their ad server.

## A Few Final Thoughts to Remember

Before any advertising campaign goes live make sure you have prepared your landing pages appropriately. A landing page is a Web page that is created spe-

**Worldwide Online Social Network Advertising Spending, 2006-2011 (millions)**

|                 | 2006  | 2007   | 2008   | 2009   | 2010   | 2011   |
|-----------------|-------|--------|--------|--------|--------|--------|
| U.S.            | $350  | $900   | $1380  | $1810  | $2110  | $2515  |
| Outside of U.S. | $95   | $335   | $530   | $745   | $970   | $1115  |
| Worldwide       | $445  | $1235  | $1910  | $2555  | $3140  | $3630  |

*Note: Definition includes general social networking sites where social networking is the primary activity; social network offerings from portals such as Google, Yahoo! and MSN; niche social networks devoted to a specific hobby or interest; and marketer-sponsored social networks that are either stand-alone sites or part of a larger marketer site; in all cases figures include online advertising spending as well as site or profile page development costs.*
*Source: eMarketer, May 2007*                                    www.eMarketer.com

**Figure 19.7.**   eMarketer's worldwide online social network advertising spending projections for 2011.

cifically to respond to a marketing campaign you are running; when done properly it can greatly increase conversions, or the number of customers who act on your offer. For more information on landing pages see Chapter 7.

Now more than ever it is important to track your ROI, or return on investment. ROI will help you determine whether or not an ad campaign has generated more, or less, revenue than it costs. The Web metrics software systems available today allow you to track your ROI pretty easily. They even allow you to track the different ads you have running at the same time. For more on Web metrics see Chapter 28.

## Internet Resources for Chapter 19

I have developed a great library of online resources for you to check out regarding online advertising. This library is available on my Tourism Internet Marketing University Web site *http://www.TourismInternetMarketingU.com/max* in the Resources section where you can find additional tips, tools, techniques, and resources.

I have also developed courses on many of the topics covered in this book. These courses are also available on my Tourism Internet Marketing University Web site *http://www.TourismInternetMarketingU.com/max*. These courses are delivered immediately over the Internet or can be ordered as a CD.

# 20

## Maximizing Media Relations

Your online media strategy can be extremely effective in building targeted traffic to your site. The travel and tourism industry has lots of news, and news release distribution can be done easily. Build the right list of e-mail addresses or make use of one of the online news release distribution services. All reporters and writers have e-mail addresses. There are still a few that don't like to receive e-mailed news releases; many others prefer the e-mail versions. When e-mail news releases are sent out, reporters reply by e-mail. They will expect your response within 24 hours. Develop a media kit that you can e-mail out to editors. In this chapter, we cover:

- Developing your online media strategy

- Public relations versus advertising

- Online public relations versus traditional public relations

- Effective news releases

- News release and distribution services online

- How to distribute news releases online

- Providing an area for media on your site

- How to find travel and tourism reporters online

- How these reporters want to receive your information

- Encouraging re-publication of your travel-related article with a direct link to your site or the article

- Providing press kits online

- Electronic newsletters.

## Managing Effective Public Relations

Media relations can be very important to your marketing efforts. The best results are achieved when you integrate both online and offline publicity campaigns. News release distribution can be accomplished easily if you have an established list of reporters and editors that cover the travel and tourism beat, or if you make use of a news distribution service.

Maintaining effective public relations delivers a number of benefits to your company. Your company, your destination, and your travel-related offers gain exposure through news releases. Your relationship with current customers is reinforced, and new relationships are formed.

## Benefits of Publicity versus Advertising

Media coverage, or publicity, has a major advantage over paid advertisements. Articles written by a reporter carry more weight with the public than ads do because the media and reporters are seen as unbiased third parties. The public gives travel-related articles printed in media publications more credibility than they do paid advertisements. Another advantage of distributing news releases is that it is more cost-effective than advertising. You have to pay for advertising space on a Web site or time on the radio, but the costs of writing and distributing news releases are minimal.

One of the disadvantages of news releases compared to advertising is that you don't have control over what is published. If the editor decides to cast your company in a negative light, there is nothing you can do to stop him or her. If the writer of the piece does not like your company, for whatever reason, this might come across in the article. Basically, after your news release is distributed, you have no control over what will be written about your business.

It is important to note that when generating publicity, you might lose control over the timing of your release as well. For example, you might want an article released the day before your festival or event, but the editor could relegate it to a date the following week. There is nothing you can do about this. It is not a good idea to rely exclusively on publicity for important or newsworthy events, because if the release is not reviewed or is not considered newsworthy, you might be stuck with no promotion at all.

## What Is a News Release?

Before you begin your media campaign, you should know what news releases are and how to write them. News releases are designed to inform reporters of events concerning your travel offers, your travel business, or your destination that the public might consider newsworthy. News releases can get your company free public attention. A news release is a standard form of communication with the media. News releases must contain newsworthy information. Companies that continually send worthless information in a blatant attempt to get their name in the press do not establish a good relationship with the media.

### Writing a News Release

Journalists are bombarded with volumes of news releases. To improve the chances that your story will interest the journalist enough to publish it, you must make the journalist's job easier by presenting your news release in an appealing format and style. Your news release should be written as if it were prepared by an unbiased third party. The news release should follow a standard format, which is described in the following paragraphs.

**Notice of Release**

The first thing the reader sees should be . . .

FOR IMMEDIATE RELEASE

. . . unless you have sent the information in advance of the time you would like it published. In that case, state it as follows:

FOR RELEASE: Wednesday, December 12, 2007 [using the date you want it released].

Remember that no matter what date you put here, the publication can release the information before or after that date. If the news is really big, it is unlikely that the publication will hold it until the date you have specified.

## Header

The header should be in the upper-left corner. It should contain all of the contact information for one or two key people. These contacts should be able to answer any questions regarding the news release. If reporters cannot get in touch with someone to answer their questions, they might print incorrect information or even drop the article altogether.

Contact:
Susan Sweeney
Connex Network, Inc.
(902) 468-2578
susan@susansweeney.com
*http://www.susansweeney.com*

## Headline

Your headline is critically important. If you get it right, it will attract the attention you are looking for. Your headline should be powerful, summarizing your message and making the reader want to continue reading. Keep the headline short—fewer than ten words.

## City and Date

Name the city you are reporting from and the date you wrote the news release.

## The Body

Your first sentence within the body of the news release should sum up your headline and immediately inform the reader why this is newsworthy. With the number of news releases reporters receive, if you don't grab their attention immediately they won't read your release. Begin by listing all of the most relevant information first, leaving the supporting information for later in the article.

Ask yourself the five W's (who, what, where, when, and why) and answer them up front. Write the news release just as if you were writing a newspaper article for publication. Include some quotes from key individuals in your company and any other relevant, credible outside sources. If there are any statistics that support your main message, include them as well, providing references.

Your last paragraph should be a short company description.

**The Close**

If your release is two pages long, center the word *more* at the bottom of the first page. To end your release, center the word *end* at the end of your message. A sample news release is shown in Figure 20.1.

## Advantages of Interactive News Releases

Online news releases take the same standard format as offline news releases, but the online news release can be interactive, with links to a variety of interesting information that supports your message. When your news release is pro-

**Figure 20.1.** This news release from Destination Hotels & Resorts contains several hypertext links, enabling a journalist to quickly access additional information and perform due diligence.

vided by e-mail and you provide a hypertext link in that e-mail, the journalist is just a click away from accessing all the information he or she needs to complete the story. Helpful links to include in your interactive news releases are:

- A link to the e-mail address of the media contact person in your organization so that with the click of the mouse a journalist can ask a question via e-mail.

- A link to the company Web site so that the journalist can quickly and easily access additional information as part of his or her due diligence, or can find required information.

- Links to articles that have been written about the company and related issues, both on the corporate Web site and on other sites. Don't provide a link to the site of a magazine that has written the article; rather, get a copy of the article and place it on your own Web site to ensure a live link.

- Links to graphics and pictures for illustration. If your story relates to your destination, have a link to a graphic that can be used.

- Links to key corporate players, their biographies, their photos, and possibly some quotes. Journalists usually include quotes in their stories.

- A link to an FAQ section where you can have frequently asked questions and a few that you wish were frequently asked.

Figure 20.2 is an example of an online news release.

## Sending News Releases on Your Own versus Using a Distribution Service

When distributing news releases on your own, you save the money it would cost to have a service do it. You can also be more targeted in your efforts than a service would be. Some services' lists could be outdated or incomplete. Their lists of reporters and editors might not be comprehensive and might not have been updated. On the other hand, some services could make sure your news release is taken more seriously. A reporter who recognizes the name of the service might be more receptive than if the release were to come from an unknown company. Using a service is bound to save you a lot of time.

**Figure 20.2.** Best Western provides great news releases on a regular basis on its Web site.

If you decide to send your news releases on your own, you have to build a list of journalists who cover the appropriate travel and tourism beats. When reading publications that you'd like to be covered in, look for the names of reporters and find out their contact information. If you don't know whom to send a news release to at any publication, you can always call and ask for the name of the appropriate editor. Subscribe to a personalized news service to receive articles about your industry. This is a great way to find the names of journalists who might be interested in what you have to say.

There are a number of online resources to assist you in building your news-distribution list, such as the one shown in Figure 20.3. Mediafinder (*http://www.mediafinder.com*) is a Web site that provides access to a database of thousands of media outlets including magazines, journals, newspapers, newsletters, and catalogs. Bacon's (*http://www.bacons.com*) is a public relations resource that has detailed profiles on more than 20,000 media contacts, including their phone numbers, fax numbers, e-mail addresses, and work preferences (Figure 20.4). They also have editorial calendars that tell you who will be writing a scheduled story, what the topic of the story is, and when it will be written.

There are a number of news release distribution services online (Figures 20.5 and 20.6). Several of them are listed in the Internet Resources section of my Web site, referenced at the end of this chapter.

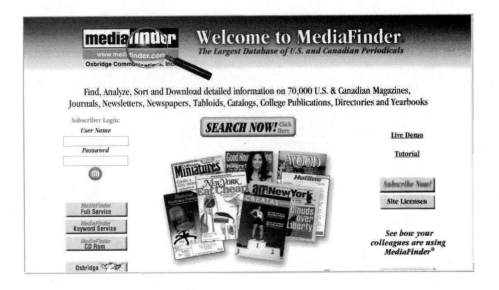

**Figure 20.3.** Use MediaFinder.com to locate appropriate magazines, journals, newspapers, newsletters, and catalogs.

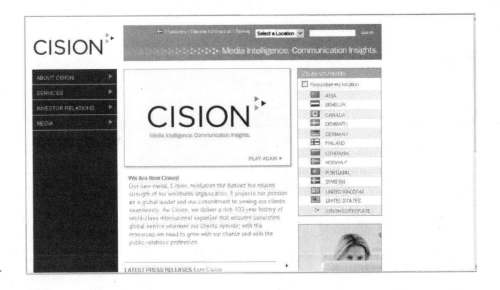

**Figure 20.4.** Cision is a media information company.

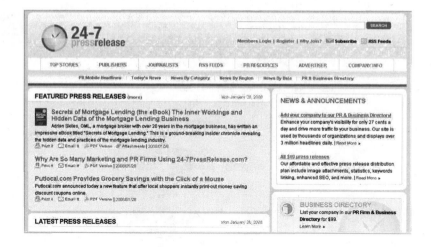

**Figure 20.5.**    24-7pressrelease.com is an e-mail news release service company.

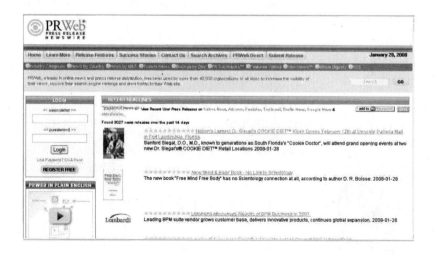

**Figure 20.6.**    You can submit your news release to PRWeb.

## Golden Tips for News Release Distribution

When distributing your news releases, don't send them to the news desk unaddressed. Know which editor handles the travel or tourism type of news in your release and address the news release to that person. Don't send the news release to more than one editor in any organization unless there is more than one angle to the information in the news release. Call ahead, if possible, to discuss and solicit the editor's interest in your news release before sending it. Also, follow up with a phone call a few days later to make sure that it was received and to answer any questions. Be sure to review editorial calendars of travel-related publications to see if there are upcoming articles where your story could make a contribution.

## News Release Timing and Deadlines

One of the most important things to remember when sending a news release or advisory is the deadline. Know how far in advance you should send your information for each of the media. Here are some time guidelines for your news release distribution.

### Monthly Magazines

For monthly magazines, you should submit your news releases at least two to three months before the issue you want it to appear in. Magazines are planned far in advance because it often takes a number of weeks to have the magazine printed and in subscribers' mailboxes.

### Daily Newspapers

It is a good idea to have your news release arrive on the editor's desk at least several weeks in advance. If it concerns a special holiday, you should send it even earlier.

### TV and Radio

When submitting news releases to TV and radio, remember that you might be asked to appear on a show as a guest. Be prepared for this before you submit the release. TV and radio move very quickly; a story that has been given to the news director in the morning might appear on that evening's news.

## Formatting Your E-mail News Release

Your news releases can be e-mailed. Some reporters prefer e-mailed releases; others say they prefer mailed or faxed releases. Check the reporter's preference before you send your news release. If you e-mail your news releases, make sure that your e-mails are formatted properly. Refer to Chapter 10 for guidelines on how to create effective e-mail messages.

Keep your e-mailed news releases to one or two pages with short paragraphs. It is best to insert the news release in the e-mail. Do not send your news release as an attachment. You don't know which platform or word-processing program the reporter is using. You might be using the latest Microsoft Word program on a PC, but the reporter could be using an incompatible program on a Mac and may not be able to open the file. There could also be problems downloading, which would prevent your release from being read. The person on the receiving end of your e-mail could be using an old computer with a slow dial-up connection, so what might take you two minutes to transfer might take the recipient 20 minutes or two hours to download. In addition, you may be using a PC platform, but the reporter may be using a MacOS-based computer. Someone who spends 20 minutes or longer downloading your e-mail only to find that it's useless won't be impressed—great start to getting the journalist to do a positive story on you!

Make sure the subject line of your e-mail is compelling. Journalists can easily delete e-mailed releases unopened, and quite often they do, because they receive large volumes of these daily. Make sure your e-mail is clear and concise. Get to the point with the first sentence. If you don't grab the reader's attention at the beginning of the release, the recipient might not keep reading to find out what your news is.

It's important to be able to send news release information in digital format within the body of the e-mail. With a quick copy-and-paste, the journalist would then have the "first draft" of the story. You have made it easy for him or her to then edit the draft and have a story quickly. Everybody loves to save time, and nearly all journalists are under tight deadlines.

## What Is Considered Newsworthy

Your news release has to contain newsworthy information for it to be published. One of the main concerns for public relations representatives is figuring out what is considered newsworthy and what isn't. You have to have a catch, and, if possible, the story should appeal to some sort of emotion. Here is a list of newsworthy items:

- The appearance of a celebrity at a company event or upcoming online promotions

- A special event your destination is hosting

- A charitable contribution by your company

- History-related information on your destination for certain magazines

- A milestone anniversary that your business is celebrating

- An award presented to your company

- Holiday event tie-ins

- Tips, articles, or advice

- Stories with a human interest element.

## What Isn't Considered Newsworthy

Some things that aren't news to the general public might be news to targeted trade magazines and journals. Use your own judgment when trying to determine if your news release is news or just an excuse to get your company's name in print. If your release focuses on any of the following, it is probably not newsworthy enough to publish:

The launch of a new Web site has not been news for a number of years now. Unless the site is based on a breakthrough in Internet technology or serves the public interest in an innovative way, you won't get a mention in the news. Nor is a new feature or change to your Web site newsworthy information. Even if your site has undergone a major overhaul, this is not news to the general public.

Specials or packages you are offering generally don't make the grade as newsworthy.

## Developing an Online Media Center for Public Relations

If publicity is a significant part of your public relations strategy, you should consider developing an online media center as part of your site (see Figure 20.7). The media center should be easily accessible from your navigation bar. It would include all the components a journalist needs when doing a story on your com-

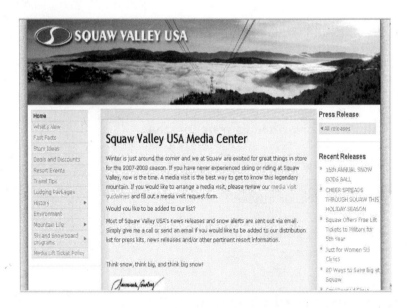

**Figure 20.7.**   Squaw Valley provides a great media center on its site.

pany. Journalists should be able to find pictures to include in the story and all the information necessary to do their due diligence. They should be able to send a question to the appropriate media contact within the organization with one click. The media center should include:

- A chronology of news releases distributed by the company. Make sure you put the latest news release at the top.

- The company or destination history and background information

- An electronic brochure

- Links to other articles written about your operation or destination. Make sure you have these on your site and not as a link to the magazine site that published the article.

- Links to story ideas for future articles

- Links to pictures that can be used by journalists in their stories. Perhaps have a gallery where journalists can choose the pictures they want to include in their story. If you want to take this seriously you might consider using an online media service like CleanPix (*http://www.CleanPix.com*). With CleanPix you store all of your media and marketing materials, such as pictures, logos, videos, and ad templates online. All material can be catalogued and searched by keyword or with thumbnail previews. All media and marketing materials, along with caption information, are delivered in multiple formats so that "the right file, in the right format, is instantly available, at the right time." See CleanPix in Figure 20.8.

- Background information on key company personnel, along with their pictures, bios, and quotes

- A link to your company's media contact and contact information

- FAQs and answers to anticipated questions.

**Figure 20.8.** CleanPix is a brand management software which converts media files to the most commonly used formats, and stores and distributes them in the right file format.

By having a media center on your site, you are sending a clear message to the journalist. You are saying, "You're important to me! I want to provide you with everything you need to quickly and easily complete your story on our operation or our destination." With the media center you are providing all the information, in a format that journalists can use, to enable them to do the story no matter when they choose to do it.

You will want to encourage permission marketing by offering visitors the opportunity to be notified to receive your news releases "hot off the press." Place a "Click here to join our media list and to receive notification of our news releases" link on your Web site. In addition, make it easy for visitors to send a copy of your news release to a friend. Sometimes journalists work on stories together, so give the journalist the option to send the news release to a colleague, or even to his or her editor, through viral marketing.

## Internet Resources for Chapter 20

I have developed a great library of online resources for you to check out regarding online media relations. This library is available on my Tourism Internet Marketing University Web site *http://www.TourismInternetMarketingU.com/max* in the Resources section where you can find additional tips, tools, techniques, and resources.

I have also developed courses on many of the topics covered in this book. These courses are also available on my Tourism Internet Marketing University Web site *http://www.TourismInternetMarketingU.com/max*. These courses are delivered immediately over the Internet or can be ordered as a CD.

# 21

## Increasing Traffic Through Online Publications

More than 60 percent of Internet users frequently read online publications, or **e-zines**. You can identify marketing opportunities for your travel and tourism business by searching for and reading e-zines that are relevant to your business. In this chapter, we cover:

---
**e-zines**
Electronic magazines.
---

- What electronic magazines are

- Finding online sites on which to advertise or arrange links

- How to find appropriate e-zines for marketing purposes

- Submitting articles to e-zines

- Advertising in e-zines

- E-zine resources online

- eBrochures and iBrochures—the latest in online publications.

## Appealing to Magazine Subscribers on the Net

Many Web users frequently read e-zines. This is one of the reasons they are among the most popular marketing tools on the Internet. Five years ago there were a few hundred e-zines in publication. Now there are thousands of e-zines dedicated to a wide variety of topics such as family travel, adventure travel, backpackers, Caribbean travel and life, destination travel, you name it. For any travel and tourism topic you are interested in, there quite likely are several e-zines dedicated to it.

## What Exactly Are E-zines?

E-zines, or electronic magazines, are the online version of magazines. They are content-rich and contain information regarding a certain topic in the form of magazine articles and features. Many e-zines display ads as well. Some e-zines are Web site-based and others are e-mail-based.

Many offline magazines provide a version online as well (Figure 21.1). *Southern Living, Coastal Living, Business Travel News* and *National Geographic* are all accessible via the Internet. Some of these sites provide the full version of

**Figure 21.1.** *Southern Living* is an example of an offline magazine that has an online version.

their traditional magazine; others are selective about the articles they provide; and still others provide the previous month's edition.

## Web-Based E-zines

There are many travel and tourism Web-based e-zines that have only an online presence (Figure 21.2). These e-zines are accessed through Web sites by browsing from page to page. They have the look and feel of their traditional magazine and include lots of pictures and advertisements. Usually there is no charge to view Web-based e-zines, but some do charge a subscription fee. These Web-based e-zines tend to be as graphically pleasing as offline magazines.

## E-mail E-zines

Although e-mail e-zines can come as text or as HTML, these days we are seeing more and more in HTML as they get a much higher readership and most e-mail viewers have no problem displaying HTML e-mails, which look like a Web page.

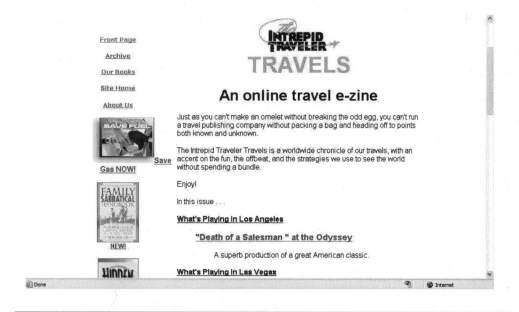

**Figure 21.2.** Destinations2Discover provides a great e-zine of interest to travelers, travel professionals, and destination marketing organizations.

Today we are seeing a blur between newsletters and e-mail e-zines as most newsletters now are sent as HTML and most are content-rich on a specific subject.

E-mail-based travel and tourism e-zines tend to be very content-rich and, as such, tend to be more of a target-marketing mechanism. Travel and tourism e-mail e-zines tend to be several screens in length with one main article or several short articles and, sometimes, they include classified advertising. The benchmark is that these e-zines should be able to be read in about five minutes. Circulation is often in the thousands. Most run weekly or biweekly editions and are free to subscribers.

People interested in the subject of the e-zine have taken the time to subscribe and have asked to receive the information directly in their e-mail box. Once you have found an e-zine that caters to your target market, that e-zine could be a valuable marketing vehicle.

Every subscriber to an e-mail-based e-zine has access to the Internet. These people regularly receive and send e-mail and quite likely surf the Net. If you advertise in this type of medium and place your Internet address in the ad, your prospective customer is not more than a couple of clicks away from your site.

People subscribe to travel and tourism-related e-zines because they are interested in the information that is provided. Even if they don't read it immediately when it is received, they usually read it eventually. Otherwise, they would not have subscribed. No matter when they take the time to read it, if you advertise in these e-zines or have your destination profiled, subscribers will see your URL and product advertisements. For this reason, travel and tourism-related e-mail e-zines are a great marketing tool.

## Using E-zines as Marketing Tools

Online publications are superior marketing tools for travel and tourism organizations for a number of reasons. They can be used in a number of ways to increase the traffic to your Web site. You can:

- Advertise directly

- Be a sponsor

- Submit articles

- Send press releases

- Be a contributing editor

• Start your own.

## Finding Appropriate E-zines for Your Marketing Effort

There are many locations online to find lists and links to both Web-based and e-mail e-zines. A number of these resources are listed in the Internet Resources section of my Web site, referenced at the end of this chapter.

You evaluate an e-zine's marketing potential by its audience, reach, and effectiveness. The most important element of choosing an e-zine is to find one that reaches your target market. E-zine ads are effective because there is a high correlation between the target customer and the magazine's subscribers. If you advertise in an e-zine simply because it has the largest subscriber rate, you will probably be disappointed unless your destination, getaways, or travel packages have mass-market appeal.

You should review a number of the e-zine-listing sites, such as the one shown in Figure 21.3. Some of these sites have keyword search capabilities. Others have their e-zines listed by category. Once you have a list of e-zines you feel fit well with your marketing objectives, you should subscribe and begin reviewing these e-zines.

**Figure 21.3.** eZINESearch.com provides a searchable directory of e-zines.

## The Multiple Advantages of E-zine Advertising

One of the major advantages of e-zine advertising is the lifespan of your ads. E-zines that are delivered to e-mail addresses are read by the recipient and sometimes saved for future reference. Many e-zines archive their issues with the ads intact. Advertisers have received responses to ads that are several months old!

When you place an ad in an e-zine, you see it in a relatively short period of time, perhaps the next day or the next week, depending on how often the e-zine is published. Most traditional magazines close out their ad space months before the issue is available on the newsstand.

Your ad in an e-zine is also much more likely to be noticed because there are so few of them. In a traditional magazine every second page is an ad, whereas e-zines have a much greater focus on content and far fewer ads.

When your ad appears in an e-zine, your customer is just a click away because your ad is usually hyperlinked to your Web site. This brings your customer that much closer to being able to purchase your golf getaway package, your three-day spa package, or a stay at your hotel or destination.

Another advantage of e-zine advertising is that they are often shared with friends and associates. Most e-zines use viral marketing effectively, encouraging readers to send a copy to a friend. Your ad might be passed around a number of times after it first enters the mailbox of the subscriber. You are being charged for the ad based on the number of e-mail subscribers. Therefore, the extra viewers of your ad cost you nothing.

One of the most tangible advantages of e-zine advertising is the relatively low cost, due, in part, to the low overhead for development, production, and delivery. E-zines need to fill all of their available space. If an e-zine advertising section has empty spaces, the publisher might be willing to negotiate. Some will even barter with you—advertising space at a discounted price in exchange for their e-zine promotion on your Web site.

E-zines provide a very targeted advertising medium. People subscribe to various travel and tourism-related e-zines because they have a genuine interest in the topics covered. This provides a major advantage over other advertising mediums. E-zine ads have been shown to have very high response rates due to their targeted nature.

Because they are distributed via the Internet, e-zines reach a far wider audience geographically than most traditional magazines. It is not uncommon for an e-zine to have subscribers from all around the world.

There are thousands of e-zines out there related to the travel and tourism industry. Most e-zines have thousands of subscribers. When you couple the low cost to advertise in these e-zines and the many e-zines that might reach your target market, it is no wonder that many travel and tourism companies are allocating more and more of their advertising budgets to online activities.

## Guidelines for Your Advertising

Once you have found e-zines that reach your target market, you should consider a number of other factors before you make a final decision on placing your ad.

- Check the ads displayed in the e-zine for repetition. If advertisers have not advertised more than once, then they probably did not see very positive results.

- Respond to some of the ads and ask the advertisers what their experiences were with advertising in that particular e-zine. Be sure to tell them who you are and why you are contacting them. If you are up front, they will probably be receptive to your inquiry.

- Talk to the e-zine publisher and ask questions (for example, how many subscribers there are). Ask what other advertisers have had to say about their results. Find out what types of ads they accept and if there are any restrictions. Check to see if the publisher has a policy of never running competing ads. Maybe the e-zine has a set of advertising policies that you can receive via e-mail.

- Find out if the publisher provides tracking information and, if so, what specific reports you will have access to.

- Find out if your ad can have a hyperlink to your Web site. If the e-zine allows hyperlinks, make sure you link to an effective page—one that is a continuation of the advertisement or a page that provides details on the getaway package you were advertising. Provide a link to your reservation or order form from this page to assist with the transaction.

- In some cases e-zines have an editorial calendar available to assist you with the timing of your ad. The editorial calendar will tell you what articles will be included in upcoming issues. If an upcoming issue will have an article relating to your destination or packages you could choose to advertise in that issue. You might contact the editor regarding a review of the services you offer or submit an article relevant to the issue topics.

- Make sure that the advertising rates are reasonable based on the number of subscribers, and ask yourself if you can afford it. Find out the "open" rate, or the rate charged for advertising once in the e-zine. Ask what the rate is for multiple placements. If you are not in a position to pay for the advertising now ask if there are other arrangements that could be made. For example, the publisher might accept a link on your Web site in exchange for the ad.

- Develop your ads with your target customer in mind. They should attract your best prospects. Wherever possible, you should link to your site or provide an e-mail link to the right individual within your travel and tourism organization.

- Develop a mechanism to track advertising responses. You could use different e-mail accounts for different ads to determine which ads are bringing you the responses. You can also use different URLs to point viewers to different pages within your site. If you have a good traffic-analysis package, you can track the increase in visitors as a result of your ad.

- Make sure you are versed in the publication's advertising deadlines and ad format preferences.

## Providing Articles and News Releases to E-zines

Besides advertising, a number of other marketing opportunities can be explored with e-zines. Once you have found the e-zines that cater to your target market, these e-zines could be fruitful recipients for your news releases. Refer to Chapter 20 for recommendations on news release development and distribution. The editors might also accept articles of interest to their readers. You might be able to incorporate information on your travel and tourism organization, your destination, or packages in an interesting article that would fit the editor's guidelines.

There are many e-zines looking for great content. If you can write articles for them that provide great content for their readers and at the same time provide a little exposure for your travel and tourism organization, it's a real win-win situation. You'll want to target those e-zines that have the same target market you do and have a broad subscriber base. You'll want to make sure the e-zine includes a resource box at the end of the article crediting you as the author and providing a hyperlink to your Web site or your e-mail address. Having articles published enhances your reputation as an expert, and people like to do business with people who are experts in their field. You might see if you can be a contributing editor or have a regular column or feature in their e-zine.

Besides sending your articles directly to targeted e-zines, you can also submit them to "article banks" online. Article banks are online resource sites for e-zine publishers. E-zine publishers search through these banks for appropriate articles for their e-zine and, if they use one, they include the resource box of the author.

## Reasons You Might Start Your Own E-zine

Today, it is relatively easy to start your own e-zine. There are lots of resources online regarding e-zine development and administration. Don't make this decision without much thought, though, as you can damage your reputation if you don't deliver consistent, valuable content.

There are a multitude of reasons that you should consider developing and distributing your own e-zine. E-zines can be an extremely effective online marketing tool for the following reasons:

- You become established as an "expert." By providing your readers with valuable articles related to your area of expertise, you become, in their eyes, a valued and trusted expert.

- You establish trust. The first time someone visits your Web site, he or she has no idea who you are, how capable you are, or how professional you are. Sure, visitors get an impression from the look and feel and content of your site, but are they ready to do business with you? By providing them with free, valuable content over a period of time, you earn your visitors' trust, and they are more likely to turn to you when they are ready to plan their vacation.

- You generate significant traffic to your travel and tourism Web site. Your e-zine should always reference and provide a hyperlink to something available from your Web site. Once your visitor links through, there should be elements that encourage him or her to stay awhile and visit a number of pages on your site. The more often people visit your site, the more likely they are to do business with you.

- You build loyalty. Relationship marketing is what it's all about on the Web. You want to build relationships over time, and your e-zine will help you do just that. Your subscribers receive something free from you every month. Whom are they going to do business with when they have a need for your travel services or packages? People prefer to spend their money with businesses they know and trust.

- You stay current with your customers and potential customers. When you are in front of your subscribers every month, you're not too easy to forget. You can keep them up to date on what's new with your company, your products, packages, and services, or what's new in the travel and tourism industry.

- You grow your database. See Chapter 14 for tips on how to build your database.

## Developing Your Own E-zine

If you do start your own e-zine, you should spend sufficient time planning and testing before you publish to ensure that you do it right. You don't get a second chance to make a first impression, and you want your readers to subscribe and tell others about the great e-zine they found. You want them to be excited to read your e-zine every time it is delivered to their e-mail box. The following tips will help you in your e-mail-based e-zine planning and preparation:

- Provide great content. This goes without saying. If you have content that people want to read, they will remain subscribers. Don't think that shameless self-promotion is great content; your target audience certainly won't. As a rough guide, make sure your e-zine is 80 percent rich content and no more than 20 percent promotion and ads. Your e-zine should be full of what your target market considers useful information.

- Consider the length of your e-zine. You want your e-zine to be read relatively soon after it has been delivered. You do not want it consistently put aside for later because it is always too long to read quickly. In this case, less is more. Subscribers should be able to read your e-zine in five minutes or less. If you do have a lengthy article, you might give a synopsis in the e-zine with a hyperlink to more detail on your Web site.

- Limit your content to four or five dynamite articles for an e-mail-based e-zine. Provide a brief table of contents at the beginning of the e-zine. Keep the copy short and to the point.

- Keep your line length under 60 characters including spaces to avoid word-wrap issues.

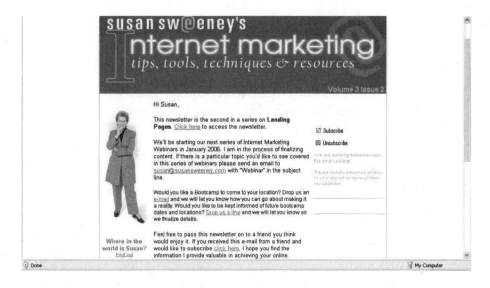

**Figure 21.4.**   Encourage readers to send a copy of your e-zine to a friend and provide subscribe instructions for those who receive forwarded copies.

- Encourage your readers to send a copy to others they feel might be interested in your great content. Make sure you provide subscribing instructions as well for those who receive these forwarded copies (Figure 21.4). You should also provide instructions on how to opt out, or unsubscribe.

- Test your e-zine with different e-mail programs to ensure that your e-zine looks the way you designed it no matter which e-mail program your reader uses. Send test copies to friends with different e-mail readers such as Outlook Express, Netscape Mail, Pegasus Mail, and Eudora. See how it looks, make sure that word-wrap is not an issue, and make sure the hyperlinks work.

- Make sure you run your e-zine through a current spam checker to ensure that your e-zine will not be seen as spam by the spam filters.

- Have an unsubscribe button at the bottom of every e-mail enabling anyone in your database to opt out.

- Keep your subscriber addresses private and let subscribers know your privacy policy.

As word about your e-zine spreads, a large community of people who fit your target market will be reading it.

Once you have your own e-zine, you'll have to:

- Promote it to your target market through newsgroups, mail lists, your Web site, and your e-mail signature file. If you do promote your e-zine in newsgroups and mail lists, be sure it is appropriate to advertise your e-zine in a given newsgroup or mail list before you post. You do not want to be accused of spamming. However, promote your e-zine shame-lessly on your own site (let people subscribe to the e-zine on your site) and in your signature file.

- Provide an opportunity for subscribers to let others know about your ezine. In your online e-zine, have a form that allows subscribers to e-mail a copy of the e-zine to their friends and colleagues. Use a call-to-action statement such as "Do you know someone who might be interested in this e-zine? Click here to send them a copy." This is a great way to pick up additional subscribers because some of the nonsubscribers who read your e-zine might then become subscribers if your content is interesting to them.

- Make it easy for people to subscribe to your e-zine. Provide clear sub-scription instructions in each e-mail version of your e-zine and on the online version. Have a form handy on your site to collect e-mail ad-dresses from people who wish to subscribe. Always ask for the first name so that you can personalize your e-zine.

- Provide an archive of past issues on your Web site so that visitors can sample your wares before subscribing. Make sure you provide an op-tion for visitors to subscribe from that page as well.

- Don't provide your list of subscribers to anyone. This protects your subscribers' privacy and keeps your list spam-free. People will not be happy if they start receiving spam as a result of your e-zine.

## eBrochures and iBrochures—The Latest in Online Publications

Madden Preprint Media is in the forefront of electronic brochures for the travel and tourism industry. Madden Preprint offers three tiers of electronic brochures,

**Figure 21.5.** Madden Preprints' iBrochure for Tucson, AZ.

with different levels of interactivity—eBrochures, iBrochures, and iBrochures with interactive maps and calendars.

An eBrochure is similar to a paper brochure. It contains all of the information you want your target market to read.

An iBrochure is similar to the eBrochure except that it implements elements of macromedia flash and page turning capability. iBrochures also use a simple point-and-click format, as if turning the pages of a brochure or magazine.

Madden Preprints iBrochure for Tucson, AZ, featured in Figure 21.5, is an excellent example of how to get the most out of an iBrochure. There is the option of clicking on the specific parts of the iBrochure you are interested in reading or you can flip through and read all pages. They have also integrated other Internet marketing techniques into their iBrochures as well, such as viral marketing with their "tell a friend" button. They have integrated the reservation software with the "book a room" button so that those who are ready to purchase do not have to go to a separate Web site. They have also used the call to action "bookmark this site" element we talked about earlier in this book. They are also giving something away for free with their "free visitor info" button.

Some iBrochures use interactive maps and calendars. Madden Preprints' tier III iBrochure, featured in Figure 21.6 for example, implements the interactive calendar.

**Figure 21.6.** Madden Preprints' iBrochure for Chicago which includes the interactive calendar.

eBrochures and iBrochures may, depending on the file size, be easily downloaded from your site, sent to customers or prospective customers via e-mail, or handed out on CD or DVD. Both complement your existing Web site and branding strategy and open up a whole new way of communicating with existing and prospective customers. Both eBrochures and iBrochures have the advantage of being easily updated or corrected.

## Internet Resources for Chapter 21

I have developed a great library of online resources for you to check out regarding e-zine marketing. This library is available on my Tourism Internet Marketing University Web site *http://www.TourismInternetMarketingU.com/max* in the Resources section where you can find additional tips, tools, techniques, and resources.

I have also developed courses on many of the topics covered in this book. These courses are also available on my Tourism Internet Marketing University Web site *http://www.TourismInternetMarketingU.com/max*. These courses are delivered immediately over the Internet or can be ordered as a CD.

# 22

---

# Really Simple Syndication

RSS, or Really Simple Syndication, provides Webmasters and content providers a distribution vehicle for their content that is guaranteed to be delivered. This distribution channel makes it easy for individuals to access the most current information, but also for other site owners to publish the syndicated content on their sites as well.

In this chapter, we cover:

- What is RSS?

- How does RSS work?

- What to send via RSS

- Benefits of RSS

- How to promote your RSS content

- Getting the most out of your RSS

- RSS versus e-mail.

## What Is RSS?

One of the earliest forms of content syndication is the Dear Abby column. As most of you know, Dear Abby writes one column and it appears, or is syndicated, in many different publications. That was the "old school" way; today we have RSS readers and feeders. RSS is an acronym for Really Simple Syndication. RSS is a format for syndicating news and other content that can be broken down into discrete items. RSS is really a delivery channel which allows you to send content to subscribers and also to other Web sites. Once information is in RSS format on a site, an RSS reader can check the feed for updates and react to the updates in a predefined way. RSS can deliver many different types of content including text, audio, or video files and can distribute them quickly and easily.

## How Does RSS Work?

To publish your travel and destination promotional material and make it available to the masses for their review or publication on their Web site, you first need to create an RSS feed. To do this you need to develop an **XML** file structured in the proper format, upload it to your server, and then provide a link to that file on your Web site. There are many tools online that make this an easy process. There are RSS software programs that enable the user to quickly and easily create and publish syndicated content.

---

### XML
Extensible Markup Language
Its primary purpose is to facilitate the sharing of data across different information systems, particularly via the Internet.

---

Once you have your RSS feed developed, you need to develop your content and update it on a regular basis—be sure to include a catchy headline and a link to your site in your content. Usually you will provide a summary letting the subscribers to your feed know about the new content, with a link directly to it. Alternatively, you could provide the full content in your feed.

Your subscribers need an RSS news reader or news aggregator that will enable them to access and display the RSS content. There are many different RSS readers and news aggregators available for free. You might want to provide a little education to your visitors as some may be new to RSS, and also provide links to recommended RSS readers from your site to enable new users easy access (see Figure 22.1). The news aggregator helps viewers keep up with all their favorite resources by checking their RSS feeds and displaying the new or recent items from each of them.

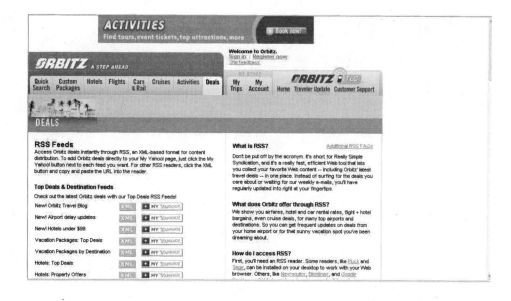

**Figure 22.1.** Orbitz provides everything a user needs to subscribe to its RSS feed—information, tools, and instructions.

There are also Web-based RSS services that work with your browser. After you run through your initial setup, you subscribe to any RSS service you want to access on a regular basis.

The RSS readers automatically retrieve updates from sites that are subscribed to, providing the user with the latest content as it is published.

## RSS Content Options

There are all kinds of content that can be sent through RSS:

- Travel coupons, deals, or travel tips (see how Travelocity uses RSS in Figure 22.2)

- Package specials

- Destination articles

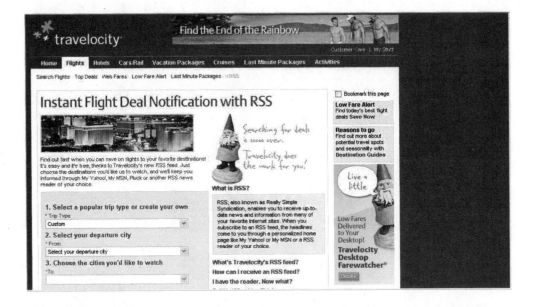

**Figure 22.2.** Travelocity uses RSS to send its subscribers instant notification of flight deals.

- Newsletters

- Travel blogs—I turn your attention to the Visit PA (*http://www.visitpa.com*) destination marketing organization Web site that hosted PA travelers' blogs on its site for all to see.

- News—company, industry, or general

- Audio content (see Chapter 24 on podcasting)

- Audio interviews

- Video content (see Chapter 24 on videocasting)

- Press releases—check out AsiaTravelTips.com

- Schedule feed for teams, corporate meetings, etc.

- Specific material for employees, association members, or customers

- Specific types of requested information or subscribed content.

What you're looking to do is get information in front of your target market on a regular basis. You'll provide the information directly to your target market or through sites that market to the same target market you do for more leverage.

We are seeing personalized or customized feeds where a subscriber might indicate that he or she would like to receive the spa and golf packages but not the ecotourism packages. There are all kinds of RSS feeds available online these days. We see travel agencies with their last-minute deals, vacation destinations with their latest articles, and resorts with their newest spa or golf packages; they can even send the content to your mobile phone! See Chapter 25 for more on mobile marketing.

Leverage your exposure by partnering with travel and tourism-targeted sites that have significant traffic and that provide branded relevant, valuable, and interesting content for their visitors. For example, a golf course might have its golf pro develop golf tips to be provided to other golf-related sites; this provides a real win-win—the partner site has great new content that is updated on a regular basis without having to do any work, and the golf course providing the tips gets valuable exposure to the target market and hopefully increased traffic to its site and more business.

There are many opportunities to use RSS feeds in the travel and tourism industry to gain exposure with your target market online.

## Benefits of RSS

The benefits of RSS are many:

1. You are guaranteed 100 percent delivery. Spam filters are not an issue. This means that your marketing and other messages to customers and potential customers are getting through.

2. You can quickly and easily get exposure on other sites that have the same target market you do by having your content published on those sites through content syndication. You immediately increase your reach.

3. Through your RSS feed opportunity, you can build your targeted database.

4.  You can improve your search engine ranking through providing keyword-rich content that is distributed to other sites with the link back to your site.

5.  You will increase targeted traffic to your site.

6.  You will increase your brand awareness.

7.  Through distribution of great content, you can establish yourself as a great resource.

8.  You have a great potential to increase revenue through your use of RSS with the delivery of coupons, specials, and promotions with the links back to your site.

9.  You don't have to worry about compliance with legislation, privacy policies, spam, or age guidelines.

10. You will build trust, your reputation, and credibility.

11. RSS feeds are significantly less work than maintaining and promoting through private mail lists. You don't have to worry about cleaning lists, running your content through the spam checker, or removing bad e-mail addresses. This does not mean that you should switch everything previously provided through permission-based e-mail to RSS. See Chapter 14 for more on private mail lists.

12. RSS content is seeing significant click-through rates.

## How to Promote Your RSS Content

Once you have an RSS feed, you will want to maximize the number of subscribers who read your feed and you will want to develop a strategy to have as many sites as possible post your syndicated content on their sites. Of course, you will always look for sites that are selling to the travel and tourism market.

You will want to create a page on your site specifically for your RSS information. On that page, or linked to that page, you will provide a little education on RSS—what it is, how it works, and how one would subscribe. You'll also provide links to some recommended RSS readers along with step-by-step instructions on how to subscribe. Provide your visitors with all the benefits of subscribing to your RSS feed—sell the sizzle! Incorporate viral marketing (see Chapter 5) and make it easy for them to tell their friends about your RSS feed.

Promote your RSS feeds in your signature file with a link to the page on your site with all the details. Signature files are discussed in Chapter 11.

There are many RSS directories online to which you can submit your RSS feed for inclusion. With some you ask to be included, and others allow you to add your feed information yourself. Many of these directories provide lists of feeds under a number of categories. You can search "RSS directories" in Google or Yahoo! Search to find these.

There are RSS submission tools that will submit your RSS feed to a variety of RSS directories. Again, searching Google or Yahoo! Search for "RSS submission tools" will provide you with everything you need.

Many Internet browsers provide easy access to RSS feeds for their users. These browsers provide information on their Web sites as to how to make this happen. Yahoo! provides a Publisher's Guide to RSS (see Figure 22.3). In the Publisher's Guide (*http://publisher.yahoo.com/whatis.php*) is information on auto-discovery, which is a way to let applications know that you have an RSS feed and makes it easy for those browsers to let their users subscribe directly to your feed.

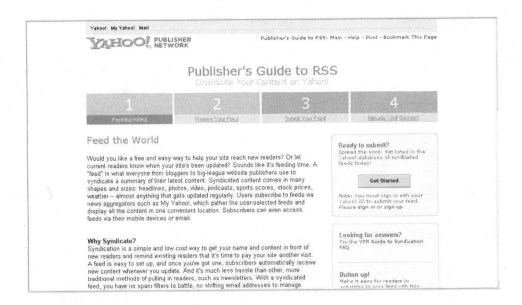

**Figure 22.3.** Yahoo! provides a Publisher's Guide to RSS.

## What is Social Bookmarking?

Social bookmarking allows users to store links to Web pages, otherwise known as bookmarks, that they find useful. Rather than saving these bookmarks on your computer, as was normally done through the "Favorites" button on your Internet Explorer toolbar, these new social bookmarking sites allow users to save their bookmarks to a Web page. They allow users to save their favorite articles, blogs, music, reviews, RSS feeds, and more, and allow users to access them from any computer on the Web.

To create a collection of social bookmarks you must register with a social bookmarking site—and there are many to choose from. Once you have registered you will be able to store bookmarks, share them, and categorize them with the use of keywords or tags. These sites allow users to search for other Internet bookmarks saved by others and add them to their own collection and subscribe to the lists of others.

Social bookmarking has created a new way for Web site visitors to organize and categorize information and resources. They represent the user's personal library and when combined with other personal libraries, they allow for many social networking opportunities.

## Why is Social Bookmarking Important?

Social bookmarking makes it easy for your Web site visitors to bookmark your Web site, your blog, and subscribe to your RSS feeds. If your Web site visitors add your site, blog, and/or RSS to their bookmarks, they are essentially promoting you, generating more traffic to your site and more subscribers to your blog and RSS feeds.

Because of the increase in popularity and the increase in competition, many social bookmarking services offer more than just the ability to share bookmarks. Many now offer the ability to rate and comment on bookmarks. They have also added the ability to import and export, add notes, reviews, e-mail links, automatic notification, feed subscriptions, create groups, and of course, social networks.

Make it easy for your Web site visitors to add you to their social bookmarks by providing Chicklets on various pages of your site. Chicklets are the tiny social network bookmark icons, and they allow your Web site visitors to quickly and easily add you to their bookmarks. Be sure to provide Chicklets to all of the most popular social bookmarking sites. See how Topix (*http://www.topix.net*) gets its Web site visitors to bookmark its travel and tourism articles in Figure

22.4. There are a number of tools on the Web, like TopRank (*http://www.toprankblog.com/tools/social-bookmarks*) or Blogger Social Bookmarking Tool (*http://social.front.lv*) as seen in Figure 22.5, that help you create and choose which Chicklets you want to add to your site. Below is a list of some of the most popular social bookmarking sites available on the Web right now:

- Del.icio.us (*http://del.icio.us*)

- Google Bookmarks *(http:// www.google.com/bookmarks)*

- Technorati (*http://technorati.com*)

- Stumble Upon (*http://www.stumbleupon.com*)

- Yahoo! Bookmarks (*http://www.bookmarks.yahoo.com*)

- Slashdot (*http://slashdot.org*)

- Netscape (*http://www.netscape.com*)

- Reddit (*http://reddit.com*)

**Figure 22.4.** Topix (*http://www.topix.net*) gets its Web site visitors to bookmark their travel and tourism articles by providing links to social bookmarking sites.

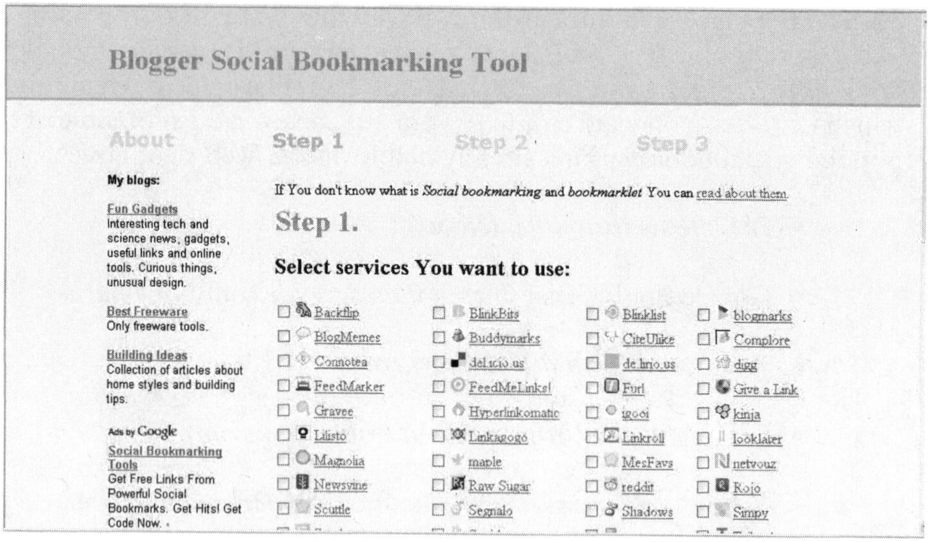

**Figure 22.5.** Sites such as Blogger Social Bookmarking Tool make it easy for Web site owners to add chiclets to their sites.

- Facebook (*http://www.facebook.com*)

- Blogmarks (*http://blogmarks.net*)

- Digg (*http://digg.com*)

- Squidoo (*http://www.squidoo.com*)

- NewsVine (*http://www.newsvine*)

- Furl (*http://www.furl.net*).

## Getting the Most out of Your RSS

As with everything in Internet marketing, you need to develop content after giving consideration to:

- Your objectives with this Internet marketing technique

- Your target market(s) for this technique

- The specific products and services you want to promote with this technique

- You will want to give consideration to the terms of use for your content. Do you want to limit the content to noncommercial use on others' sites, or is it okay if they use it for commercial purposes?

Always make sure that you have mandatory source identification. When others use your content and want to publish or distribute it, you will want a resource box identifying you as the provider and, more importantly, a link to your Web site.

For the content that will bring you the most business, you want to publish it on a Tuesday, Wednesday, or Thursday. Tuesday is the most active day for RSS readership. The time of day is important as well. Morning scanners view the most content, whereas the midnight cowboys tend to have a higher click-through rate.

## RSS versus E-mail

There are many opportunities to use RSS feeds in an Internet marketing capacity in the travel and tourism industry. However, as with everything in Internet marketing, you need to always refer back to your objectives and target market. With the introduction of spam filters, mass e-mail campaigns, declining open and click-through rates, list fatigue, and legislation, some people are thinking that e-mail marketing is dead and that RSS is the new alternative. However, unlike RSS, with e-mail campaigns you can track open rates, click-through rates and ROI. E-mail campaigns can be personalized and segmented, and they can

| RSS Pros | RSS Cons |
|---|---|
| Streamlines communication | User adoption is still quite small |
| No list to maintain | Hard to get prospects' attention and click-through |
| No privacy, spam, or age guidelines | Takes extra click to get the information to visitor |
| No spam filters, firewalls to pass | Can't track |
| Hands-off way to upgrade | Can't build the profile of the readers |
| Seen as "out in front" | Can't personalize the message or content |

be highly targeted, designed and branded with rich content. They also allow you to incorporate viral marketing campaigns.

There are many things to consider before making the decision to go solely with RSS. Listed previously are a few pros and cons of RSS that must be considered.

A better alternative is to incorporate both e-mail and RSS as part of your marketing mix. See Chapter 14 for a more detailed discussion on this topic.

## Internet Resources for Chapter 22

I have developed a great library of online resources for you to check out regarding RSS. This library is available on my Tourism Internet Marketing University Web site *http://www.TourismInternetMarketingU.com/max* in the Resources section where you can find additional tips, tools, techniques, and resources.

I have also developed courses on many of the topics covered in this book. These courses are also available on my Tourism Internet Marketing University Web site *http://www.TourismInternetMarketingU.com/max*. These courses are delivered immediately over the Internet or can be ordered as a CD.

# 23

## Blogs & Wikis

Blogs can help you keep your travel and tourism Web site current, and they are an easy way to add new content to your site. They can be used to provide your potential and existing customers with the latest news on your travel and tourism products and services, industry news, updates, tips, or other content relevant to your target market. But be careful. Always go back to your objectives and target market to determine the proper use, if any, for your tourism operation. Many people jumped on the blog bandwagon when it first came out and since then many have fallen off as 82 percent of blogs have been abandoned.

In this chapter, we cover:

- What are blogs and wikis and how do they work?

- How do I create my blog or wiki?

- To blog or not to blog?

- Benefits of publishing a blog on your travel and tourism Web site

- Blog promotion.

## What are Blogs & Wikis?

Blogs are simply Web logs on a Web site—an online journal of postings that is updated on a regular basis, with the most recent posting appearing at the top. Sometimes they look like an ongoing diary or a journal on a site. Blogs have one author and are usually written in more conversational or informal style than most business materials and can include text, images, and links to other content such as podcasts, video files, or even other Web sites.

Writing the actual content for your blog is referred to as blogging. Each article that you add to your blog is called a blog post, a post, or an entry in your blog. You are a blogger if you write and add entries or posts to your blog.

Blogs usually focus on one topic or area of interest or at least they *should* focus on one type or area of interest. For example:

- A person might have a personal blog on his or her trip through South Africa.

- A market analyst might have a blog on his or her findings in the travel and tourism industry—what's happening in the industry, news, or articles on his or her latest research.

As with many marketing techniques, blogs have many offshoots. The most popular and most similar is the wiki. A wiki uses the same technology as a blog. However, while blogs have only one writer and each post is presented in chronological order, a wiki allows anyone to post and it is not necessarily in chronological order.

When setting up your blog, you have several options:

1.  There are a number of free blog hosting sites. An example of this type would be Blogger.com (see Figure 23.1), which was acquired by Google in 2003. Other popular blog hosts include LiveJournal, TypePad, and Xanga.

2.  You can set up your blog using blog software or a blog publishing system and host it yourself. Popular blog software packages include WordPress (*http://wordpress.org*) and Movable Type (*http://www.sixapart.com/movabletype*).

3.  You can also create your own blog using HTML.

**Figure 23.1.** Blogger.com, a free blog hosting site, was acquired by Google in 2003.

## How Do I Create My Blog or Wiki?

Blogs are a great way to keep in front of your Web site visitors with new regularly updated content. Following are a few tips, tools, and techniques to help you establish your first blog.

### Do Your Research

Search the Web for blogs that interest you. Visit blog directories and search engines such as Google, Blog Search, Technorati, and Blogorama. Find out what other people are doing with their blogs.

### Determine Your Objectives for Starting a Blog

Just like everything related to your Web site and marketing initiatives, you must go back to your objectives and your target market. A successful blog takes much planning and must be relevant to your online objectives. Focus on other travel and tourism blogs to determine what you like, what you don't like, and what you can do to differentiate yourself from them.

### Decide on the Content and Tone of Your Blog

Blogs can range from very professional and in-depth to very casual and chatty. Probably the best tone for your blog is professional, since it is a representation of your business, yet informal.

### Choosing Blog Software

It is not hard to find free blog software on the Internet. The key is to find one that suits your needs. Most blog software is based on templates, with many templates to choose from, which allow you to add a post without having to know HTML. Many of these templates allow you to customize the look and feel of your blog by adding your logo or links to other Web sites or blogs, or by adding photos.

### The Legalities

If you are going to allow posts to your blog from your Web site visitors, you must have a disclaimer, in a visible spot, stating that you are not responsible for the accuracy of the information posted by others.

### Schedule Your Posts

It is very important to update your blog on a regular and consistent basis. Choose a schedule and stick to it. It doesn't matter if you choose to update your blog once a day, once a week or once a month, as long as your visitors know when to expect it. The ideal schedule would be two or three times a week, since a blog is meant to be updated on a regular basis.

### Writing Your Blog

Blogs are meant to be both educational and entertaining. Add a few pictures and links to your posts to make them more interesting. Keep your posts short, 200 to 300 word posts are fine; and remember to write for scanability as most Internet users do not read, they scan. It is a good idea to write two or three posts in advance and save them so that you are always on top of things. If you are finding it difficult to come up with new entries, find a blog partner and take turns adding posts.

### Search Engine Ranking for Your Blog

Blogs should be written for the reader not the search engines. However, there is no point having a blog if no one can find it. Use your most important keyword phrases throughout your blog to give it a boost in the search engines. Another way to increase its search engine friendliness is to link it to other blogs with related content. Visit other travel and tourism-related blogs and post a comment with your name and a link to your blog.

### Organize and Archive Your Entries

As mentioned earlier, blog posts are presented in chronological order. However, after a while you will want to consider organizing your blog entries so that they are easier to navigate through. With many of the blog software programs you have the option to archive your blog by topic or date.

### Track Your Blog's Readership

As with any of your marketing and advertising initiatives, you will want to track visitors to your blog. Tools such as Google Analytics (which is free) allow you to track visits to your blog so that you can see how many visits you had, where they came from, and which blog entries they visited. Some blog software programs, such as TypePad, have this feature built in. We talk more on analytics in Chapter 28.

Blogs take time and effort, but they may be worth the effort if they bring you extra business and fit with your objectives and your target market.

## To Blog or Not to Blog?

Blogs were probably one of the first new entries into Internet marketing in the third generation. Because of this there was a lot of buzz created around them and just about everyone jumped on the bandwagon. Since then about 82 percent of blogs have been abandoned.

As with everything related to your Web site content, you must go back to your objectives and your target markets when trying to determine whether a blog is right for your travel or tourism business.

What are you hoping to accomplish with your Web site content? Who are you hoping to interact with on your site? Is a blog the most effective technique to "speak to" your target market and get them to do what you want them to do? Is there a more effective mechanism? How much work is involved? Is this time well spent, or are there other techniques that would be more effective given the time commitment?

You don't add Web site content just because it is the latest trend or because you can. Always go back to your objectives and your target market to see if this type of content is the most effective and most efficient way to accomplish what you want to online.

A great example of blogs being used in the travel and tourism industry is the Visit PA (*http://www.visitpa.com*) destination marketing organization Web site (see Figure 23.2). They had individuals from six different target markets update blogs on their Web site for all visitors to read—giving the impression of a third-party endorsement. These blogs were very well written and they described all of the things the bloggers saw and did in Pennsylvania. The idea behind this was that if, for example, the family of four from Pittsburgh shared the amusement

**Figure 23.2.**   Visit PA is a great example of blogs being used in the travel and tourism industry.

park-filled adventure they had in Pennsylvania, then other families looking for an amusement park-filled vacation would be encouraged to visit PA for the same type of vacation. Or if the Harley-loving open roader from Butler, PA gave a mile-by-mile description of his bike tour across the state, some other motor-cycle enthusiasts would take this trip as well.

## Pros and Cons of Blogging

Some pros of blogging are:

- Blogs are an easy way to add new content, thus keeping your Web site current.

- Blogs can be used to provide your potential and existing customers with the latest news on your travel products and services, industry news, updates, tips, or other relevant content.

- Using keyword-rich content can help your search engine placement.

- Blogs can be updated from anywhere. You can even send camera phone photos straight to your blog while you're on-the-go with Blogger Mobile.

- You can create an RSS feed to syndicate your blog, giving you instant access to your subscribers and the opportunity to have your blog content appear on relevant sites. See Chapter 22 for information on using RSS feeds to distribute your blog content.

Some of the cons are:

- Blogs need to be constantly updated, at a minimum of three times per week. You need to have the discipline to keep it current.

- You have to have enough news or new content to make it worthwhile for both you and your readers.

- Updates usually get done on your own personal time.

- The time spent updating blogs could be used toward something more productive.

- The time to update is often under-estimated.

- The marketing impact is often over-estimated—how many times have you bookmarked a blog and gone back on a regular basis?

Again, it is important to be cautious when considering whether or not a blog is right for you. Don't jump on the blog bandwagon—just because it's easy doesn't mean it's right.

## Avoid Classic Blog Mistakes

While blogs can be an easy way to communicate with your target audience, there are still many common mistakes that people make when taking on such an endeavor.

### Underestimating the Time Commitment

One of the biggest mistakes people make when deciding to start a blog is under estimating the time commitment. While it's convenient to know that blogs *can* be updated from anywhere, it is more important to know that they *have to* be updated.

Blogs should be updated at least three times per week, and you need to have the discipline to keep it current. That means at least three times per week you have to research your topic or put your thoughts into words in a way that is interesting to read (both very time consuming tasks), and post them online.

### Overestimating the Marketing Impact

The second biggest mistake people make when deciding to start a blog is over-estimating the marketing impact. It takes time and effort to build an audience for a blog—again, when was the last time you bookmarked a blog and went back to it on a regular basis? And if you did—did it influence you to make a purchase?

### Irregular or Infrequent Updating

Users must be able to anticipate when and how often updates to your blog will occur. People are busy and they do not have the time to keep checking your blog to see if it has been updated—always provide an RSS feed (see Chapter 22).

Your readers need to know that every day, or every two days, or what ever the case may be, there is going to be a new post that they can read. Otherwise you will lose many of your readers. Pick a posting schedule and stick to it—a blog that isn't updated regularly will simply be ignored.

### Writing for the Search Engines and Not for the Blog

There is the growing tendency by many bloggers to write for search engines rather than focusing on the needs of their "human" readers. Putting search engines first rather than putting your readers first will almost certainly lead to bad decisions that will make your blog less usable, even if it is optimized for search spiders.

While blogs can be a great way to speak to your target market and keep them up-to-date on all the latest news on your travel and tourism business products and services, you must determine if there is a more effective, time efficient way to communicate.

## Promote Your Blog

Just like your Web site, once you have a blog, you want to maximize its exposure; you want to have as many of your target market reading or reviewing your blog on a regular basis as possible.

There are many ways to get your blog noticed. The most obvious place to start is your own Web site. However, there are many other ways to promote your blog:

- Generate links to your blog from other related sites.

- Promote your blog in your e-mail signature file.

- Submit your blog to all of the major search engines.

- Send out press releases and media alerts about your blog.

Another way to promote your blog is to register it with all of the major blog directories such as Yahoo! and Blogorama. These blog directories profile blogs by category where you can usually search by keyword. Great portals like BlogCatalog (*http://www.blogcatalog.com*) (see Figure 23.3), RSSTop55 Best

**Figure 23.3.** Blogcatalog is one of many great blog resources online.

Blog Directory, and RSS Submission Sites (*http://www.masternewmedia.org/rss/top55*) would be great starting points.

Get your blog listed and high in the search results for your important keyword phrases in the Blog Search Engine (*http://www.blogsearchengine.com*), Bloogz (*http://www.bloogz.com*), and other popular blog search engines.

It is also a good idea to offer your blog as an RSS feed and get as many of your target market as you can subscribe to your blog RSS feed (see Chapter 22 for more on RSS). Remember when you provide the RSS to also include links to social bookmarking sites, also covered in more detail in Chapter 22.

## Resources for Chapter 23

I have developed a great library of online resources for you to check out regarding blogs. This library is available on my Tourism Internet Marketing University Web site *http://www.TourismInternetMarketingU.com/max* in the Resources section where you can find additional tips, tools, techniques, and resources.

I have also developed courses on many of the topics covered in this book. These courses are also available on my Tourism Internet Marketing University Web site *http://www.TourismInternetMarketingU.com/max*. These courses are delivered immediately over the Internet or can be ordered as a CD.

# 24

# Podcasting & Videocasting

Podcasting is a term that was coined a few years ago and comes from combining the terms *broadcasting* and *iPod*. Podcasting is the distribution of audio content via the Internet and is distributed for listening on personal computers, MP3 players, iPods, or other mobile devices.

Podcasting is all about creating content for a demanding audience that does not want to be marketed to, but rather wants to listen to what they want, when they want, and how they want.

In this chapter, we cover:

- What is podcasting and videocasting?

- Setting up your podcast

- Equipment necessary to produce a podcast

- Podcast content for your travel or tourism Web site

- Promoting your podcast

- Podcast pros and cons.

## What Is Podcasting?

The term *podcasting* is a little misleading because, although it comes from the terms *broadcasting* and *iPod*, it has nothing directly to do with Apple iPods. Podcasting, in its simplest definition, relates to audio content that can be listened to on a Web site, on your personal computer, any MP3 player (not just the Apple iPod), and many mobile devices.

When you make podcasts available on your travel and tourism site, your Web site visitors can listen to the content on your site, you can allow the podcasts to be downloaded on an individual basis, or you can allow visitors to subscribe to them through an RSS feed. As you upload new audio or video files to your site, subscribers get notification in their RSS reader; the reader will download the content to a location the subscriber has specified on his or her hard drive. When a subscriber connects a mobile device or MP3 player to his or her computer, the files can be added to that device for future listening or viewing. See Chapter 22 for more on RSS.

We are seeing podcasting take off in the travel and tourism industry because there is so much great content that can be provided in this format. It also enables listeners to enjoy the audio content where they want, when they want—they can listen to a tour of the Amazon rainforest while on a 10:30 a.m. flight to Brazil, they can enjoy a podcast on how to plan a destination wedding while on the treadmill first thing in the morning, or they can listen to information on the new spa packages while tanning by the pool.

## What Is Videocasting?

The term videocasting refers to video content that can be downloaded and viewed at your convenience. A videocast can be distributed as a file or as a **stream** from a Web server. By downloading videocasts, the user will be able to play the videocast offline on a portable media player. Once the videocast is downloaded it can be watched many times at the user's convenience. A streaming videocast even allows the user to download only the portions of the videocast they want to see. Of course there may be pauses in the playback if it is downloaded this way.

### Stream
Video or audio transmitted over a network that users can begin to play immediately instead of waiting for the entire file to download.

## Advantages of Podcasting

- Having a podcast is like having your own radio channel. Your customers and potential customers can automatically receive your valuable broadcasts.

- Videocasts or video podcasts enable you to send virtual tours of your hotels, destinations, or products to customers and potential customers.

- Podcasts, as long as you produce them frequently, will keep you in front of your target market and can easily establish you as an "expert" with your valuable content.

- RSS technology enables your subscribers to automatically receive your new podcasts as you make them available.

- With your mobile device you will be able to show your virtual tours to consumers.

## Setting up Your Podcast

Podcasts are a great way to keep communications with your target market open and also a great way to establish yourself as an authority in the travel and tourism industry. Podcasts take planning and commitment but with the following tips, tools, and techniques you will be able to establish a professional and informative podcast.

### Decide on Content and Frequency

There are any number of subjects travel and tourism professionals can use to develop podcasts. You should decide whether you want to record audio reports that do not require constant updating or if you want to provide the latest information on your packages, destinations, or services.

### Develop the Format

The most basic and most successful format for any podcast is to first have a great opener that grabs the readers' attention. Then provide the content. Always make sure the content is informative, relevant and useful to the listener. And last, but not least, is the close. Always close with a reference to your Web site, contact information, and of course a call to action.

## Gather Your Podcasting Equipment

Podcasting is a relatively easy process. You need your content, a few pieces of equipment, and a Web site or host for distribution, and you're in business.

The equipment you need includes:

- A laptop or desktop computer with an Internet connection and a sound card.

- A microphone. For good audio quality, you will usually want to purchase an external microphone that plugs into your computer.

- Audio recording software. There are lots of downloadable, free and paid, audio software programs online. Be sure to pick one that will satisfy all of your needs as some of the cheaper recording software does not offer many editing options, while the more expensive ones allow you to edit the audio, enhance the sound quality, and even add music.

- An MP3 encoder which will convert your audio into an MP3 file. For example iTunes can convert audio content to an MP3 file, or there are a number of popular free encoders online.

## Recording Your Podcast

Once you have your content prepared, you will plug your microphone into your computer, start your audio recording software, and record your podcast. Always record your podcast in a quiet location. When you are finished, you can use the editing tools in your audio recording software to make any changes or enhancements to your content. You can remove that cough or the pause, add music as background, or add special sound effects.

Save your podcast as an MP3 file. When naming your file, consider including your important keyword phrase, where appropriate, for search engine optimization purposes.

### Publishing Your Podcast

Once you have finished recording and editing your podcast you can upload or FTP the file to your Web site host and make it available online. You will then make your podcast available through your Web site as an individual podcast or as a series of podcasts available to subscribers through your RSS feed. See Chapter 22 for details on how to develop your RSS.

## Outsourcing Your Podcast

If you're not entirely comfortable developing a podcast on your own, or if you'd like to have a professional quality podcast, there are many companies out there that offer services such as developing, publishing, and distributing podcasts and videocasts, for example, WhatIWantPodcasting.com (*http:// www.whatiwantpodcasting.com*) (see Figure 24.1). There are a number of com-

**Figure 24.1.** Whatiwantpodcasting.com is one of many companies out there that offers services such as developing, publishing, and distributing podcasts and videocasts.

panies that will help you design and create your podcast. Some of these companies will help with the podcast form, style, and format. Some companies will record and edit your podcast for you, host it on their server, create RSS feeds, and even submit your podcast to podcast directories for you. I have actually had the pleasure of working with one such company, Allan Hunkin's Podcast.Biz Consulting (*http://www.podcast.biz*) with great results.

## Podcast Content

There are all kinds of content suitable for travel and tourism podcasts—there can be as many podcasts as there are target markets. A few examples include:

- Vacation or cruise planning tips

    - What to expect upon arrival

    - What to pack

    - Where to stay

    - What to see and do

- Golfing in North Carolina (or your destination)

- Self-guided walking tours. Many destination marketing organizations provide downloadable:

    - Audio walking tours of the area

    - Audio tours of museums

    - Parks tours

    - Art gallery tours

    - Driving directions

    - Tours of particular places of interest

- Industry news

- Suggested itineraries

- Things to see and do in your destination

- Testimonials from your guests.

## Promoting Your Podcast

Once you have developed your audio or video content, you will usually want to get as wide a distribution as you can. The most obvious place to promote your podcast would be right on your Web site.

If you are going to put your podcast on your site, make sure it stands out; you can even have a whole page dedicated to it (or them!). Remember to make it easy for people to subscribe by way of an RSS feed or give you permission to e-mail them when you have new podcasts available. Be sure to provide information on your podcast content. For example, instead of saying "download my podcast" say something like "download my podcast full of great tips and information on what to see and do in Colorado"—you've got to sell the sizzle!

Since podcasting is still relatively new it is important to make sure you provide your visitors with the tools and education they need to be able to access and download your podcast. Make it easy for them to do what you want them to do.

It's also a good idea to include viral marketing as well—tell a friend about this podcast—to enable your Web site visitors to spread the word.

| Podcast Do's | Podcast Don'ts |
| --- | --- |
| Make it professional. | Don't ramble. Make a point and move on. |
| Provide content that is informational, educational, and entertaining. | Don't stray too far from the topic. |
| Skip long introductions. | Don't forget to include meta data—include keywords in feed title and descriptions. |
| Provide a transcript or detailed show notes. | Don't ignore your audience—find out what they want to hear and give it to them. |
| Subscribe to your podcast to see and hear what your audience hears. | |
| Offer new podcasts frequently. | |

Other ways to promote your podcast include:

- Promote your podcasts in your e-mail signature file.

- Promote your podcasts on partner sites.

- Promote your podcasts on popular podcast directories. There are many great podcast directories online like Podcast.net (*http://www.podcast.net*), Podcast Alley (*http://www.podcastalley.com*), Podcast.com (*http://www.podcast.com*), iTunes (*http://www.itunes.com*) and Yahoo! Podcasts (*http://podcasts.yahoo.com*) (see Figure 24.2).

- Submit your podcast to podcast search engines like Podcast Alley (*http://www.podcastalley.com*) (see Figure 24.3).

We are seeing podcasting take off because it enables listeners to enjoy the audio content when they want, where they want, and how they want.

**Figure 24.2.**   Promote your podcast through Yahoo! Podcasts.

**Figure 24.3.** Submit your podcast to Podcast Alley for greater exposure.

## Internet Resources for Chapter 24

I have developed a great library of online resources for you to check out regarding podcasting. This library is available on my Tourism Internet Marketing University Web site *http://www.TourismInternetMarketingU.com/max* in the Resources section where you can find additional tips, tools, techniques, and resources.

I have also developed courses on many of the topics covered in this book. These courses are also available on my Tourism Internet Marketing University Web site *http://www.TourismInternetMarketingU.com/max*. These courses are delivered immediately over the Internet or can be ordered as a CD.

# 25

## Mobile Marketing

With mobile devices we can do all kinds of things, like check flight schedules, transfer money from one account to another, pay bills, make hotel reservations, check the local MLS, and the list goes on and on. Today's consumer is very demanding—they want what they want, when they want. There are over 1.8 billion people with mobile devices capable of voice, text, image, and Internet communication. That's a huge market already, and one that will escalate in the coming years as we see less-developed countries go directly to wireless for their telephones. We are beginning to see location-based services (or LBS) really take hold. Every new advancement in Internet-based technology provides new marketing opportunities.

In this chapter, we cover:

- What is mobile marketing?

- Benefits of mobile marketing.

### What Is Mobile Marketing?

Mobile marketing is using a mobile or a wireless device for marketing purposes. Mobile marketing is a travel and tourism organization's dream come true—it enables an agent to communicate directly, one-on-one, to the target market with the opportunity for a direct response in real time.

There are a number of mobile marketing opportunities for the travel and tourism industry that are becoming commonplace:

- SMS (short messaging service)

- MMS (multimedia messaging service)

- Mobile search

- Instant messaging

- LBS (location-based services)

- Profile-specific advertising

- Mobile blogging

- Subscribed content.

## SMS—Short Messaging Service

SMS is a service that allows text messages to be sent and received on your mobile phone. The messages can also be sent to a mobile device from the Internet using an SMS gateway Web site. With SMS, if the phone is turned off or is out of range, the message is stored on the network and is delivered the next time you power on.

An example of an SMS campaign would be a "text to win a free vacation package" contest. There are many SMS services springing up for the travel and tourism industry. Resort Marketing launched a text messaging service that enables advertisers to communicate directly with subscribing visitors (see Figure 25.1). Clickatell (*http://www.clickatell.com*) provides you with a simple, high-speed messaging service. Their "any message, anywhere" solutions allow travel and tourism businesses to talk to their customers in an immediate and personal way, no matter which communication device they use. Clickatell allows travel and tourism businesses to alert customers of delays, confirm bookings, and send schedule changes and update arrival times, so that pick-ups can be there at the correct time.

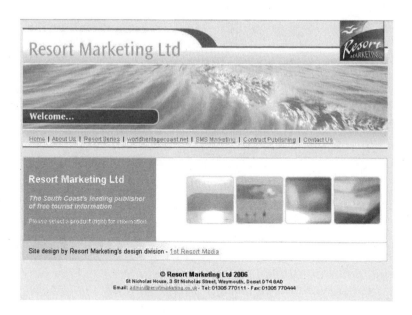

**Figure 25.1.** Resort Marketing launched a text messaging service that enables advertisers to communicate directly with subscribing visitors.

## MMS—Multimedia Messaging Service

MMS brings a whole new dimension to mobile marketing with its enhanced transmission service that enables video clips, color pictures, text, and audio files to be sent and received by mobile phones. The marketing opportunities are endless for the travel and tourism industry using this technology, and the benefits are plentiful—immediate contact, immediate response, and multimedia capacity. With MMS, virtual tours of your destination can be provided to potential customers.

Combine MMS with the ability to know where your subscriber is physically as well as having a profile of the subscriber—and the possibilities are endless!

## Instant Messaging

Wireless providers are now including instant messaging as part of their services, and according to the AOL Instant Messaging Survey, 59 percent of Internet users use instant messaging on a regular basis, and at least 20 percent of instant messaging users send mobile instant messages or SMS text messages through a mobile device. Microsoft, AOL, and Yahoo! all offer instant-messaging products that enable quick and easy access to over 200 million consumers with text, audio, and video content.

## LBS—Location-Based Services

Location-based services use location as a key element in providing relevant information to users, and there are many mobile marketing applications for this type of service:

- Finding the nearest hotel because your flight has been cancelled

- Finding the closest Thai restaurant in a strange city, including the directions on how to get there from where you are.

Location-based services will change the way we do lots of things. With technology being developed that is able to identify the specific geographic location, within 5 to 10 yards of the device, opportunities arise to send highly targeted location-based advertising.

## Profile Specific Advertising

Each mobile phone has a unique identifier in the telephone number making it possible to build a profile of the owner. Once you have permission and a profile, you can send very targeted advertising messages to that profile. You must be careful when using this type of advertising that messages are permission-based and not considered spam or unsolicited.

## Mobile Blogging

In a matter of seconds, color pictures, video, and audio files can be instantly added to a blog through a mobile device.

## Subscribed Content

Travel and tourism operations should always be looking for permission-based opportunities where they can send weekly package discounts, upcoming contests, Web site updates, and news announcements along with targeted advertisements and promotions to subscribers. Mobile devices are another avenue for such permission-based marketing. You can provide targeted content to subscribers through RSS from your site to a mobile device. You can also send ski conditions, travel coupons, or e-specials to subscribers.

## Benefits of Mobile Marketing

The different mobile marketing applications provide a variety of benefits to the travel and tourism industry:

- Mobile marketing allows direct, personal communication in real time with the opportunity for immediate, direct response.

- By building a customer profile, you can be very targeted with your vacation packages, campaigns, or offerings.

- Brand awareness can be increased.

- Messages can be sent through this medium very cost-effectively.

- Traffic to Web sites can be increased.

- Customer loyalty can be enhanced.

- Sales can be increased when you provide the right vacation package at the right time to the right customer.

- Interactivity—the target customer is engaged using this technology.

- The number of potential customers you can reach with this medium is staggering. There are over 1.8 billion consumers with access to this technology.

- Two-way dialogue between marketer and target market allows one-on-one marketing.

- Immediate impact.

- Personalized messages get a much higher response rate than generic messages.

- Sponsored messages can be provided.

- Messages are delivered instantaneously.

- This medium makes it easy for people to spread the word quickly and easily.

With the increase in the number of 3G devices that are becoming more mainstream and the number of marketers becoming more savvy, the mobile marketplace is significant. We have seen a quick uptake on most mobile marketing opportunities, like voting for your favorite American Idol. We're already seeing a number of travel and tourism businesses implement mobile marketing applications, such as BlueMountain (see Figure 25.2). With BlueMountain you

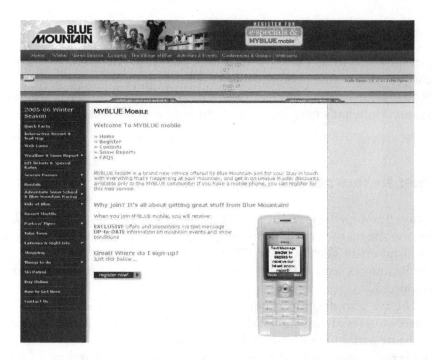

**Figure 25.2.** BlueMountain uses mobile marketing for exclusive offers, promotions, and up-to-date information on mountain events and snow conditions.

**Figure 25.3.** The Scottsdale, Arizona CVB uses mobile marketing and RSS feeds to update visitors on what's new, celebrity sightings, wedding planning, and much more.

can subscribe to MYBLUE mobile and get up-to-the-minute ski conditions, exclusive offers and promotions, and information on upcoming events. The Scottsdale, Arizona CVB (see Figure 25.3) also uses mobile marketing to update visitors on what's new, celebrity sightings, wedding planning, and much more.

## Internet Resources for Chapter 25

I have developed a great library of online resources for you to check out regarding mobile marketing. This library is available on my Tourism Internet Marketing University Web site *http://www.TourismInternetMarketingU.com/max* in the Resources section where you can find additional tips, tools, techniques, and resources.

I have also developed courses on many of the topics covered in this book. These courses are also available on my Tourism Internet Marketing University Web site *http://www.TourismInternetMarketingU.com/max*. These courses are delivered immediately over the Internet or can be ordered as a CD.

# 26

## Interactive Mapping

Studies show that the more interactive your Web site is, the longer your Web site visitors will stick around. Interactive maps are a great element for travel and tourism operations to feature on their sites because they allow you to showcase listings on your Web site like never before. In this chapter, we cover:

- What is interactive mapping?

- Why is it important to the travel and tourism industry?

- How do you do it?

- How do you leverage interactive maps?

### What is Interactive Mapping?

An interactive map is a map your Web site visitors can interact with. It is a map of a specified region, city, town, or neighborhood that has integrated interactive multi-media functionality. These interactive multi-media capabilities give users the ability to explore the map in much more depth and give the map, and the location of your destination, your resort, and/or your hotel, much more meaning.

Interactive maps give users a visual of where your destination or resort is located. Interactive maps give your Web site visitors the ability to view surrounding neighborhoods and all of the available amenities therein on one map. They can also provide layers of information about a particular area. Along with your hotel listing information for example, interactive maps can show visitors where the shopping centers are in relation to your hotel, where the parks are, and where the restaurants and golf courses are located in relation to your hotel. Interactive maps can link to content, which could be useful to the consumer who is making a final decision on visiting a particular destination.

Interactive maps can link to visual images, a voice-guided tour, or videos. Add text, slide shows, animations, and panoramas to give your consumers a full view of the surrounding area and the most information they will need for their purchasing decision.

Interactive maps visually and geographically organize visual content. They allow your Web site visitors to get a feel for the layout of a particular area or property listing. More advanced maps provide users with a legend and categories and sub-categories of information. Check out the map Down South Publishers Inc. developed for its Web site HiltonHead360.com in Figure 26.1. This map offers users the ability to see many different color-coded categories and sub-categories, including golf courses, private or open golf courses, restaurants, beaches, shopping centers, and spas. Users can select a category of their choice, for example spas, to see where on the map all of the available spas are located.

**Figure 26.1.** HiltonHead360.com's interactive map.

The yellow dots on the map represent all of the vacation rental properties, and as the users drag their mouse over those dots they are given the street address (see Figure 26.2) and if they click on the dot they are given a picture of the vacation rental along with other links, such as a virtual tour like the one shown in Figure 26.3.

## Why is Interactive Mapping Important to the Travel and Tourism Industry?

The first thing people do when they decide to take a trip or a vacation is begin their search online. It is for this reason that interactive mapping is very important to the travel and tourism industry. Interactive maps make it easy for prospective customers to see the physical location of the interested vacation destination in conjunction with the surrounding area.

Interactive maps are still quite new, and by providing an interactive map you are providing leading edge information and tools to your customers and potential customers. This will help set you apart from other travel and tourism organizations and help reinforce the fact that you are a leader in your field—the industry expert.

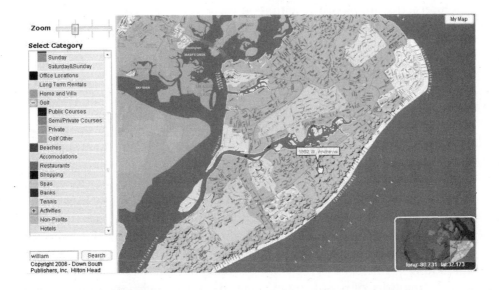

**Figure 26.2.** The yellow dots on the map for HiltonHead360.com represent all of the vacation rentals, and as users drag their mouse over those dots they are given the street address.

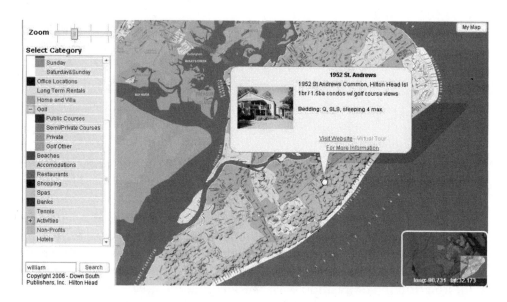

**Figure 26.3.** If users click on a dot they are given a picture of the vacation rental along with other links, such as a virtual tour.

Interactive maps are just that—they are interactive. The more interactive your travel and tourism site is, the more likely your Web site visitors are going to stay longer and the more likely they are going to return again and again. The longer your Web site visitors stay, and the more often they visit your site, the more your brand is reinforced, the more your target market feels a part of your community, the more they feel like they know and trust you and, as I've said before, people do business with people they know and trust.

Once you have established the trust of your Web site visitors, the more likely they are to give you permission to stay in touch through your e-club, newsletter, or new package updates, and the more likely they are to tell others about your destination, your packages, and your services. By offering your Web site visitors leading edge tools and content, the more likely you will be first in mind when they go to research or purchase their vacation. When visitors see how you go above and beyond to help them, either in their purchasing decision or help them research all of their options, they will come to you again and again.

The majority of people focus their attention on visual components of a Web site first, such as images, maps, or charts, before they process any text. Interactive maps serve as a visual trigger. They create interest in non-visual information—"A picture is worth a thousand words" as the saying goes.

## How Do You Do It?

Although interactive maps are still in the early stages, there are a number of options available to you for providing this service to your Web site visitors. Each option has its own unique bells and whistles and functionality. Each option has its own technology, ease of development, and varying costs. Therefore, it is important to research each option carefully and decide which is going to be the right choice for you, your Web site, and for your target market.

Depending on the model and the technical capabilities you want your interactive map to have and if you have the right expertise, you can build your interactive map in-house or use Google Maps. Either way, you must be sure that it will provide the type of information your target market is looking for. Google Maps is a product, offered by Google, which allows you to view maps in your Web browser, and offers user-friendly mapping technology.

Google Maps will show you where you want to go, how to get there, with driving instructions, and will also show you what you'll find when you get there, with local business information, including location, contact information, and driving directions. Google Maps allow you to do local searches. If you want to find coffee shops in a particular neighborhood, simply navigate to that area and type in "coffee" and coffee shops will appear at the various locations on your map. It also gives you phone numbers and a link for each location on the left side of the page (see Figure 26.4). If you click on the link for one of the listed coffee shops, Google Maps gives you the shop's name, address, phone number, links for driving directions, reviews, and much more.

With Google Maps you can view an aerial perspective of any location on Earth with its satellite view (see Figure 26.5), and in certain locations you can view and navigate street-level imagery (see Figure 26.6). You can even create your own personalized, customized maps complete with explanations, footnotes, place markers, photos, and videos.

Another option available to travel and tourism professionals who want to offer their Web site visitors interactive maps on their Web sites is to use an **ASP**. The ASP provides you with the basic infrastructure or the software you need to develop your interactive map. In other words, the ASP provides you with the technology you need to upload your map and populate it with all of the information you want to provide your Web site visitors—including your destinations, restaurants in the area, beaches, shopping centers, golf courses, and parks.

**ASP**

Application Service Provider—an organization that hosts software applications on its own servers within its own facilities.

As with many software programs available today, the variety of interactive mapping software that is available is broad. Some are really simple while others offer robust options. It is important that the ASP you choose will be able to

**Figure 26.4.** Google Maps provides phone numbers and a link for each location on the left side of the page.

**Figure 26.5.** Google Maps allows you to view an aerial perspective of any location on Earth with its satellite view.

**Figure 26.6.** Google Maps allows users to view and navigate certain locations through street-level imagery.

meet your needs, the needs of your Web site objectives, and the needs of your target market. Research each one carefully to be sure it has the ability to offer all of the information you want your Web site visitors to see, such as virtual tours, podcasts, videos, links, and other listing information.

It is extremely important that all of your listing details are up-to-date. If something is sold out or no longer available, it must be removed from your interactive map immediately. You may choose to update your map in-house or you may choose to outsource that activity to the ASP or to someone else who provides that as a service.

Igemoe (*http://www.maps.igemoe.com*) pictured in Figure 26.7 is an ASP that allows you to add highly interactive self-managed maps to your site. Go to the Resources section of my Web site *http://www.TourismInternetMarketingU.com/ max* for more interactive mapping solutions.

## How Do You Leverage Interactive Maps?

I am a big proponent of leveraging everything you do for maximum marketing results. By offering interactive maps on your Web site you are opening up many avenues for online marketing success.

**Figure 26.7.**   Igemoe is an ASP that allows you to add its highly interactive self-managed maps to your site.

You can leverage interactive maps to get reciprocal links and increase your link popularity with the search engines. If you are featuring the shopping centers in the area and the restaurants and fitness centers, provide a link to their Web sites from your map and ask for a link back from their site. The more links you have, the higher your search engine ranking. Links are discussed more in Chapter 16.

Another way to leverage your interactive map is through viral marketing. Provide a "Tell a friend about this map" button (see Chapter 5). Use permission marketing to your advantage here as well by asking Web site visitors if you can send them notifications of new features added, new package listings, or new resources (see Chapter 4 for more on permission marketing).

Some travel and tourism companies are using interactive maps as a source of revenue generation. This can be done several ways depending on the software you are using. For example, for each category of resources you have available on your map, schools, restaurants, or shopping centers, you can offer different types of listings at different fees—a free listing, a basic listing, and a premium listing. Let's take golf courses as an example. You can offer all the golf courses in the area a free listing. This could include simply the name of the golf course. The basic listing would have more enhanced features like a link to their Web site, their address and phone number, a picture, and a list of tee-off times, and would have an associated cost. The premium listing could incorporate links to their specials and promotions page, a podcast, video, or a virtual tour, and again have an associated fee that is higher than the basic listing.

Another way to use your interactive map as a source of revenue generation is to offer advertising on the results page. If your interactive map had golf courses listed in the legend, you could sell those golf courses advertising on the results page.

Stay tuned. Interactive mapping is very important for the travel and tourism industry and I expect over the next year a number of new players will be emerging on the market with added features, bells and whistles and there will be a few emerging leaders in the field.

## Internet Resources for Chapter 26

I have developed a great library of online resources for you to check out regarding interactive mapping. This library is available on my Tourism Internet Marketing University Web site *http://www.TourismInternetMarketingU.com/max* in the Resources section where you can find additional tips, tools, techniques, and resources.

I have also developed courses on many of the topics covered in this book. These courses are also available on my Tourism Internet Marketing University Web site *http://www.TourismInternetMarketingU.com/max*. These courses are delivered immediately over the Internet or can be ordered as a CD.

# 27

---

# The Power of Partnering

We have talked about many different online marketing opportunities through the course of this book. Often there are great opportunities that are overlooked because of their simplicity. Partnering is one of those often-overlooked opportunities. There are many other sites that are selling to your target market. Quite often they are selling non-competing travel and tourism packages, products, or services. Quite often they have significant traffic to their sites or significant databases that they communicate with on a regular basis. If you can find a win-win opportunity to partner with these sites, you can have significant results.

In this chapter, we cover:

- Ideal partner sites

- Partnering opportunities.

## Ideal Partner Sites

When you look for sites to partner with, you are looking for:

- Sites that have your ideal target market as their site visitor

- Sites that have significant targeted traffic

- Sites that have a significant permission-based database

- Sites that have non-competing travel and tourism related products or services.

Once you identify the types of partners or the types of non-competing products or services of potential partners, it will be easier to find and develop a list of potential partners. For example, if you have a country inn, you might identify local attraction sites as potential partners—you are both selling to the same target market, but you are selling non-competing products and services. If you have a ski hill, you might identify local hotels, attractions and restaurants as potential partners. Once you have identified the types of partners you are looking for, you will be able to do research on-line to find specific potential partners.

## Partnering Opportunities

Once you have found potential partners, next you need to look at win-win ways to partner with these sites. There are all kinds of ways to work together to do cross-promotion, leverage the exposure on each other's site, or provide exposure through each other's database.

> *Cross-promotion through banner advertising.* You can exchange banners on each other's site. If you have a ski hill and you are partnering with a local country inn, you can have a banner that indicates that any customer of yours can get a 10 percent discount on a stay at the inn upon presentation of their lift ticket, and the banner ad would link back to the country inn's Web site. The country inn can provide the quid pro quo—your banner on their site can provide their customers with a 10 percent discount off their lift ticket at the ski hill if they stay at the inn and the banner would link back to your ski hill.

> *Co-operative banner advertising.* Drop-down ads provide the viewer with the option to click on different parts of the banner ad and be taken to different sites. You could partner with four others who are all selling to the same target market to develop and place this type of drop-down menu ad. The result is either the same amount of advertising you did previously at 20 percent of the cost, or spending the same amount and getting five times the exposure.

*Partner with others on contests.* Find sites that are selling to the same target market and offer your packages, a stay at your destination or your products as part of the prize for their contest as long as the other site provides some details on your packages, your destination, or your product and a link to your site. Leverage the link by getting your most important keywords in the text around the link pointing to your site to increase your link relevancy score and your search engine placement. You can also partner with others on your contests. The greater the prize, the more exposure you'll see through the contest.

*Partner with others' e-specials.* Look for sites that provide e-specials to their target market and see if you can provide them with a great e-special. This works great for industry associations and also travel agencies. If you have a spa or resort, providing a great package at a great price to a travel agency that has a significant database could result in not only significant new business but also new visitors to your site and, if you develop the landing page properly, new members to your e-club.

*Partner with directories or meta-indexes that provide links to your type of site.* Look for a mutually beneficial opportunity. At the very least look for an opportunity to have your listing appear at the top of the page, have it stand out in some way, or have your banner ad appear on the most appropriate page of their directory.

*Partner with your industry associations.* If you have a listing, make sure that your description is as appealing as it can be. Provide a call to action in your description. Have the link go to the most appropriate page of your site—it's not always the home page! Look for areas on their site where you can gain a little extra exposure. Do they have sections like:

- Top 10

- Featured

- Recommended

- Site of the day/week

- Suggested.

These all provide an opportunity for added exposure. Another example is that if you have a tourist attraction, look for all the destination marketing organizations in your geographic area for things like "Suggested Itineraries" to get your attraction included—even if you have to write it yourself. There are lots of these opportunities out there.

Partner with industry associations to get your press releases or story ideas in front of the media. Most travel and tourism industry associations have a media center. If you've got a press release or a story that would be of interest to the media, the travel and tourism industry association's media center would be a great place for exposure. Perhaps they'd be interested in a joint press release to their media list.

Be a contributing journalist to e-zines that have your target market as their subscribers. Make sure you have your contact information in the resource box, with a link back to your Web site.

Sites such as VacationFun.com (*http://www.vacationfun.com*) and Destinations2Discover (*http://www.destinations2discover.com*) are great travel and tourism partnering sites. These sites get a significant amount of traffic that is very targeted. People using these sites are planning a vacation. They are researching where they are going to go, where they are going to stay and what they are going to do when they get there—better still, many of their visitors are ready to buy. Why do all of the work trying to get hoards of traffic to your site when sites such as these are already doing it for you.

With your iBrochure posted on VacationFun.com Web site visitors can view your iBrochure online, order your iBrochure as an electronic version or in print, or click through to your Web site for more information on your organization, destination, getaway packages, etc. (see Figure 27.1).

Destinations2Discover, pictured in Figure 27.2, is an online travel resource portal. It provides Web site visitors with a searchable database of destinations, activities, events, and attractions worldwide. Destinations2Discover is designed as an information resource for both domestic and international travelers.

There are all kinds of partnering opportunities available; you just have to do a little brainstorming. Think about who is selling non-competing products or services to the same target market you are and figure out a win-win opportunity.

## Internet Resources for Chapter 27

I have developed a great library of online resources for you to check out regarding partnering. This library is available on my Tourism Internet Marketing University Web site *http://www.TourismInternetMarketingU.com/max* in the Resources section where you can find additional tips, tools, techniques, and resources.

I have also developed courses on many of the topics covered in this book. These courses are also available on my Tourism Internet Marketing University Web site *http://www.TourismInternetMarketingU.com/max*. These courses are delivered immediately over the Internet or can be ordered as a CD.

**Figure 27.1.** VacationFun.com features various travel and tourism business iBrochures.

**Figure 27.2.** Destinations2Discover is an online travel resource portal.

# 28

## Web Traffic Analysis

You had 50,000 unique visitors to your Web site this month? Up from 35,000 last month? Wow! That must have had quite an impact on your bottom line! Oh, you don't know...

Unfortunately, most travel and tourism companies that monitor their Web site traffic are in this very position, though at least they're doing something. Even more unfortunate is that many more travel and tourism companies don't give any attention to Web site analytics at all.

To make your online presence a valuable part of your travel and tourism business, you need to be paying attention to Web site analytics.

In this chapter we look at:

- Web analytics defined

- Common measurements of performance

- Monitor what matters to your business

- Determine what works—A/B testing as a start

- Go deeper—use it or lose it

- Bringing it all together—use what you've learned from other sources

- Segmenting your target market

- Choosing a Web analytics solution

- Closing comments on Web analytics.

It is not our goal in this chapter to tell you step by step how to roll out Web analytics in your organization; it would take far more than a chapter to do that. What we do want you to walk away with is a good understanding that this can help your business, and we want you to question how you can make it work for you. Everyone needs to start somewhere. This is where you should start.

## Web Analytics Defined

Any time you're watching over what happens with an online marketing campaign or your Web site, you're technically partaking in Web analytics. Since there was so much controversy over what exactly Web analytics was, the Web Analytics Association (*http://www.webanalyticsassociation.org*) was founded, and it offers this concise definition:

> *Web analytics is the measurement, collection, analysis, and reporting of Internet data for the purpose of understanding and optimizing Web usage.*

Basically, it encompasses all that is involved in measuring the success of your online activities.

When speaking of Web analytics, you will commonly speak of both qualitative and quantitative research. Qualitative research, usually accomplished through interviews, surveys, or focus groups, offers insights into a person's motivation—why did they do what they did? Think of it as feedback or opinions. Quantitative research, on the other hand, offers results that you can measure, such as the number of unique click-throughs to a Web page, the number of people in North America with broadband Internet access, and so on.

When speaking of Web analytics, most of the time you're talking in terms of quantitative data—"this happened 2,000 times over 24 hours." Qualitative research is often used with quantitative research to help explain what happened by providing insight into an individual's motivation, attitude, and behavior. Together they provide very useful insight.

### Key Performance Indicators

*Key performance indicators (KPIs)* is a common phrase in the business world and you will see it come up often when discussing Web analytics. Key performance indicators are also known as key success factors.

A KPI is measurable and reflects the goals of a company. KPIs are used in everything from measuring the average time that customer service representatives spend on the phone with a customer to the graduation rate of a high school. When thinking in terms of Web analytics, your KPIs concern those measurements that make a difference to your business in relation to the Internet. In the next section we cover some of the more common measurements of performance.

## Common Measurements of Performance

The first thing you need to do is establish what key performance indicators are important to your business model. What questions about your Web site visitors do you want an answer to? Following are some of the more common measurements for you to evaluate.

### Click-Through Rate

Your click-through rate pertains to how many people actually followed your online advertisement to your Web site or landing page out of the total number of advertising impressions delivered. This measurement is very basic and cannot tell you a whole lot except for an approximation of how much overall interest there is in a particular online marketing campaign you are running. Think of this as a general measure of popularity. This measure is general in scope because it could contain hits by search engine spiders, a single potential customer who makes multiple visits, and competitors who decide they want to exhaust your click-through budget.

### Unique Visitors

"Unique visitors" pertains to how many individual people came to your Web site or landing page from a current marketing promotion over a specific period of time. This is a very basic measurement as well, but it offers a more accurate look at just who has taken an interest in you by filtering out double data and irrelevant visits. Make sure you remove the search engine spiders and crawlers from your statistics so that they are not mistaken as potential customers.

### Time Spent

With your Web site you want people to stay for a while—to have a "sticky" Web site. You can look at time spent per page or spent during an overall visit. If a lot of people are leaving within a matter of seconds of hitting your landing page, they are likely dissatisfied with what they see. On the other hand, if the target market is spending an inordinate amount of time on your landing page, they are likely confused, or having a good time, or maybe they got up to go to the kitchen to make lunch. Time is only one indicator. You need to monitor the click stream of your visitors.

### Click Stream Analysis

What paths do the target market follow when they hit your Web site or landing page? Is the target market hitting a particular page and then leaving your site? Monitoring the behavior of your target market on your Web site enables you to refine the navigation and lay out a simple trail of bread crumbs to lead your customer down the intended path.

### Single-Page Access

Look at the number of one-page visits to your Web site or landing page. This is where the visitor comes to your page but takes no action other than to leave. If that is happening on a frequent basis, you undoubtedly have a problem. It could be that your landing page is not effective at converting, that the page the client hits does not show a direct relationship to the ad or link the target clicked on to reach you, or perhaps a shady competitor is trying to exhaust your ad campaign. Understand what percentage of your visitors are coming to your site and are immediately taking off. If you have a very low percentage of single-page accesses then you are fine; however, if you see a lot of single-page accesses that should throw up an immediate red flag that you need to do some further research.

### Leads Generated or Desired Action Taken

Every travel and tourism organization wants to know how many leads a particular advertising campaign generated over a specified period of time. This is also a very basic measurement. How many leads did you get through your Web site during, say, the month of May? When tracking the number of leads generated through your landing page or Web site, you should also look at the number of those leads who become customers down the road. You may also want to measure how many people signed up for your newsletter or e-club or downloaded those coupons.

## Customer Conversion Ratio

Of all the potential clients, how many followed through on the action you wanted them to take? Here you are looking at the effectiveness of your ability to convert customers. Make sure you are looking at unique visitors so that you are not counting the person who came back 10 times as 10 different people. The higher your customer conversion ratio, the better—the average conversion rate for a travel and tourism Web site falls between 2 and 5 percent.

## Net Dollars per Visitor

This is simply a look at how much each visitor is worth to your business. How much money, on average, is each Web visitor worth to your bottom line?

## Cost per Visitor

This information pertains to all visitors to your Web site or landing page, not just to consumers who make a purchase. It is important to understand how much each visitor to your Web site costs you so that you can work toward bringing that cost down to maximize profits. This information is also useful for forecasting and budgeting.

## Form Abandonment

The average online form abandonment rate is around 40 percent. How many people gave up somewhere along the line in the process or on the second page of a three-page information request form? You have to know where the process fails in order to improve it. Do everything in your power to understand your market and make the intended objective as easy to accomplish as possible.

Do not just look at the number of people who gave up, but be sure to look at where they gave up so that you can pinpoint where the potential issue lies and fix it.

### Impact on Offline Sales

Do not neglect the impact your online marketing campaigns have in the offline environment. Your landing page might be converting customers and you do not even know it, unless you are watching for it. How? Your Web site or landing page will likely include other methods of contact the target market can use to do business with your company.

This can be a difficult thing to track; however, you can make it manageable. You might consider setting up a phone number that is only available from your Web site, so that when a call comes through you know it is because of the phone number that rests on your landing page.

### Return on Investment (ROI)

ROI is a measure of overall profitability. Take your profit from an activity, particular promotion, month, and so on, and then factor in the total capital you invested to accomplish your activity to figure out the ROI.

It came to my attention recently that nearly 75 percent of online advertisers don't monitor their ROI. They could be spending $60 to make $50. Boy, that seems like a great idea.

Ultimately the most relevant key performance indicators for your business depend entirely on what you are trying to accomplish with your online marketing initiatives.

## Monitor What Matters to Your Business

What do you want people to do? That's a question you should be asking yourself. Travel and tourism operations have Web sites that are focused on generating sales. Measurements that matter to most of you will:

- Produce accurate and cost-effective information

- Be supported by and for company stakeholders

- Reflect and drive business results through positive change.

As an e-commerce Web site, you're going to be interested in critical data like the total sales conversions, how easy it is to go through your site's purchase process, and how well a promotion sold during a specific period of time. For example, how many of those 25 percent off spa packages did we sell during the promotion week of December 3 to December 9? That's good stuff to know.

What you monitor will be unique to your business. For a brand-new company, your efforts might be on getting as many new acquisitions as possible, whereas a more established company might focus more of its efforts on customer retention. Monitor what matters.

## Determine What Works—A/B Testing as a Start

If you're going to make Web analytics work for you, then testing is one thing you cannot live without. Direct marketers obsess over testing to see what changes generate the best responses. Why is it, then, that typical online marketers don't measure and test their efforts? It is the most measurable medium out there!

A/B testing is a common approach to testing different creatives in order to make incremental improvements. Let's explore this a bit more here. You might want answers to questions like:

- Is short or long copy more effective?

- Is it better to use bulleted lists to emphasize key points as opposed to paragraphs of information?

- Does separating content with taglines or headers increase the number of responses?

- What happens if I bold or emphasize key points in the copy?

- What impact does changing the writing style, or tone, of your copy have on a page's ability to convert?

- What impact does changing the presentation of the offer itself have on results? "50% off," "1/2 price" showing the original $200,000 price tag with a strikethrough and the new price next to it emphasized in bold red font as $100,000, are all different ways of presenting the same offer. Which method generates the best response from the target market?

- Does your offer perform better with a lot of pictures, only a few pictures, or no pictures?

- What colors on the page elicit the most favorable responses? Does the contrast between the page copy and the background influence the response rate?

- What font types, styles, and sizes are most effective?

- How many navigation options work best? Am I providing the target market with too many navigation options such that they get distracted, or would the page be effective with more navigation options?

- Where is the best position on the page to place the "Contact me" or "Request information" button? When the target market completes the request form, the first thing you want them to do is submit their request, not cancel it. This means putting the "Submit" button as the obvious next step, before the clear or cancel option. Actually, don't put the clear or cancel option there at all—they're just distractions.

- Does the wording of the request information button generate more of a response if I play with the wording? For example, "Request a Free Vacation Guide Now!" versus "Submit."

- Have I tested different approaches for completing the action I want the target market to take? Does a short or long form work best? Does the same request form perform better if it is split across two steps on two different pages?

- Have I tested variations of my offer to see what generates better results? Maybe a free gift will help boost the response rate.

A/B testing helps you address answers to questions like those mentioned above. There is always something you can do a bit better to maximize your results based on your page goals and what you have determined as the basis for measuring success. There are any number of tidbits you can test and tweak to refine your campaigns—some things will work, some things will not, but you obviously want to find out what does work the best and do more of it. Even the smallest changes can have a big impact. When running a marketing campaign, employ A/B testing to see which landing page techniques generate the best responses from your target market.

Here is a simplified way to think about A/B testing. Say you have an e-mail promotion you want to send out to your house list of 10,000 subscribers. What you're going to do is send 5,000 of those subscribers to one landing page and the other 5,000 subscribers to another landing page to learn which version is more effective (landing pages are discussed more in Chapter 7).

When running a new campaign for the first time, it is difficult to say what will trigger the best response, so you might test two, three, or even five dramatically different e-mail campaigns, landing pages, PPC ads, or whatever it is you are testing. You would use the one that performs the best as your starting point for future refinements.

## Keep It Simple

It is best to test one element at a time during refinements so that you can measure results and determine the effectiveness of the new change. If you change too many items at once, it will be difficult to determine how much of an impact the items you changed had on the effectiveness of the page. If you made three adjustments to your landing page at once, it might be that two of the three components have increased the response rate, but the third might have dragged it down a bit, so you are not quite reaching your potential. If you change just one element at a time, you can tell what impact your change has on the landing page's ability to convert.

## Give It Time

When running a test, you must let it run long enough to enable you to pull accurate results. You need to gather enough responses and give people enough time to respond to your campaigns. If you're curious about the immediate responses, you might look at some preliminary results a couple hours after your e-mail campaign launch, but a 1 percent sample is not really an accurate representation of the total campaign success. How much time you give a campaign ultimately depends on what you're testing; it could need days or even weeks to paint the complete picture.

## Tracking Your Tests

There are many ways to make tracking your test results easier. If you want to get people to sign up for your e-club, test a couple of different offers to entice them to do so. You might issue a different code for each offer that the customer must enter at the time of sign up. This makes it quite easy to determine the offer that was more appealing. Alternatively, you can use scripts or send people to different servers or different pages. As mentioned above, you might test two variations of a landing page to see which one more people respond to.

If A/B testing is something you would sooner not have any part in, there are companies out there that can help you run tests and conduct performance measurements. Optimost (*http://www.optimost.com*) and Offermatica (*http://www.offermatica.com*) are two reputable sources that can help you with A/B testing and other types of testing such as multivariate testing.

Web analytics will tell you how well you did, but you must conduct tests to cause change. One test alone will not give you all the answers. Using Web analytics and testing together will help you measure and improve your results and is an ongoing process. Capitalizing on any great campaign requires a great closing, so keep at it!

## Go Deeper—Use It or Lose It

For lead-generation Web sites, such as your travel and tourism Web site, knowing the conversion rate is a big deal. No doubt, knowing your site's conversion rate is hugely important, but here's the kicker. Knowing your conversion rate is like getting a grade on your high school report card. It will tell you how well you're doing, but not what happened between start to finish getting to that score. Did people get freaked out by the length of your contact form? Was the call to action not properly worded? Heck, did you go after the wrong people altogether?

When monitoring your results, analyze what happens at every stage of the process your potential client engages in. If nine out of ten people are dropping out of your "Contact me" form or your e-club sign up form at the same step in the process, you know something is clearly wrong and you can investigate it further.

When measuring your performance online with Web analytics, compare and contrast the information you gather with historical information. By looking at historical information, you can see the results of your current efforts against the past to identify trends and variations in the results. If you notice a new landing page has not performed as well as your previous landing page, then you know that little tweak you made did not benefit you and you can eliminate it from your next online marketing effort. If the little tweak you made to your landing page paid off, then you keep it and try something else to further improve your conversions and return on investment.

It helps to track the differences in behavior between first-time buyers and repeat clients. What motivates a first-time buyer, in comparison to what motivates a return client, is different. With repeat clients, you have less convincing to do in most cases. You can use the knowledge you learn about new clients and repeat clients to tailor the experience to each market segment's needs.

Now, you've gone through all this effort to find out how you're doing, but in order for that knowledge to make a difference you have to be proactive and encourage positive change. Test different changes to watch their impact on your results. In the previous section we covered the topic of A/B testing and a variety of things you can test on your own. The whole purpose behind monitoring your performance is so that you can use what you've learned to change the future—you know, that old adage "learn from your mistakes,"—don't lose sight of the big picture.

## Bringing It All Together—Use What You've Learned From Other Sources

When deciding what actions you are going to take to make updates to your online initiatives, the more you know, the better. You can use information from other sources along with your Web analytics to paint a more complete picture of the situation at hand. Let's look at a few examples:

- Industry studies and metrics—Studies by market research companies, such as Forrester Research (*http://www.forrester.com*), JupiterResearch (*http://www.jupiterresearch.com*), nielson/netratings (*http://www.nielsen-netratings.com*), and eMarketer (*http://www.emarketer.com*), provide great industry benchmarks that you can use to sit back and ask, "Okay, how is my travel and tourism business performing in comparison to the industry as a whole?"

- Usability studies—By conducting usability studies you can pinpoint a problem and find out what to test to make improvements. Usability studies are labor-intensive and require skills that are highly sought after. For more information on usability studies, we recommend you check out Jakob Nielsen's Web site at *http://www.useit.com*. Jakob is a highly regarded usability expert.

- Eyetracking studies—These allow you to look at your Web site through the eyes of your Web site visitors. An eyetracking analysis produces heat maps that show you where a person's eyes are drawn by tracking eye movement on a page. A company like Eye Tools (*http://*

*www.eyetools.com*) can provide you with eyetracking analysis services. The results of the studies then allow you to better position, add, or remove items on your Web site that you want your customers to see and act on.

- Competitive studies—To make sure you do not neglect the online activities of your competitors, perform an online competitive analysis. Look at what they are doing and how you can do it better.

- Clients, partners, and affiliate studies—Simply ask the people you deal with on a daily basis for their input. Interviews or online surveys or feedback forms can be set up as part of your site. Ask a simple question about your Web site visitors' experience. If they like what you are doing, great, if not, then follow up to find out what you can do better.

- Site performance studies—Don't neglect the basics. Your Web site might have exactly what the client is looking for but it takes 20 minutes to load, so they simply can't be bothered. Look at everything that could cause problems and potentially tarnish your image, such as errors on the Web site, the speed of the server you're hosting with, the load time of your pages, and cross-browser compatibility.

There is a challenge in getting your offline and online data together, but you're not alone. Everyone struggles with this. Make use of other sources to try to close the gap on some of your unknowns.

## Segmenting Your Target Market

Get to know who uses your site and why. The next leap in getting the most out of your online presence is to know how to speak to people and get them to respond—not everyone responds the same way when put in the same situation.

As an example, what we are asking you to do is to think beyond sending everyone on your e-mail list the same newsletter and look beyond sending everyone in your database all the same vacation packages. You will get more bang for your buck if you can segment your target market to appeal to their specific interests and needs. Someone looking for a weekend golf getaway will not be interested in your white water rafting package.

You will find with your newsletter that certain content is of interest to group A, but not to group B, and that group B responds very well to certain words that group A ignores, and so on. Confused? Think of it this way. Client A's name is John and John has been your client for years. John has purchased many vacation packages from you, from two-day mini getaways to two week excursions. Customer B's name is Jane, and she is in the market for her first ever real vacation, but has no idea who you are or how you stack up against the competition. Jane is at a different stage of the cycle and is going to react differently to a call to action than John might. John knows you offer what he wants and likes dealing with you, so he just wants to make his purchase. Jane, on the other hand, isn't so sure about you and wants information that will persuade her into becoming a first-time client.

How does all this tie into Web analytics? You can monitor the behavior of your visitors and establish segments based on that. Very basic segments might include:

- People who are new or are repeat visitors

- People who are new or are repeat customers

- People from marketing campaign X, Y, or Z

- People who subscribe to your newsletter

- People who are bargain hunters and book at the last minute

- People who are booking online for the first time

- People who arrived at your site from search engines, or e-mail, or through partner networks. (You would be surprised in the behavioral differences of people depending on how they find out about you.)

You really could go on and on, but again it depends on what you need to know. For your travel and tourism business, it might be important to segment your target market first by geographic region and then by another qualifier to get more specific.

Segmenting your target market allows you to get into targeted ads and customized content that appeal to the different characteristics of the segments. The more you adapt your message to your target market, the more likely they are to respond favorably.

## Choosing a Web Analytics Solution

According to JupiterResearch (*http://www.jupiterresearch.com*), over $450 million was to be spent on Web analytics solutions worldwide in 2005. It is clear that the value of Web analytics is starting to get recognition.

Travel and tourism companies effectively using Web analytics know that marketing plans are just paperweights unless you can measure performance. They know that if they do not measure their performance, they increase their risks; and they know that by measuring performance, it helps them make informed business decisions that result in a better return on investment, more client satisfaction, and in turn, more customer loyalty. Another perk of Web analytics is that travel and tourism marketers are able to prove that their efforts actually do something—a great thing when trying to justify one's job or when asking executives for funding.

### Look at Yourself

The very first thing you need to do is figure out what you're going to use the Web analytics package for. What are you going to measure and how does it relate to your travel and tourism business objectives? There are solutions that exist that offer far too little and solutions that offer far too much. There is no need to pay for what you will not use until you are ready for it, but be sure to choose a solution that will grow with you as your needs grow.

What reporting capabilities will you need and who will be using the package? If you need to be able to produce real-time reports, add it to your requirements. If different reports are needed for different departments such as marketing, make a note of that too. If you do a lot of historical comparisons, you will want to make sure you choose a solution that will let you compare data over time. Perhaps you want to be able to group visitors into specific segments. Assess the reporting needs of your travel and tourism business or organization.

What can you afford? There are open source solutions that will cost you nothing, to more complex Web analytics packages that will cost tens of thousands of dollars. If you know what you need it for, you will be in a much better position to spend the right amount of money for your needs.

### Look at Technology

There are many traffic analysis solutions to choose from ranging in price from free to thousands of dollars per year. One great free solution is Google Analytics.

Google purchased the popular Urchin Software Corp. in 2005, renamed it, redesigned it and improved its functionality. Now Google Analytics offers over 80 distinct reports, each customizable (to some degree), and offers three dashboard views of data: Executive, Marketer and Webmaster.

Google Analytics now provides more advanced features, including visitor segmentation and custom fields. It also provides integration with its own Google Adwords (Google's pay-per-click campaign), so that users can see their PPC campaign performance as part of their reports (see Chapter 9 for more on pay-per-click). Users can now add up to 50 site profiles—each profile corresponds to one URL.

Other Web analytic packages are typically ASP-based (hosted or on-demand) or stand-alones (software). ASP-based applications will use a snippet of code, such as a Java tag, to label every page of your Web site that must be measured. A stand-alone application is often a program you install on a local system to analyze log files.

WebTrends is a very popular Web analytics vendor that offers an on demand version as well as a software version of its popular analytics package.

What are your internal technology capabilities? Do you have the ability to install, run, and maintain an application in-house?

Is the Web analytics solution compatible with your current Web site? Some Web analytics packages have trouble with dynamic content—content generated on the fly and usually with longer addresses that include database query strings. A dynamic address often will look something like: *http://stores.skipjack.com/dells/Search.bok?no.show.inprogress=1&sredir=1&category=swiss+maid+caramel+apples*. What about pop-up window content or content that spreads across different servers?

Is the Web analytics solution compatible with your Web server? A package that can be installed on a UNIX box will not work on a Windows box.

Do you require integration with third-party software? For example, you might want to link the Web analytics package with your customer relationship management package. Think about the uniqueness of your travel and tourism business and its infrastructure to determine how you want a Web analytics package to fit into the picture.

Is the Web analytics package easy for you...

1. To set up—will they install it for you?

2. To maintain—are upgrades easy to handle?

3. To customize for a unique situation—a flexible solution is good to have.

4. To use—are the reports easy to generate and do they make sense?

If a solution is going to cause more headaches than benefits, you don't want it. There is something out there for every business, and it is just a matter of taking the time to find the solution that works best for you.

Many Web analytic packages offer evaluation copies for you to try out. Take advantage of it!

## Look at the Vendor

Look beyond the technology and the functionality of the Web analytics package and look at the vendor.

Does the vendor keep on top of changes in Web analytics and how often are offerings upgraded or improved? This will give an indication of how current the vendor is and what is invested in research and development. You want to deal with a company whose focus is Web analytics, not 20 other things with Web analytics as a side dish.

What is the vendor's track record like?

1. Does it have a history of happy, loyal customers?

2. What are some of the results the vendor has helped companies achieve?

3. How long has the vendor been in operation and has there been a recent merger or acquisition?

Look at the stability of the company and customer satisfaction. You want to deal with a company that is well respected. ClickTracks makes no bones about promoting its recent awards—and well deserved ones at that (Figure 28.1). Here are some questions to consider.

1. What is the vendor's training and support like?

2. Do you have to pay for support? If so, what does it cost?

3. What are the support hours?

4. What support options are available? Examples include an online knowledge base, e-mail, and toll-free phone support.

4. What training does the vendor provider (online courses, manuals, etc.)? Is their a cost for the training?

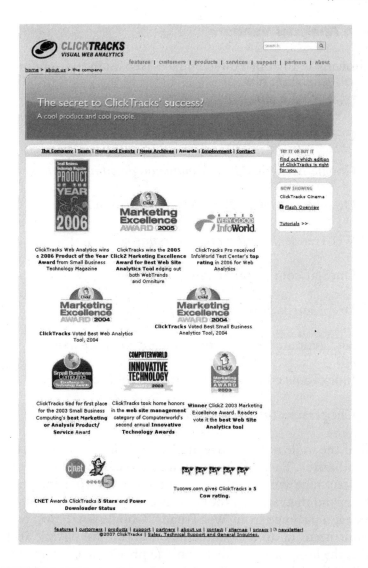

**Figure 28.1.** ClickTracks prominently displays its recent, well deserved awards on its Web site.

5. Does the vendor have community support? Packages that are widely adopted often will have a community of users that support each other to work out solutions. Odds are, if you're having an issue, someone else has already encountered and solved it. Take a look around for support groups and online communities.

### Popular Web Analytics Vendors

The following is a list of 10 recognized Web analytics vendors:

- WebSideStory (*http://www.websidestory.com*)

- CoreMetrics (*http://www.coremetrics.com*)

- Google Analytics (*http://www.google.com/analytics*)

- Omniture (SiteCatalist) (*http://www.omniture.com*)

- WebTrends (*http://www.webtrends.com*)

- OneStat.com (*http://www.onestat.com*)

- DeepMetrix (*http://www.deepmetrix.com*)

- MyComputer.com (*http://www.mycomputer.com*)

- IndexTools.com (*http://www.indextools.com*)

- ClickTracks (*http://www.clicktracks.com*).

All of the tools noted above are valuable in monitoring the success of your online initiatives. Each offers its own approach to Web analytics, so it is up to you to determine what analytics make sense for your business and marketing objectives and then select a tool that is compatible with your budget. For most businesses, a package from WebTrends, Google Analytics, or ClickTracks will meet your needs at an affordable price. If you are paying an ISP to host your Web site, the host may already be able to provide some sort of analysis software which is included with the fee of hosting your site. In some cases they might charge you an additional fee for this service.

## Closing Comments on Web Analytics

To measure the key performance indicators for your Web initiatives, you are going to rely on a number of assistive tools and old-fashioned analysis. Many e-mail marketing solution providers, pay-to-play search engine sites, and companies offering ad placement services, offer detailed reports and self-service tools for monitoring your campaigns that can be used along with your Web analytics package to give you more information about your efforts than any other marketing medium.

There are statistics packages available that can track everything from click-throughs, your ROI, the lifetime value of a customer, the pay-off between organic and paid search engine marketing campaigns, whether your static ad or flash ad is performing better, and even the effectiveness of a link positioned at the top of a page versus one near the bottom. If you are running an online marketing campaign, then it is important to know if your efforts are justified.

At the end of the day, remember that no marketing measurement is exact, but they provide you with insight on how well your travel and tourism Web site is doing and offer guidance so that you can make positive changes in the future. Strive to make your clients' lives better and you will reap the benefits.

## Internet Resources for Chapter 28

I have developed a great library of online resources for you to check out regarding Web traffic analysis and Web metrics. This library is available on my Tourism Internet Marketing University Web site *http://www.TourismInternetMarketingU.com/max* in the Resources section where you can find additional tips, tools, techniques, and resources.

I have also developed courses on many of the topics covered in this book. These courses are also available on my Tourism Internet Marketing University Web site *http://www.TourismInternetMarketingU.com/max*. These courses are delivered immediately over the Internet or can be ordered as a CD.

# About the Author

## Susan Sweeney, CA, CSP, HoF

Renowned industry expert, consultant, and speaker Susan Sweeney, CA, CSP, HoF, tailors lively keynote speeches and full- and half-day seminars and workshops for companies, industries, and associations interested in improving their Internet presence and increasing their Web site traffic and sales.

Susan is a partner of Verb Interactive (*www.verbinteractive.com*), an international Internet marketing and consulting firm. She holds both the Chartered Accountant and Certified Speaking Professional designations. Susan was inducted into the Canadian Speakers Hall of Fame in 2006. She is an experienced Internet marketing professional with a background in computers, marketing, and the Internet.

Susan is the author of several books on Internet marketing and e-business: *101 Ways to Promote Your Web Site* (a best seller now in its sixth edition, it has been translated into German and Spanish), *Internet Marketing for Your Tourism Business, 3G Marketing on the Internet, Going for Gold, 101 Internet Businesses You Can Start from Home,* and *The e-Business Formula for Success.* She is also the developer of a two-day intensive Internet Marketing Boot Camp. Susan offers many Web-based tele-seminars, seminars on CD, and e-books related to Internet marketing.

Susan is a member of the Canadian Association of Professional Speakers, the National Speakers Association, and the International Federation for Professional Speakers.

Verb Interactive is a marketing firm that provides Internet and international marketing consulting and training services to industry and government. Their clients range in size from single-person startup operations to multi-million-dollar international firms. Their primary services include Web site design and development, Internet marketing strategies and campaigns, SEO, Web site report cards, Internet marketing consulting, market research, and competitive analysis. The team of Internet marketing analysts at Verb is highly trained in the area of Internet marketing, and all stay up-to-date with the latest technological advancements and industry trends in the online marketing world. Every person on the team has extensive practical hands-on experience and the necessary skills to use proven tips, tools, and techniques to generate high volumes of traffic to your site.

As a result of technological change and global competitiveness, a strong Internet presence is essential. Susan instructs individuals with her enthusiastic personality combined with her vast hands-on international marketing experience, which keeps her listeners informed and captivated. Let Susan help you increase your traffic and make your business prosper!

Susan Sweeney, CA, CSP, HoF
URL: *http://www.susansweeney.com*
Phone: 1-888-274-0537
Email: *susan@susansweeney.com*
*www.verbinteractive.com*
*www.TourismInternetMarketingU.com/max*

## Susan Sweeney Is One of the World's Top Internet Marketing Experts

Susan Sweeney has been sharing her vast Internet marketing expertise with corporate and conference audiences around the globe for over 10 years. Susan's passion for the subject, depth of knowledge, and enthusiasm fuel her dynamic presentations. To discuss hiring Susan to speak for your next event or having her do a private Internet Marketing Bootcamp for your organization, contact her speaking office at 1-888-274-0537 or visit her Web site, *http://www.susansweeney.com*.

Presentation topics include:

- Past, Present, and Future Trends of Marketing Online

- Secrets of Search Engine Success

- 3G Marketing on the Internet

- The Formula for eBusiness Success.

Susan works with organizations to custom-develop appropriate presentations to meet her audiences' needs, level of knowledge, and interest.

The full agenda for Susan's Internet Marketing Bootcamp can be found at *http://www.susansweeney.com/agenda.html.*

Keep up to date on where Susan is speaking by checking *http://www.susansweeney.com/booksusan.html.*

Find out about Susan's upcoming webinars, her Internet Marketing Bootcamps, as well as her latest CDs, e-books, and podcasts at *http://www.susansweeney.com/store.html.*

Sign up for Susan's free Internet marketing newsletter at *http://www.susansweeney.com.*

Check out *http://www.TourismInternetMarketingU.com* for a full range of tourism online courses.

# Index

## Reader Feedback Sheet

Your comments and suggestions are very important in shaping future publications. Please e-mail us at *moreinfo@maxpress.com* or photocopy this page, jot down your thoughts, and fax it to (850) 934-9981 or mail it to:

**Maximum Press**
Attn: Jim Hoskins
605 Silverthorn Road
Gulf Breeze, FL 32561

**101 Ways to Promote
Your Web Site,
Sixth Edition**
by Susan Sweeney, C.A.
432 pages
$29.95
ISBN: 978-1-931644-46-4

**101 Internet Businesses
You Can Start From Home
Second Edition**
by Susan Sweeney, C.A.
336 pages
$29.95
ISBN: 978-1-931644-48-8

**Marketing on the Internet,
Seventh Edition**
by Susan Sweeney, C.A.,
Andy MacLellen & Ed
Dorey
216 pages
$34.95
ISBN: 978-1-931644-37-2

**Podcasting for Profit**
by Leesa Barnes
376 pages
$34.95
ISBN: 978-1-931644-57-0

To purchase a Maximum Press book, visit your local bookstore,
call (850) 934-4583 or visit *maxpress.com* for online ordering.